CULTURE IS NO LONGER A FACTOR IN THE HIGH PERFORMANCE EQUATION
IT *IS* THE EQUATION

We are in the midst of a seismic shift in leadership and company culture—one accelerated by the recent pandemic. Throw in the increasing competition for talent, and the growing desire for employees to find a shared purpose or connection with their employer, and it's clear that true leadership requires a new set of skills and a new way of thinking. Leaders must become *culturepreneurs*—putting culture at the centre of business strategy.

Global expert on human capital Marty Parker takes you through what it means to be a culturepreneur and how you can implement a Culturepreneur Operating System that drives culture transformation resulting in significant growth. You'll emerge with a new culturepreneurial mindset that will give you a corporate culture supported by planning, leadership alignment, measurement, and the right human systems.

An essential resource for current and future leaders who realize a new cultural order is upon us, *The Culturepreneur* will help you and your organization reach new levels of performance that exceed even your own expectations.

THE
CULTUREPRENEUR

THE
CULTUREPRENEUR

How High Performance Leaders
Craft Culture as
Competitive Advantage

MARTY PARKER

PAGE TWO

Cataloguing in publication information is available from Library and Archives Canada.
ISBN 978-1-77458-081-3 (paperback)
ISBN 978-1-77458-082-0 (ebook)

Page Two
pagetwo.com

Edited by Kendra Ward
Copyedited by Crissy Calhoun
Proofread by Alison Strobel
Cover and interior design by Jennifer Lum
Interior illustrations by Jennifer Lum and
Setareh Ashrafologhalai

waterstonehc.com
martyparker.ca

To Tanya, my incredible wife and partner in life.

Thanks for coming to the Canada's Most

Admired Corporate Cultures Awards Gala that cold

Toronto day in February and making all my dreams

come true. No one won bigger than me that day!

CONTENTS

INTRODUCTION

I was not born a culturepreneur. Far from it. My own leadership journey has been more Dickensesque: a tale of two leaders.

In my first book, *Culture Connection*, I described myself as an observer, someone who spent my youth carefully watching the behaviour of people who were older and wiser than me, including my five older siblings. By observing, I learned how to take the best of what they did and adapt it to my own abilities. It was the 1970s and I was raised to be "well rounded" and to "exercise sound judgment," and I took great pride in striving toward those goals. That is how leader number one was born.

My good judgment, particularly in assessing people, prepared me well for a career in executive search, but I always felt that being well rounded (as a leader and as a person) made me a jack of all trades and master of none. At times, trying to be good at everything felt overwhelming. And, of course, I was not always good at everything. I tried to learn all I could about leadership and apply the skills demonstrated by those who I thought were it doing well: I had structured meetings; I developed clear agendas; I gave constructive criticism when needed; I helped others achieve their own goals;

1

I studied leadership books; and I went to conferences. I valued my role as a leader of others and took seriously the job of ensuring I got the best out of my team as often as possible.

Then something changed.

It started the day I received the results of a behavioural profile that I completed with my Entrepreneurs' Organization group. The profile, the first of its sort that I'd completed, said I was ambitious, pioneering, competitive, inspiring, enthusiastic, and persuasive. "You bet!" I thought. It also characterized me as impatient, restless, independent, and self-willed. True enough.

I'll never forget the first paragraph of the report: "Marty displays a high energy factor and is optimistic about the results he can achieve. The word 'can't' is not in his vocabulary. He can be aggressive and direct but still be considerate of people. Other people realize that directness is one of his great strengths. He is extremely results-oriented, with a sense of urgency to complete projects quickly."[1] As I learned more about these results, I felt a great sense of relief, like this tool validated everything I thought to be the true me. At home, I excitedly told my wife: she thought the answers were accurate and obvious, but they were a revelation to me. I had finally found something that gave me licence to pursue my own strengths and made it okay for me to rely on others to pick up for my weaknesses. I no longer needed to be a jack of all trades! I was now on a path to be the master of my own strengths and, in doing so, I could help others do the same. That is how leader number two came into being.

I could now also see clearly in others the patterns of behaviours outlined in these types of profiles, and over time I could more clearly see that behaviours were often somehow linked to what people loved. Leading my own entrepreneurial business at Waterstone Human Capital, I could adjust people's roles to take advantage of their strengths and create opportunities around my team members' passions. It was powerful stuff.

By 2010, a clear relationship between culture and performance had emerged. *Culture Connection* set out to validate that relationship and to identify the steps organizations were taking to ensure their culture positively impacted performance. Through my work with high performance teams across North America, I noticed that a growing group of leaders were building their organizations around their unique corporate cultures. Others were attempting to evolve their existing organizational cultures.

The real trend that stood out for me was that the unique cultures of companies were becoming a core element of business strategy and the centre of their organizational platforms. *How* things were getting done was paramount and driving *what* was getting done. In other words, culture was the competitive advantage trumping everything else. In these organizations, results were exceptional (outpacing the S&P/ TSX 60 by an average of 600 percent).[2] And just as importantly, these organizations were retaining and attracting great talent. Employee Net Promoter Scores (eNPS), culture, and engagement and retention scores were now as prevalent in boardroom discussions as return on investment, revenue, and asset or earnings growth. Culture was influencing corporate social initiatives, giving rise to social enterprise and B Corporations. Organizations like Google, McKinsey, and Gallup were spending money researching culture and its impact on their teams' performance. New generations were entering leadership roles and creating cultures where organizations and individuals shared purpose. Leaders were creating psychologically safe environments and allowing for the flow of ideas. Innovation and collaboration were accelerating at levels I had never before seen in such organizations—and technology facilitated this. The rise of the employee-centric organization was growing fast and culture reigned supreme.

In March 2020, COVID-19 arrived in North America. This awful global pandemic required almost all organizations adapt in some way to a digital or hybrid workplace, with all or some of their team members working from home. Culture shifted at an astonishing pace—in many cases overnight—to support this changing world. The silver lining of COVID-19 has been that leaders and organizations are now recognizing that placing culture at the centre of business strategy is a must. And so the culturepreneur and culturepreneurial organization were born.

The Culturepreneur reflects this new era of entrepreneurial leaders who are driving our economies and society forward with culture at the centre of organizational design. These leaders understand that we are in the process of a leadership renaissance that was accelerated by the COVID-19 pandemic. They know that leaders need to adapt to their team members and that a strong workplace culture is central to supporting that mindset. Culturepreneurial leaders and organizations see opportunity in using this new business model to drive unprecedented levels of innovation, competitive advantage, and performance.

One tool that drives culture transformation is Waterstone's Culturepreneur Operating System. It gives leaders a simple, proven, and measured approach to identifying and curating culture, so they can then put culture at the centre of business planning for higher human, organizational, social, and economic performance. All the tools and strategies offered in this book are based on examples set by best-in-class leaders and organizations. Some of the tools and strategies are new, others not, but they are all effective in this new workplace culture.

Culturepreneurs have changed the landscape of leadership forever. Adopting a culturepreneurial mindset will give you the corporate culture you desire—one supported by planning, leadership alignment, measurement, and the right human systems. And when your culture is supported with exceptional and contemporary culturepreneurial leadership, your results will exceed your expectations.

PART 1

THE PAST TO
THE PRESENT

1

A BRIEF HISTORY OF CORPORATE CULTURE

"Study the past, if you would divine the future."

CONFUCIUS, Chinese philosopher, teacher, and politician

I've been very fortunate in my career to speak with, and learn from, some true trailblazers in the field of corporate culture. One such person is Michael McCain, president and CEO at Maple Leaf Foods. I've admired McCain and his approach to corporate culture for years—he has not only built a culture that is the definition of competitive advantage, but the level of stickiness in that culture is amazing. In my work in executive search, and through the Canada's Most Admired Corporate Cultures program that Waterstone Human Capital founded, I often encounter Maple Leaf Foods alumni, all of whom speak passionately about the role of culture at the company. The last time I spoke with McCain, I asked him what influenced his approach to culture. He told me a great story that captures, in a nutshell, the evolution of corporate culture over the past half century or so:

I came out of a private enterprise [McCain Foods Limited] that my father and his brother built over a very long period of time and in the forty-plus years that they operated that business together they never once used the C word of culture; they never once talked about company values, never crossed the radar. There were no posters on the wall ... yet they had a profoundly well-understood culture in their organization. All of which leads you to the conclusion that the behaviours of the leaders is the single most important attribute to culture development in an organization. And they were very clear over that forty-year history about their own behaviour and the behaviours they expected of their teams in defining that culture.

When we acquired Maple Leaf in 1995, one of the first observations I made with the board was that I believed as a long-term owner/operator that our success was going to be defined by the people in our organization and the environment that they worked in and how they behaved together. But, at the time, there really was no strong culture at the Maple Leaf organization. It was a disparate federation of businesses, if you will, as the result of a siloed structure. And I remember identifying at least half a dozen unique cultures throughout the organization, all defined by the divisional heads, not one common bond.

And I believed, back in the late '90s, that what was going to define our success was having the bond, the glue of a really powerful culture that was magnetic to the people inside the organization, or people coming to the organization, and defined how we would work together.

Because we were re-engineering, if you will, a common bond of an organization that we'd come into as opposed to built brick by brick from the very first day. It was a different approach to building culture . . . We needed to manage it overtly, proactively, to achieve the outcomes that we wanted. So we started that journey in the late 1990s and we've been at it ever since.[1]

McCain's story highlights not only how he and the Maple Leaf Foods team emphasize culture but also how far we've come in terms of recognizing the critical importance of putting culture at the centre of business operations.

Do your job well, keep your head down, don't question authority

Despite the fact that corporate culture is now such an ingrained part of organizations, it has only been "a thing" since the 1950s. Prior to that, corporate culture certainly existed, but its value in terms of organizational success wasn't necessarily recognized. It also wasn't something employees were looking for.

With the Great Depression and two World Wars still fresh in the minds of many, a certain "be happy to have a job and money in your pocket" mentality drove the actions of several organizations and employees. In the Western world at least, significant infrastructure development and the growth of cities led to a shift in society, while in the business world, the sense of "clock in, do your work, clock out" was prevalent.[2] The idea of job mobility, of having the option to change jobs or find a new job if you lost work was certainly on the rise, but for many (if not all) organizations, people were viewed as units of work. And for most employees, work wasn't about liking your job or connecting with the goals of your organization. It was a means to an end—putting food on the table, buying a home, building a life.

Over the next thirty years or so, the corporate culture conversation ramped up thanks, primarily, to the pursuit of the American Dream: "a happy way of living that is thought of by many Americans as something that can be achieved by anyone in the US especially by working hard and becoming successful."[3] After World War II, the world was in shambles, but the US was ready to spend money and to innovate. Unlike much of the world, the US had found a way to make consumer goods accessible (somewhat evenly) across locations and classes, giving organizations the means and the time to look beyond the products and begin to focus on the environment in which those products were produced.[4] An aspirational mindset began to creep into organizational planning, with leaders moving to a "let's make the workplace better" approach.

People like Edgar Schein, from the MIT Sloan School of Management, "embarked on what he calls 'an exciting quarter century of model building,' which helped define how people thought about and engaged with organizations."[5] And then, of course, there was Peter Drucker.

"Culture eats strategy for breakfast" is an axiom most often attributed to Drucker, a management consultant and successful author from the 1940s, who eventually published thirty-nine books on management. Drucker was driven to c reate "a functioning society." To do that, he looked to the development of "effective and responsible institutions, including those that by the 1940s were emerging to be the most powerful in the world: big American corporations. Management, practised well, was Drucker's bulwark against evil." Although widely considered the inventor of management as a practice or system, Drucker most notably "focused this discipline on People and Power; on Values, Structure and Constitution; and above all on responsibilities—that is, focused the Discipline of Management on Management as truly a liberal art."[6]

So, even before culture ate strategy for breakfast, Drucker suggested that people and values were central to performance. It was an important shift in thinking—from "clock in, do your work, clock out" culture to one in which people could be much more than just units of productivity.

The next evolution

The 1980s saw the rise of mission, vision, and values. Management theorists Robert Waterman Jr. and Thomas Peters, who wrote the seminal book *In Search of Excellence*, "knew that common management theories played an important role in how anxious or afraid people were in their workplace. Therefore, they developed a self-analysis tool for corporations to assess their standing, which often decreased fear and anxiety because corporations were in much better shape than originally thought."[7] Central to this work was that organizations needed to ensure that vision and values stay at the core of an organization's thinking and strategy.

The work that flowed from that, in my opinion, took culture and leadership to new heights. By the late 1980s and into the 1990s, writers and theorists were getting behind the idea that culture could drive performance. And you had the rise of "knowledge work" (a term coined by Drucker in 1959, "foreshadowing a new economy in which brains would trump brawn").[8]

Even before culture
ate strategy for
breakfast, people and
values were central
to performance.

I entered the workforce in the early 1990s. At that time, in North America, the economy was still in recovery, but investment in people development was on the rise. Corporate culture was on the radar for some leaders, but performance and results still dominated.

In the 1990s and early 2000s, another change occurred. This time, it was less about the role of culture and more about the role that people play in culture. In *Corporate Culture and Performance*, published in 1992, authors John Kotter and James Heskett argue that "strong corporate cultures that facilitate adaptation to a changing world are associated with strong financial results. We found that those cultures highly value employees, customers, and owners and that those cultures encourage leadership from everyone in the firm."[9]

This is when we first started to see people move from units of work to organizational capital—a shift from human resources to human capital. Leadership was considering employees as chief in importance and as assets of great value that could be grown or developed. In fact, Waterstone was among the first companies in our country to brand itself using the term "human capital." It sounds amazing now, but when I started the company in 2003, that shift in thinking was just beginning. That, combined with my personal interest in the idea of corporate culture, led me to the idea of culture by design. The thinking being that every organization has a culture and even when you don't believe it's important, culture will happen. Leaders of high performance organizations realize they can affect culture.

The war for talent

The book that tipped the balance was *The War for Talent* by Ed Michaels, Helen Handfield-Jones, and Beth Axelrod. It came out of a 1997 McKinsey study of 13,000 executives and 120 companies and said, for the first time, that getting the right people (and all the work around finding those people) was going to be the number one reason for business success. Strategy, leadership, and first-hand knowledge were important, but people usurped them. Michaels, Handfield-Jones, and Axelrod were the first to say that in the next twenty years, you would have to win the war for talent. They discuss attracting, developing, and retaining highly talented leaders, the strategic importance of human capital, and the direct correlation between better leadership talent and better organizational performance. They talk about making companies uniquely attractive to talent, moving beyond recruiting hype, and looking for patterns of job experiences to find ways to coach and mentor and to cultivate better managers.[10]

The impact of technology

Access to information and to knowledge also changed the way culture was viewed within organizations. In the 1990s, home computers flourished, the internet became a public tool, and suddenly people could access information at an astounding rate. Shortly thereafter, candidates began to have a different kind of access to information about potential employers, not simply relying on employers or recruiters—they could read reviews and learn from third parties about their potential new boss or company. Everything changed. This began a significant shift in power from the employer to the employee: more access to information meant more choice and flexibility about where and how employees worked.

As the internet, and our use of it, has evolved, so has the depth and breadth of information available to candidates, clients, and competitors alike. It is now a platform for employees and former employees to discuss an organization publicly—what do they like about working there, would they recommend the company, why did they leave? Thanks to LinkedIn, potential candidates are one direct message away from all of your current and former employees; Glassdoor gives them insight into your hiring process and an unvarnished view of what it's like to work at the organization. Suddenly, your employee value proposition has been reduced in importance next to your Glassdoor rating and Net Promoter Score (NPS). And just as suddenly, your culture is doing double duty as your brand.

Culture becomes a business system

When culture becomes brand, we need to go beyond simply understanding and communicating culture to actively curating an aspirational culture. Leaders today are taking the time to look at culture and ask, "Where do I want to be, culture-wise?" When culture becomes a deliberate goal—as opposed to an organic evolution—developing a business system around it, curating it, is possible.

This is the future of high performance leaders and teams— a future where we put culture at the centre of the system. I will delve deeper into the idea of culture as a business system in the coming chapters. But it's important to understand from the start that when we treat culture as a system, that culture (the values and behaviours that define who we are as an organization) can drive higher levels of innovation, performance, and success.

Those of us who recall the pre-internet days know what it was like to have to actively search for information about the world and to live in a smaller, less-connected bubble—buying newspapers from outside your community, coveting that set of encyclopedias your parents bought in the 1960s (or '70s or '80s), thumbing through issues of *National Geographic* at the local library. Over the last twenty or twenty-five years, we've seen incredible change in the way we access and process information, in the way we raise our children, and in how we interact with the world around us. We rely on smartphones, Zoom calls, and the internet. We work in an era of high collaboration, instant feedback, gender-neutral pronouns, #MeToo, Black Lives Matter—the list goes on.

For many of our team members, unprecedented adaptability and agility are native to the way they work. The speed at which they hop and jump until they find something that connects to their passion and their purpose is incredible, especially for those of us who have had to develop adaptability as a skill over the course of our careers. It's not that our younger colleagues are flaky or anxious or lack grit—it's that they were raised in a world of constant change and so change comes naturally to them. That's a big factor in how we approach work and it's making corporate culture more important than ever.

As leaders, our challenge is to grow and sustain a culture that reflects our organization and what's happening in the world—as well as how it's happening. For many of us, that may mean adjusting our definitions of work, performance, and success to accommodate ideas like shared passion, individual purpose, and diversity. For most of us, it's going to mean taking time to reflect on our own skills as leaders and to develop new expertise in soft skills that will help us better lead teams that think in ways that don't always come naturally to us.

As leaders, we need to put culture at the centre of how we do things. In the coming chapters, I'll outline this new era and style of leadership, the benefits of putting culture at the centre, and how to leverage your own personal skills and style of leading in doing so. That doesn't mean putting culture before performance or placing less importance on the bottom line; it means understanding what drives you and your team, understanding what connects those passions to the organization's purpose, and placing that at the centre of everything you do to drive performance and success.

The takeaway:
The marriage of culture and strategy
has been a long time coming

- Today, people understand and accept that culture drives performance, and they are starting to recognize that culture needs to be central to (versus supportive of) business strategy and its support systems.

- Every organization has a culture; high performance organizations realize they can affect, change, and even create their ideal culture.

- When culture becomes a deliberate goal—as opposed to a natural evolution—developing a business system around culture and curating the culture you want is possible.

- When you treat culture as a system, it can drive higher levels of innovation, performance, and success.

- The challenge is to grow and sustain a culture that reflects your organization and also what's happening in the world.

- We need to put culture at the centre of how we do things to drive performance and success; we also need to understand how to adapt and change to reflect this new approach.

2

THE ERA OF CULTUREPRENEURSHIP

"Culture isn't just one aspect of the game, it is the game."
LOUIS V. GERSTNER JR., former CEO of IBM

Culture is all about behaviour—the collective behaviours of your organization. It is the one thing about your organization that cannot be copied. You can replicate ideas from other organizations or from other leaders and you can find new people to join your team, and both can positively impact your culture and your results, but every other organization can do the exact same thing. The one thing that can't be duplicated is the unique combination of behaviours that make your corporate culture yours alone.

Entrepreneurs are people who innovate or create solutions to problems and who are willing to take the risks associated with that type of activity. They are critical in any economy because they anticipate needs and bring solutions to the market, they innovate, and they help power the economic engine of society. Our world has been built by entrepreneurs. Imagine it without the entrepreneurial spirit of Steve Jobs, Richard

Branson, Oprah Winfrey, Bill Gates, Cher Wang, Jeff Bezos, Sara Blakely—and those are only examples from the past few decades. But the definition of entrepreneurship has expanded. Entrepreneurship has become an ethos, a mindset. Many professional managers or leaders in functional areas would say they are entrepreneurs, and they would be right in doing so. And now we have the concept of social entrepreneurs—people who work with or within organizations to do good for the broader community.

Combining culture and entrepreneurship to help drive performance to new heights only makes sense. I call it "culturepreneurship," and at its most basic, it's about innovative leaders putting culture at the centre of business strategy to drive higher performance, whether in a business unit, group of people, organization, or the broader society or economy. Culturepreneurs understand that culture is not just an organization's competitive advantage, but that placing culture at the centre of strategy can drive an organization's cause, purpose, and economic and social impact. Culturepreneurship, then, becomes a system that drives innovation, competitive advantage, and higher levels of success for a variety of performance markers.

Putting culture at the centre of strategy

For years, we've talked about culture as supporting business strategy. In fact, it's the other way around. Your innovation and your impact on society need to be centred on how you do things and linked to both your culture and your purpose. Culture is no longer one factor in the equation: it *is* the equation because it is what distinguishes an organization from the

Culturepreneurship
makes culture the
hub and everything
else the spokes.

others in its competitive set. Culturepreneurship refers to the mindset, the ethos, and the operating system that makes culture the hub and everything else the spokes. Culturepreneurs are those leaders who say things like, "It's all about culture," "It starts with our culture," or "They would not fit with our culture."

Every so often, in business, art, music, sports, or any endeavour, something comes along that completely changes the way we do things within that field. As a former athlete and a passionate sports fan, I can think of two great examples from the sports world that have fundamentally changed the way these sports are played: the West Coast offense (from football) and the neutral-zone trap game (from hockey). Bill Walsh, as head coach of the San Francisco 49ers, introduced and used the pass-oriented West Coast offense to great success in the National Football League (NFL) of the 1960s, '70s, and '80s.[1] And the neutral-zone trap game was perfected in the 1990s by the New Jersey Devils under coach Jacques Lemaire.[2] These were significant innovations to their respective sports and have stood the test of time—in fact, virtually all coaches in football and hockey run elements or variations of these operating systems today because they drive results. Both need a commitment from leadership, the right talent, and support systems to make them work. And, of course, coaches need to consistently measure their impact to evaluate their effectiveness.

Culture today is the same: it is an operating system that has fundamentally changed the game of organizational behaviour and development. Leaders who understand this have adapted their styles accordingly, and many up-and-coming leaders are now naturally developing their style in a culture-centric world.

The theory that culture drives performance has been proven repeatedly. Culture went from something not talked about to something interesting to consider to a central part of organizational tactics that was widely viewed as having a direct impact on performance. Culture is now the key differentiating element of a company's competitive advantage and business strategy. So, we can stop trying to prove the theory and start leveraging the data we already have to take things to the next level. The question today is not "Does culture drive performance?" Rather it is "How can we create or adapt our own unique culture to drive performance?" This requires the kind of leader who commits to putting culture at the centre of organizational strategy. Enter the era of the culturepreneur and the culture operating system.

We know that using culture to drive performance works, can be adopted and replicated, and has proven to be sustainable over time. The best part, however, is that as a culturepreneur, you can customize how you use culture to drive performance, based on your organization's unique corporate culture. Waterstone's Culturepreneur Operating System (which is discussed extensively in chapter 8) will drive results, and because your unique culture will be at the centre of the equation, the results will be specific to the purpose and processes of your organization. Just as there is no universally correct culture, there is no universally perfect way to transform culture. Knowing your culture and aligning your systems to it ensures you're doing what's right for you and your team. Waterstone's Culturepreneur Operating System will also enable your organization to build a sustainable competitive advantage because your culture is completely unique to your organization—it can never be exactly duplicated!

When your outcomes are a direct result of your culture, they can't help but support your hiring and retention efforts. Especially following the rapid changes to the way we work that were ushered in with the COVID-19 pandemic, people want to be the best they can be; they want to be happy, enjoy what they're doing, and find success on their own terms. And more than ever before, success is being defined as happiness. Individuals are realizing that happiness isn't solely found in high performance organizations, those that pay more or offer the best benefits or work environment; happiness can also be found in organizations that align with an individual's interests and passions. An individual who knows their own passion and who can link that passion to an organization's purpose (as we'll explore later in this book) will seek out that connection almost every time—and because their commitment is deeper, their performance will be greater.

Shared purpose between you and your organization creates higher levels of personal satisfaction. This connection is better for mental health, families, and possibly even gross domestic product; more importantly, it spurs higher levels of innovation and success because your actions and your decisions are directed by the unique cultural abilities of the organization.

As a leader, being a culturepreneur signals that you truly believe your role is to help others and the organization be successful, and to align the organization around how you do things. Over the years, I've had the good fortune to know several great culturepreneurs who put culture at the centre of everything they do. One such leader is Mike Wessinger, co-founder and CEO of PointClickCare and a 2017 Canada's Most Admired CEO award winner. Based in Mississauga,

Ontario, PointClickCare provides cloud-based health information systems to the long-term and post-acute care industry. Wessinger believes that with the right culture and the right team, the organization can develop the right strategy—and then execution becomes easy. He and his team recognized early on that while they had developed a strong culture organically, the expectation that it would not change as the company grew was unrealistic. "There are core elements that really haven't changed," says Wessinger. "Today, we have a mantra, three cultural pillars we call passion, people, and performance. I have a definition of what that means and that was far more engineered than what we had originally put together."[3]

Wessinger made embodying the culture at PointClickCare central to his role as CEO. "When I think of my job, it's culture number one, team number two, strategy and vision number three, and then execution is the last piece," he says. "The reason I've put them in that order is I believe that if you really get the culture right, then you can attract the very best team and get the best work out of that team."[4] Wessinger believes that by making culture his top priority—by scheduling time to reflect and focus on it in his calendar, and actually working on it—he ensures that culture is an integral part of the business cycle. And the results speak for themselves—PointClickCare has outperformed its nearest competition tenfold.[5]

Kat Cole, former chief operating officer and president, North America, for Focus Brands, is another great example of a culturepreneur. Her story so inspired me that I asked her to speak at a Young Presidents' Organization (YPO) event back in 2016. She started working at Hooters while she was still in high school, eventually being promoted into an executive

People who feel more connected have a much higher probability of doing better in a more enjoyable way.

role; she earned the title of vice president by the age of twenty-six and helped the company open up operations in Australia. After completing her MBA, she was recruited by Focus Brands and was the driving force behind the transformation of Cinnabon from a struggling brand to a billion-dollar business. But what's inspiring about Cole's story isn't just the way she's built her career, it's also the way she's put people at the core of her process. She focuses on people development and listening, and she actively works to leverage the individual strengths of her team members. Her role also "enables her to advance youth and women's causes through work with the United Nations Foundation, the World Economic Forum, and the Women's Foodservice Forum."[6]

What Wessinger and Cole have in common is their commitment to their culture and their people—creating connections between themselves, their people, and their unique aspirations.

People who feel more connected have a much higher probability of doing better in a more enjoyable way. I liken it to when you meet a special person in your life (whether it's a friend or a romantic partner) and it just feels right. Over a lifetime, that relationship can require a lot of hard work, because a lot of interference comes along (life happens), but your values and what you hold dear as you go through life together connect you through thick and thin. And, of course, the trust you develop allows for more freedom and expression of thoughts and feelings. That connectedness happens much more easily when your behaviours and values align. In the same way, when your purpose and values connect with an organization's, it's easy to say, "I want to be a part of that." If it's a place where you can express yourself and be yourself, all the better.

Culturepreneurship in practice

David Ossip, chairman and CEO at Ceridian, a global human capital management software company, is what you might call a serial entrepreneur. He's led five companies over the course of his career and has learned a thing or two about corporate culture and its role in strategy and performance.

Early on in his career, Ossip, who won the 2017 Canada's Most Admired CEO award for transformational leadership, learned that the focus had to be on the team. "With decades of experience, you learn to effectively identify the leverage points that help build a culture of engagement, leading to operational performance. An employee-first approach that prioritizes the employee experience translates into performance and creates value for customers."[7]

In 2018, with Ceridian hitting new levels of growth and success, Ossip and his team looked at how they would sustain scale. One of their areas of focus was leadership. A founder-led culture made sense for a time, but Ossip was feeling the need to evolve the business: "We always knew we would have to evolve our organization when the time was ready. We had reached a level of revenue, global growth, and employees that it made sense to take our company to the next phase of growth."[8] In April 2018, Ossip took his company public on the New York and Toronto Stock Exchanges.

Ossip and his team fostered a culture driven by Ceridian's Our Way values. The team was purposeful in what they wanted to create, bringing in the right leadership, systems, measurement, and communications to achieve operational goals as Ceridian continued to scale. They built a culture of equality, which "starts with very clear job descriptions and key performance indicators that measure success—all aligned to Ceridian's organizational goals."[9] In effect, Ossip designed a culture operating system. He was purposeful in what he wanted to create and was prepared to bring in the right leadership, systems, measurement, and communications to achieve the operational goals.

By putting culture at the centre of strategy and transforming systems and processes to better align with culture, Ossip not only demonstrated what it means to be a culturepreneur, he also led a successful cultural and organizational transformation. You need only look to the success of Ceridian's stock since the company went public in 2018—opening at US$22 per share and trading at around US$100 per share as of December 2020.[10]

What does all this mean for leaders? It means that by becoming a culturepreneur and putting culture at the centre of strategy (by building a culture operating system), you can make culture more than your competitive advantage. As a business system, culture can drive your team's performance and it can become the engine behind your organization's economic and social impact.

The takeaway:
Culturepreneurs put culture
at the centre of strategy

- Culture is the one thing about your organization that cannot be exactly copied by others.

- A culturepreneur combines corporate culture and an entrepreneurial mindset to drive high performance.

- Culturepreneurs believe that their role is to help others (people and organizations) to be successful and they adapt their style to support their team members.

- A culturepreneur puts culture at the centre of their organizational strategy through an operational model like Waterstone's Culturepreneur Operating System that drives competitive advantage and sustained performance.

PART 2

AN INTRODUCTION TO CULTUREPRENEURSHIP

3

PURPOSE IS YOUR
NEW MISSION

"The only way to do great work is to love what you do. If you haven't found it yet, keep looking. Don't settle."

STEVE JOBS, co-founder, chief executive, and chairman of Apple

---

I didn't wake up in 2003 and start Waterstone Human Capital knowing the company's purpose—in fact, Waterstone didn't have a properly defined purpose for many years. We did have a belief in the idea that recruiting the right people for an organization would drive great corporate culture and that corporate culture was at the heart of sustained business performance.

Over time, we cultivated our understanding of and expertise in culture and its role in building high performance organizations. Through our work in the executive search business and through the unprecedented access we were given to the cultures of some of Canada's top organizations through the Canada's Most Admired Corporate Cultures and Canada's Most Admired CEO award programs, that understanding grew into a passion for the topic. We kept following that passion, saying no to projects that may have been interesting or profitable but that would have moved us away from the central idea of corporate culture driving success; if a job didn't feel like it was furthering the link between culture and performance, it wasn't for us. We were always following our purpose, we just didn't realize it. Like so many other organizations, Waterstone was still explaining what we did through the lens of a mission and vision.

Mission and vision have their places in business planning. Together, they drive you toward achievement and define what you want to accomplish. But they connect you to an output, and that output can be achieved in any number of ways, by anyone who possesses the skills and motivation to do so. Purpose, on the other hand, is about emotion—how you connect to the work being done. Purpose drives specific people toward your mission and vision, and it makes them want to achieve on your behalf. As Simon Sinek put it in his excellent article "The Science of WHY":

> Every organization—and every person's career—operates on three levels: *what* we do, *how* we do it, and *why* we do it. We all know *what* we do: the products we sell, the services we offer, or the jobs we do. Some of us know *how* we do it: the things that we think make us different or stand out from the crowd. But very few of us can clearly articulate *why* we do what we do.
>
> The WHY is the purpose, cause, or belief that drives every organization and every person's individual career. *Why* does your company exist? *Why* did you get out of bed this morning? And *why* should anyone care?[1]

Emotion and connection are at the heart of purpose.

What's different about Sinek's work is that he uses the idea of "why" to identify the reasons certain leaders are more effective than others. The connecting thread: purpose.

Finding the right words to express your purpose might take time, but the emotions that get you there are typically easy to pinpoint. And emotion and connection are at the heart of purpose. Certainly, in the civil rights movement many people were great orators, many had a great message—but there was only one Martin Luther King Jr. He spoke to a dream and in doing so connected to powerful emotions shared by millions of people. He used emotion to inspire people and rally them around a shared mission and vision. When you start from purpose, people who share that mindset—employees, suppliers, customers, clients, and so on—will be drawn to you because they understand that they can be part of something bigger.

The emotions that drive me and the team at Waterstone have been part of the company since 2003. It just took close to twenty years for us to articulate them as a purpose: we inspire organizations to build high performance cultures.

Building on a foundation of values

A few years ago, I implemented a Playbook for Success as part of the performance review process at Waterstone. (You can find a copy of Waterstone Human Capital's Playbook for Success at the back of this book.) It's a simple tool designed to focus people on their personal and professional goals, while also giving insight into who each team member is and helping us connect better as people. The first task you're faced with when you sit down to complete this document is to develop a list of your twenty loves. It's harder than it sounds.

By the tenth or eleventh item, most people have started listing activities or consumable items that bring them happiness or comfort but are perhaps a stretch as "loves" (for example, sweater weather, board games, Chicago-style popcorn). Look beyond the words, however, and the list gives you a pretty good sense of what drives that person—in other words, a good sense of their values.

Values are at the heart of corporate culture. If family is more important than money to an individual, they may gravitate to organizations that value work-life balance as part of their culture and may opt for family-oriented decisions over ones driven by money. For example, if I need to be at my child's soccer game, I won't schedule business meetings after four thirty p.m., and I will be looking for a corporate culture that supports those kinds of family-focused decisions. When your personal values are reflected in your organization, suddenly you're willing to give your blood, sweat, and tears to what you're doing because it aligns with you on a personal level.

A great example of how values set the foundation for culture can be found in the story of Infusion (now Avanade), a global software engineering, design, and digital strategy firm.

In 2000, Alim Somani and his roommate at the University of Waterloo, Sheldon Fernandez, accepted placements at Infusion in New York City. "It was a different kind of company, a different ethos," says Somani, the first-ever winner of the Canada's Most Admired CEO award in the growth category. "We weren't treated as students, we had a seat around the table."[2] Fast-forward to their final year of school. Somani and his roommate had set up their own business and were doing overflow work for Infusion in the US when their former bosses approached them with a proposal: let's start up a Canadian branch of Infusion.

When asked about those early days, Somani credits the culture that they experienced during their job placement as a guidepost for what they eventually established north of the border. They were young leaders, they had been treated as valued team members from the start, and they were empowered to work and think differently. Somani and his partners valued attitude and aptitude in a market geared toward experience, and they rebelled against "bureaucratic stuff," like making their small team fill out time sheets. "What we realized was what's important is values. Culture can change and that's okay. Culture can evolve and culture can mature, and I would actually argue that it needs to as an organization changes and matures," says Somani, now managing director for Hatch Digital. "The culture that we had on day one when we started Infusion was different than when we sold at 700 people... But what remained constant at Infusion was we had a set of values that was increasingly important."[3]

As the company grew, the behaviours of its people evolved, becoming more consistent with its values. As Somani explains, "When you choose the behaviours that are consistent with your values and you repeat them over and over again, that's what makes your culture."[4]

Purpose-driven cultures in action

Toronto-based Knix, a direct-to-consumer women's intimate apparel brand, defines itself as a mission-led company. What that means for founder and CEO Joanna Griffiths is that while the company sells products, its reason for being is to change the way that its customers and community feel about themselves.

Early on in her culturepreneurial journey, Griffiths (a 2020 Canada's Most Admired CEO award winner) was encouraged by a board member to align the company with a greater cause, so that when she was trying to build the business, she wasn't just working for her own financial gain but for something bigger than herself. Being a mission-led company helped Griffiths "bridge those two worlds where I could be highly ambitious about our goals and what it was that we wanted to accomplish, while still feeling as though I was making a positive impact on the community."[5] Today, Knix is a $100 million a year company, and a Knix product is sold every six seconds.[6] "We never would be where we are if we hadn't taken that approach," says Griffiths. "And certainly I never would have been able to recruit and hire the calibre of people that I have if it was not for something much bigger than me."[7]

Paramount Fine Foods has a similar story of success with purpose at the heart of the business. In 2006, Mohamad Fakih purchased a nearly bankrupt restaurant and transformed it into what is now the fastest growing Middle Eastern halal restaurant chain in North America. Right from the start, social justice and giving back to the community have been part of the company's DNA.

Fakih, who is president and CEO of Paramount Fine Foods and a 2019 Canada's Most Admired CEO award winner, says he was brought up with the mentality that nothing is worth doing unless it benefits others. It's a lesson he took with him into his business and one that he thinks more leaders need to consider as they look at evolving their organizations to meet the needs of today's world.[8]

"What [people] are attracted to is to be part of something bigger than themselves. When your company becomes a movement, when your company hits the right buttons into everyone's life and they see the impact immediately right in front of them, this is when people will actually start working harder, because they want something that is bigger than all of us, which is community—90 percent of the time—and purpose," says Fakih. "They know that working hard is automatically attached to being successful at helping the community, serving the community, and serving that purpose."[9]

The company's commitment to the values of social justice and giving back to the community are arguably the best known thing about Paramount Fine Foods (although their excellent food is right up there, in my opinion). Both Paramount and Fakih himself donate to fundraisers and events that support the people and communities with which they work. But the Paramount movement goes beyond just giving back. Fakih's vision, and commitment, is to build a country strengthened by diversity.[10] He made headlines when he travelled to Lebanon to visit the relief camps for Syrian refugees and partnered with Ryerson University for the Lifeline Syria Challenge—allowing Paramount Fine Foods to fund employment support to help new Syrian Canadians during their job searches. Paramount Fine Foods itself provided 150 jobs to refugees in Canada in 2017 alone.[11] In 2020, he travelled to Lebanon again to provide on-the-ground relief support in the wake of a devastating explosion in Beirut.[12]

Fakih has found his purpose, and he's surrounding himself with others who share that purpose. It's a winning formula for attracting and keeping talent. "Having that relationship only based on money, that will not make you keep talent. The only reason why someone will stay today, it's to have a reason bigger than just the money; [it's to be] part of something bigger than ourselves," he says.[13]

Attracting and retaining talent

I'm convinced that there are people working for Avanade (formerly Infusion), Knix, and Paramount Fine Foods who were drawn to those companies not just because of the work but because of the purpose behind it. When it comes to attracting and retaining talent, the impact of purpose can't be overstated. That's not to say that leading with purpose should be all about attracting talent. Purpose needs to be authentic, to be about "the right thing to do," and to be part of the big picture strategy of an organization. But don't underestimate the amount of heavy lifting that purpose can do in attracting and retaining high performers—especially among the next generation of leaders.

There was a time when people graduated from school, got a job that earned a decent paycheque, put their heads down and did that job for forty years, and then retired and moved someplace warm. Many people already in leadership positions came up in that type of environment—but the reality for emerging leaders looks much different. I credit the baby boomers. Their generation started to have a voice in how they approached life and work, and their children amplified that voice. I'm a Gen Xer by birth date but a boomer at heart. My siblings are all boomers; I came along later and I was raised in a boomer mentality. Boomer and Gen X parents collaborated

Recruitment is no
longer a question
of where organizations
find talent but how
and why people find
organizations.

with their kids, discussed issues, and listened to their kids' ideas in a way that was radically different from past generations. And now those kids are in the workforce and growing into management positions, and with them comes a whole new set of expectations and way of doing things.

Senior leaders are sandwiched between the old and the new—between tenure and job hopping, between profit-focus and purpose-focus. When viewed through the lens of purpose, the stereotypes of millennial employees lacking grit, commitment, and focus can be seen to be false. What this generation wants are organizations that they can get behind and work that has an impact. When they find those qualities, when they see their work overlapping with their purpose, they work as hard or harder than any generation that came before them. Their values are different, and as leaders we need to acknowledge that and harness it to drive performance.

The next generation of workers looks for fulfillment and connection more than just output. This fact needs to influence the way we approach recruitment, now and moving forward. We need to adapt, to recognize that it's no longer a question of where organizations find talent but how and why people find organizations. The power balance in the employer-employee relationship has shifted away from the organization (where the employer dictates the terms) toward the individual (where employees have more say in where, how, and why they work). That's where purpose comes into play: it is a key differentiator in the war for talent we discussed in chapter 1. This term, made popular by McKinsey in 2001 to describe the investment in human capital crucial to organizations' "ability to attract, develop, and retain managers at all levels,"[14] describes an approach that is still relevant twenty years later.

By focusing on values and putting your purpose and culture front and centre, you're empowering employees to say, "Yes, that feels like something I want to be part of," "I want this. Where can I find it?" or "No, I don't share that value. That doesn't resonate with me."

A few months ago, I was talking to a soon-to-be graduate who thought she might have an interest in the executive search business. Let's call her Anne. Anne had a reasonably good understanding of the role of a recruiter but wasn't sure if she was passionate about the industry. She explained to me that her biggest concern was getting locked into something she wasn't passionate about. Executive search can be a rewarding career; unlike in almost any other profession, you connect with people across a variety of industries and organizations. But after talking about our work at Waterstone, I could tell that executive search likely wouldn't be Anne's final destination. Not because she couldn't do the job, but because it didn't spark excitement in her. As a mentor, my job is to encourage young people to try new things and to remind them that it's okay to be a work in progress. As a leader, my job is to ensure that I give young people on my team the opportunity to find that connection by making moves within the organization when available and appropriate.

We've all been in situations where we feel disconnected. When you think about spending significant amounts of time in an environment that doesn't inspire you, it's hard. For those of us of a certain generation, we were raised to deal with it. Today's employees won't tolerate it. I coached my daughters' hockey teams for many years and I've seen a lot of great teams and great coaches, and I've also seen my fair share of teams that don't jell or don't work for whatever reason. I've seen kids say, "I love hockey but I'm not playing on this team anymore" because of this reason or that reason. As a player, I would have been too scared to speak up, move on, lose my spot. But that was around forty years ago. Now young people are much more self-actualized. They aren't afraid at ten, fifteen, or twenty years old to ask deep questions about purpose and culture and say, "I'm not connecting with what's happening here; this may not be my forever place."

Culturepreneurial leaders should consider asking themselves (and helping their team members to ask themselves) the following:

- What do I love?

- What are my passions?

- If I did not have a job, what would I do to fill that time? What would I do for free?

- What kinds of people do I most enjoy being around? Why?

- What makes me lose track of time?

- If I had a dream, what would I do to make it happen?

What does all this mean for culturepreneurs? It means finding your own purpose and helping your team members find their purpose and connection to the organizational values.

The takeaway:
Purpose drives performance

- A clearly defined purpose will help drive talent to your organization and make people want to achieve great things in support of your mission and vision.

- As a leader, your role is to deeply understand your organization's purpose and ensure that it is authentically aligned with every strategy, process, and output.

- The key is authenticity. Sticking with your mission and vision is better than championing an inauthentic purpose.

- Purpose will align your work and your team with your values, which in turn will drive the behaviours that build your culture.

4

THE RISE OF
BESPOKE LEADERSHIP

"Today, charting your own course isn't just more necessary
than ever before. It's also much easier—and much more fun."

PINK, American singer/songwriter

I meet one-on-one with each member of my management
team every Tuesday morning. The goal of each meeting is the
same: check in, give and receive updates on key projects, discuss issues, and generally ensure that we're all still paddling
in the same direction and no storms are brewing on the horizon. But because each of my team members has their own
style and their own needs, the process for each meeting is different. I must optimize the time, energy, and emotion of each
meeting around the needs of the individual team member.
For some, it's all business—a detailed agenda with questions
and action items clearly spelled out. For others, it's more of
a free-flowing discussion—an opportunity to vent or brainstorm or get a second opinion on one or two key projects. Do I
have a preferred style? Yes. But as much as these meetings are
an important way for me to connect with the team and keep

my finger on the pulse of what's happening at Waterstone, the reality is that they aren't about me. I'm going to get the best out of my team by adapting my style to their needs and styles.

With up to four different generations of employees currently in the workplace, and each generation bringing different expectations to the table, leaders must, at minimum, adjust and adapt their style when managing and collaborating by segment. Layer in the needs and patterns of each individual within those segments, and it can seem like a daunting challenge.

The world today is all about customization, and leadership is no different. We've grown used to getting what we want, when we want it, and how we want it. Whether that's ordering groceries to our home, calling a rideshare, customizing our order at a restaurant, or tailoring an educational program like LinkedIn Learning to meet our individual needs. If we want it, we can get it.

People management requires a customized approach to the individual—bespoke leadership, if you will—if leaders are going to leverage and unlock the power of our teams and cultures.

The growing popularity of self-directed work

Gone are the days of one working style fitting all. The power of individual employees to find roles that connect with their purpose and fit with their lifestyles has grown. This customization in the way we live, the catering to the individual needs of each consumer, has infiltrated the way we work, with flexible schedules and work-from-home options becoming more common. In fact, a 2020 report from Statistics Canada states that "most jobs in finance and insurance (85%), educational services (85%), and professional, scientific, and technical services (84%) can potentially be performed from home."[1] This has also started to shift the power in the employer-employee relationship.

I remember reading Daniel Pink's first book, *Free Agent Nation*, and connecting with his idea that everyone could be their own worker, working from home and being their own contractor. (In many ways, Pink was ahead of his time. I was so taken with his ideas that I brought him in to speak to my company.) Pink went so far as to write that "in the first half of the twenty-first century, the new emblematic figure is the free agent—the independent worker who operates on his or her own terms, untethered to a large organization, serving multiple clients and customers instead of a single boss."[2] This movement to customizing your approach to life, and to building a life that you find fulfilling, has been happening for many years. But historic events, and recently the COVID-19 pandemic, have accelerated our need and ability to embrace self-directed, individualized ways of working. Put another way, the world has changed, and we need to follow suit.

Leaders who do not account for their team members' needs for autonomy will quickly find themselves at the back of the pack when it comes to finding and keeping high performance talent. In our world of executive search, we often ask this question: "What leadership style do you work best with?" I'm willing to bet if you surveyed the executive search community across North America, you'd find that "I don't want to be micromanaged" is the answer 80 to 90 percent of the time. People want to be autonomous. They want support; they want coaching; they want to become the best they can be at something; they want to deliver quality work; and, frankly,

Leaders who do not account for their team members' needs for autonomy will find themselves losing the battle to find and keep high performance talent.

they want variety. (McKinsey reports that because individuals no longer stay at a firm for their lifetime, they value personal and professional growth and development as among the top criteria for joining an organization.[3])

The desire for autonomy is one of many things driving the shift toward side hustles and the gig economy. While there will always be people who want and need permanent, full-time employment within an organization, that won't necessarily be the norm for the next generation of workers. The 2017 "Freelancing in America" survey found that 50 percent of millennial workers are already doing freelance work and that by 2027 the majority of US workers will freelance. Sixty-three percent of the freelancers who participated in that survey also indicated that they began freelancing by choice—up ten points over the same survey in 2014.[4]

It goes back to customization: today's workforce is used to customizing everything about their lives to meet their personal needs and preferences and to getting instant and ongoing feedback on their efforts. Why should their work experience be any different?

I'll give you two examples of how this changes the way we lead.

The annual performance review

Gone (or soon to be) are the days where managers would sit down once or twice a year with their direct reports to provide (often one-way) feedback on progress and performance. People demand more frequent feedback. They also want a discussion rather than a review—a real conversation about what each party is looking for out of the relationship, what each party thinks is going well or needs work, and where the employee would like to go in the next six months, one year, or even three years, not where you as the leader think they should go.

Project teams

An individual's contribution to a team is closely tied to their purpose and their ability to do good work with which they connect. So, instead of dictating who's on the team, what their roles are, and how the work should be done, conversations should go something like: "Let's talk about who should be on the team and what your role might be. I think you'd be great in this role, but let's talk about where you see yourself. Do you have enough information to do the job? How can I help you succeed?" Those discussions need to happen with each team member before the team meets, and they need to happen again with the whole team as the project takes shape. You then need to step back and allow the team to work. Give them support, push them when needed, but allow them to determine their own *what* and *how*.

From "human resources" to "people and culture"

As we shift our thinking about people from resources that achieve on behalf of the organization to humans who require coaching, development, and a connection to the purpose of the organization, we are also veering away from traditional human resources teams and toward people and culture departments. These are the culture and training hubs of high performance teams.

The Oppenheimer Group (Oppy), a global produce company that grows, markets, and distributes fresh produce around the world, deliberately changed its leadership team to a people and culture team after assessing the functions of the team and the needs of the organization. The human resources function at Oppy was responsible for the talent that was brought into the organization and how that talent fit into the culture of the company. The recognition that culture and fit were core to the function of human resources was the spark that led to the transition away from human resources and toward people and culture.

"I said if... this is what's happening here, then they need to be responsible as guardians of that culture," explains John Anderson, chairman, CEO, and managing partner at Oppy and a 2017 Canada's Most Admired CEO award winner. "Obviously I have that responsibility as CEO, but I want to make sure that they are really feeling responsible for the culture of the organization. So we put the two of those together, and I think it was really well received."[5]

Fostering individuality and autonomy in the workplace while hiring people to demonstrate the behaviours that best represent the culture of an organization and allow it to succeed is no easy task. It requires a deep understanding of the organization's culture, as well as the ability to coach individuals who have their own gifts, talents, passions, and purpose. In short, it requires seeing employees as people rather than resources.

So, culturepreneurs need to look at training to develop our own leadership skills. I see this all the time with Waterstone's Building High Performance Teams and Cultures program. We use a four-module process of change management through which organizations align their culture, team, and business strategy to drive peak performance. It's hard work, and some leaders struggle more than others to incorporate transparency, trust, safety, and recognition into their style. (We'll be discussing these qualities in detail in the coming chapters.) Part of the reason that I'm so passionate about the process is that I've seen it work again and again. Leaders who put in the work get results.

For many of us, managing in a more individualized way requires a shift in thinking, and that means putting in the hard work to become a different kind of high performance leader.

The takeaway:
Culturepreneurs unlock the power of the individual

- Just as you don't approach interactions with your kids, friends, or colleagues uniformly, you can no longer approach your interactions with team members as if one size fits all. You must adapt your style to account for the individual needs of your team members or else risk losing the battle for high performance talent.

- In a self-directed, self-serve world, autonomy and variety in work are valued more than ever.

- Culturepreneurial leadership focuses on connecting each team member's purpose and meaning to the organization and vice versa.

- Leaders need to be so on top of their people's hopes, needs, desires, and passions (both in business and in life) that they become the true connectors of the organization.

5

BALANCING PEOPLE AND PERFORMANCE

"Employees these days expect less of a separation of work and personal life. That doesn't mean that work tasks should encroach upon our personal time, but it does mean that employees today expect more from the companies for whom they work."

MARC BENIOFF, founder, chairman,
and CEO of Salesforce

Mr. Lube is an incredibly successful franchise in Canada. Since opening its first location in Edmonton, Alberta, in 1976, the company has grown into "Canada's largest quick lube brand" and has become "a complete automotive maintenance service provider."[1] Early on, the leadership at Mr. Lube adopted a "one life" philosophy for their people, and it continues to be a cornerstone of the organization's culture. The idea is that people's lives include both personal and professional responsibilities—presentations need to be made and sales targets need to be met, but pets also need to go to the vet and kids need to get to lessons, and there are only so many hours in a day to do it all.

Stuart Suls, president and CEO at Mr. Lube, was ahead of his time when he introduced the one life philosophy in 2009. He understood that supporting his team in finding balance between work and life would be key to the organization's success. And it worked.

Balance versus integration

Our role as leaders is to help individuals find their own passions, give them the autonomy to do their work, and support them in achieving their goals. Why? Because it's the right thing to do. It positively impacts culture, and it helps people balance their personal and professional lives. A 2017 survey of 400 Canadians working in an office environment found that 58 percent felt job-related stress daily.[2] If we believe that work can be the cause of great stress or, on the flip side, great fulfillment, then the relationship between organizations and their people takes on a lot of importance. In fact, it makes them interdependent. We need to be careful, though, not to confuse that interdependency with a responsibility for the whole of an employee's life.

When I was a teenager, I once asked my father, "What are your passions?" His response: "I love to work." I didn't understand his response at the time, but I get it now. I'm the same way. But just because I *can* work all the time doesn't mean that I *should* work all the time; nor does it mean I can or should expect the same level of immersion in the job from my team.

The reality is that my balance is probably different from your balance. My team may look at me answering emails at

A leader's role is to help individuals find their passions, give them the autonomy to do their work, and support them in achieving their goals.

seven a.m. or taking client meetings at seven p.m., or conducting candidate interviews on a Sunday, and think, "What
is he talking about, balance?" But that's what works for me.
And it took me some time to convince people, among them
my wife, Tanya, that I don't expect that same kind of time
spent on work from anyone else. Because for me, it's not work,
it's my passion.

As people focus more on finding purposeful work that they
connect to, and as the where, when, and how of work change,
language is shifting away from balance and toward integration. Balance implies evenness—maybe that's not about work
and time off taking up the same amount of space in a schedule,
but it's certainly about designating times for work, and about
work activities not seeping into non-work hours. Integration
suggests customization to meet the needs of individuals as
well as the organization. And I include the organization here
because, in the discussion of balance versus integration, leaders must consider the impact on the organization as a whole.
Most people are not interested in choosing between balance
and integration but want the two ideas to work together in a
way that meets their needs.

At Waterstone, we have an unlimited vacation policy.
Team members can take the time they need to rest and
recharge, to attend to personal responsibilities, or to simply take a day to reset. I firmly believe that individuals know
what's best for themselves, and that our people should have
the flexibility to self-direct when it comes to time off. I also
firmly believe that time off cannot negatively affect the outcomes of the firm or other team members. Those who want
balance may have to do more pre-planning to ensure that
they can effectively turn off without disrupting their projects;

those who are comfortable with integration may check emails or take the occasional call during time off, but their planning can be more fluid. The organization as a whole supports both options, and it's up to each team member to determine what works for their style and needs.

At the root of this concept is understanding the impact that we have on others without trying to disrupt their lives. And so balance and integration are individualized. The challenge facing leaders is to understand the needs of team members and empower them to find a formula for more happiness, productivity, and fulfillment.

Modelling behaviour

Whether you personally seek balance or integration, it's key that you model the behaviours you want to see in your team—or rather that you empower your team to choose the model that works best for them. In many ways, this will get easier as work-from-home and flexible scheduling becomes the norm in offices across the globe. At the same time, transparency is even more important when behaviours cannot be observed as they are in traditional, in-person office settings.

For example, if employee wellness is a core element of your values and your culture, then your employees need to see and hear health and wellness happening around them. If employees don't see their leaders making time for health and wellness, they won't feel empowered to make that time themselves. So, it needs to become part of the conversation to say, "Hey, you know what? I feel so much better when I work out between eleven o'clock and one o'clock. So I'm going to be offline three days a week during that time."

I've been working with Greg Wells for four years. Wells is a scientist and a performance physiologist focused on helping high performance individuals (including elite athletes and CEOs of top-performing organizations) elevate their lives at work and beyond. His four books, *Superbodies, The Ripple Effect, The Focus Effect*, and *Rest, Refocus, Recharge*, have inspired me and transformed where, when, and how I work.

One of Wells's philosophies that has become core to my approach as a leader is taking radical control of my day. "So often we are on other people's agendas, and we do busy work instead of important work," he explains. "I want us to, as leaders, make sure that we are doing what is important and what we want to be doing so that we can get done what needs to get done. [That's] not to say that you shouldn't take phone calls or check your email or anything like that, but I believe we need to block things . . . When you are trying to do your best at whatever it is that you're doing—when you're trying to perform, when you're trying to focus, when you're trying to get something done, when you're trying to be creative—defend your attention."[3] Cal Newport explores a similar idea in his book *Deep Work*. A professor of computer science at Georgetown University in Washington, DC, Newport defines deep work as work done with undistracted focus on a cognitively demanding task (shallow work being non-cognitive, logistical, or minor duties that can be performed in a state of distraction).[4] And just like Wells, Newport advocates for a level of mindful flexibility when setting your day: "Your goal is not to stick to a given schedule at all costs; it's instead to maintain, at all times, a thoughtful say in what you're doing with your time going forward—even if these decisions are reworked again and again as the day unfolds."[5]

There is scientific evidence explaining why you can more easily accomplish certain tasks at certain points during the day, and I recommend picking up Wells's *Rest, Refocus, Recharge* if you're interested in learning more, but blocking out your day comes down to this: take the time to figure out when you are at your best for certain activities and when you have the ability to easily achieve certain goals, then build your day around those landmarks.

In theory, my day starts with nutrition early in the morning, followed by time for mindfulness and meditation. Early in the morning I do more creative work, because that's when I'm in a more creative frame of mind. Power work, where I add value to the projects I'm working on, happens in the late morning and early to mid-afternoon, and then I focus on projects that require less creativity but more energy in the afternoon.

As leaders, we need to understand not only our own patterns but also the patterns of our team members. We need to ask, "What works best for Judy, for Carlos, for Syd?" and then work with each of them to design schedules that play to their strengths, work around their individual rhythms and needs, and allow them to feel at their best and most productive. Yes, there will be client meetings or last-minute emergencies that won't fit the plan, but empowering yourself and your team to play into everyone's patterns and strengths will drive individual productivity and make your team feel supported.

Human and high performance

When I talk about high performance cultures and balancing the needs of the organization with the needs of its employees,

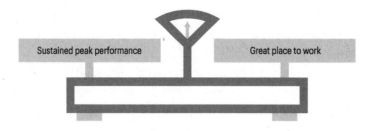

Figure 1. The High Performance Culture Scale

I will often use the image of a scale with "sustained peak performance" on one side and "great place to work" on the other. If you put too much weight on one side, you end up running a sweat shop; too much weight on the other side and you end up running a country club. The key to success is finding that sweet spot where you're meeting or exceeding the goals of the organization while also meeting the needs of your team.

One organization doing this really well is Vancouver-based Clio, a legal technology company building cloud-based and client-centred solutions that better serve lawyers and their clients. Clio has built a corporate culture that focuses equally on the needs of its people and the goals of the business—not an easy balance for many organizations. "[We aspire to be] what we call a human and high performing organization," explains Jack Newton, co-founder and CEO of Clio and a 2020 Canada's Most Admired CEO award winner. "[We want to have] one of the highest performing cultures, [and to be] one of the highest performing organizations, in the world."[6]

Unfortunately, because of stories about people crying in their cubicles or quickly burning out and being replaced by new bodies, high performance technology companies had developed a bit of a reputation for being all about the outputs and viewing their employees as commodities. That was not the culture that Newton and his co-founder, Rian Gauvreau, wanted to create. They didn't want to lose sight of the humanity of the people they brought on board.

"Our vision is that we can actually have both, a high performing, high impact organization that is accommodating the needs of its employees in the process," says Newton. "To me, what's at the heart of actually succeeding... is being a deliberately developmental organization that is really plugging in and supporting [our] staff in stepping up to the challenges... that the company is throwing at them. The idea is, we're going to throw some big audacious challenges at [our people]. We're expecting [our people] to work hard and step up to those challenges, but [we're going to provide] a whole suite of support systems to [help our people] step up and succeed at those challenges."[7]

To do that, Clio developed a series of tools, including a custom leadership development program called Basecamp. Open to everyone at Clio, Basecamp was designed to provide participants with a core set of skills that the organization determined would be essential in helping navigate its high performance environment. They also brought in a dedicated internal coach who works with team members on accelerating their growth, enhancing their performance, and tapping into new skills required for future roles.

Finally, Clio's well-established feedback process (based on a concept that Kim Scott popularized in her book *Radical Candor*, a book which every new hire at Clio receives) ensures that both employees and the organization are getting ongoing honest, actionable, and respectful feedback about where and how they can improve.[8]

As leaders, when we see people struggle, either physically or emotionally, it may be that they need a change or that they're feeling like one side of the scale is getting too much weight. One-off or occasional lapses in energy or behaviour can be addressed, although it may take time or be uncomfortable. Chronic lapses in energy or behaviour may signal that you're dealing with someone who is no longer in the right role or the right organization, and who ultimately needs to be coached up or coached out.

The focus on mental health

The topic of mental health has been shrouded in stigma for so long, but it is finally coming into the mainstream and it needs to be addressed in any high performance organization. It's been incredible to see the increase, over just a few short years, in how many of the companies nominated for the Canada's Most Admired Corporate Cultures awards now highlight what they do to support the mental health of their teams. In 2013, 7.3 percent of the nominated companies mentioned mental health in their submission to the awards program; in 2020, that number had risen to 43.7 percent.

Very few of us will become mental health experts, but we all need to educate ourselves about mental health and understand that this issue affects everyone on some level. As leaders, we need to be comfortable engaging in discussions about how we are feeling and accept that if an individual on our team needs help, we have a responsibility to help them access the resources and the support they need. And we need to understand that turning a blind eye has consequences not just for our people but for our organization. In fact, the Centre for Addiction and Mental Health (CAMH), located in Toronto, reports that 30 percent of disability claims and 70 percent of disability costs are due to mental health issues, and that by 2041, the cumulative costs attributable to mental illness will top $2.5 trillion. As CAMH's "Workplace Mental Health Playbook for Business Leaders" notes, "Prioritizing and addressing mental health in the workplace is the right thing to do for your employees, and for your bottom line. When done effectively, the potential impacts to your business include higher performance, lower absenteeism, and reduced disability costs." [9]

Start by fostering a culture that makes it safe to have conversations about mental health, one where it's okay to say, "You know what? I need a mental health day." Or "Look, I don't want to get into the details, but is there someplace I can go, resources I can access?" Then make sure that you, your human resources team, and all your people-leaders know what resources are available to your team—or at least where to look for them. Many organizations offer Employee Assistance Plans (EAPs) with anonymous access, or onsite mental health professionals. CAMH's "Workplace Mental Health Playbook for Business Leaders" is a great place to start; it provides tools for more effective solutions and better outcomes for employees and for businesses.

Most of us are not as educated as we could or should be when it comes to mental health and the impact it has on our organizations, but if we can keep an open mind, if we can look at mental health as fundamentally the same thing as physical health, our systems will catch up and our mindsets will grow and change.

For the culturepreneur, this means always remembering that your team's success is generated by its people. Your job is to empower your team to choose a model of work that best meets their individual needs while still driving organizational performance, and to build a culture of open discussions about physical and emotional challenges that are met with acceptance and support.

The takeaway:
People-first thinking drives performance

- Some team members will aim for work-life balance, while others will be comfortable with work-life integration. Leaders who can accommodate both options will empower their team members and drive higher levels of productivity and fulfillment.

- High performance leaders model the behaviours they want to see in their team members.

- Leaders within high performance organizations need to become adept at accessing, in real time, the physical and mental energy of their team members, ensuring that it's being properly directed.

- Culturepreneurs find the balance between providing a great place to work and driving sustained performance. Put another way, they find ways of meeting the needs of the organization and of the team. This balance will differ by organization and maybe even by team.

- Adopting a people-first mindset and establishing open communication channels develop a culture of positive energy, where team members feel connected to the organization and driven to perform, and where they also feel safe to share issues, whether professional or personal, when they hit a rough patch.

- Make it okay to talk about mental health in the workplace, and ensure your people-leaders know the internal and external resources available for team members.

6

THE WHY AND HOW OF MEASURING CULTURE

"Employees who believe that management is concerned about them as a whole person—not just as an employee—are more productive, more satisfied, more fulfilled. Satisfied employees mean satisfied customers, which leads to profitability."

ANNE M. MULCAHY, former chairperson and CEO, Xerox Corporation

Like many kids who grew up in the 1970s, I had what I'll call an outcome-focused upbringing. My mother was a teacher. When I came home from school, after she asked how my day was and heard my stories from the schoolyard, she would turn the conversation to academic matters: How had I done on a certain test? Did I think I could have done better? How could I have achieved more? I was also very involved in sports growing up, and so I was always looking at scorecards, win-loss records, and what I could do to improve my performance the next time I was on the ice or the field.

When it comes to my own parenting style, outcomes are important, but my wife and I also raised our kids in a contribution-focused world, where participation medals were handed out to everyone and succeeding was often secondary to satisfaction and personal contributions. So, we occasionally had to adapt the way we motivated our kids and celebrated their achievements.

If leaders are going to unlock the potential in our people and motivate them to perform, we have to adapt not only our approach but also the way we measure results. Fundamental to this change is understanding that culture measurement needs to account for both quantitative and qualitative data.

In *Culture Connection*, I dedicated a whole chapter to what I called the "Know Thyself" principle. The idea is that to meaningfully change an organization, you first need a deep understanding of what makes that organization tick. Ten years ago, I recommended that you should start with a frank assessment of your organization's existing culture, the articulation of your culture, and the identification of the behaviours that are embodied by your high performers. I call it the Four-Step Qualitative Cultural Assessment.[1] It's still an important process.

Knowing thyself is all about authenticity, and to be authentic you need to start with a diagnostic tool that will give you a good understanding of where you are today. You also need to understand where you want to be as an organization and put in place the tools and processes to measure your movement toward that goal over time. (Refer to Waterstone's Culturepreneur Operating System outlined in chapter 8 for more about assessing and curating your culture.)

The Four-Step Qualitative Cultural Assessment

Step 1: Discuss existing behaviours and practices with the CEO and the HR leader.

Step 2: Review business plans and corporate strategy documents.

Step 3: Observe behaviour. Meet with the members of the executive team and with top performers across functions, divisions, locations, and organizational events to ascertain their business practices and current behavioural themes.

Step 4: Perform gap analytics and present recommendations for moving the culture to its desired state.[2]

Beyond return on investment and key performance indicators, two key metrics have become common touchstones for organizations: employee engagement and corporate culture. Engagement is important, and it's about attitude and feeling—how your people feel at a particular point in time. When you measure engagement, you're looking at how people feel about the organization, their leader, their role, and so on. Culture, on the other hand, is all about behaviour, in particular behaviours that drive outcomes. When you measure culture, the questions tend to be more specific to what people are doing and how they believe culture is influencing their performance.

Culture is all about behaviours that drive outcomes.

At Waterstone, we help organizations measure and assess their corporate culture through a service we call Waterstone ENGAGE. The idea is to set a baseline that organizations can measure against annually and to equip leaders with actionable data about employee engagement (feelings), corporate culture (behaviours), and the level of trust (psychological safety) in the organization. Employees of Waterstone ENGAGE clients participate in one-on-one meetings with our team, during which we learn how the employees currently define the corporate culture as well as common business practices and behavioural themes (real and desired). For example, we might ask about how things are done, measured, and rewarded and about the pace of the workplace. We provide qualitative results in the form of verbatim feedback in our final report to the client. And through these interviews, we also identify areas that we can customize, or dive deeper into, in the quantitative survey.

The Waterstone ENGAGE survey emerged from years of research—specifically from a detailed analysis of the data collected from hundreds of submissions to the Canada's Most Admired Corporate Cultures awards program since it was launched in 2005. The ENGAGE survey also draws on our in-depth expertise into leading trends in employee motivation and engagement through our human capital consulting practice. The result of our ongoing research is that we have identified ten behavioural culture drivers that have the most impact on results in best-in-class organizations:

1   ownership/accountability
2   collaboration/teamwork
3   customer focus

4 competitiveness
5 innovation/agility
6 growth
7 work environment
8 clarity of leadership communication/organizational purpose
9 people focus
10 corporate social responsibility/environmental sustainability

In addition, we measure employee engagement and trust as key components of organizational health and performance.

Together the qualitative and quantitative data gathered through the Waterstone ENGAGE process provide a more holistic view of how an organization can emphasize its strengths in culture and employee engagement, and how it can close gaps to drive higher levels of performance.

The rise of the pulse survey

Traditionally, organizations have approached people measurement through employee attitude or engagement surveys that are an annual or biannual exercise. They are typically longer and primarily quantitative; when feelings and opinions are needed, qualitative focus groups might take place. The data collected is analyzed, hopefully actioned, and then reviewed and/or remeasured after twelve, eighteen, or even twenty-four months.

But when you want to transition your culture, you need more regular, diverse feedback about if and how you're moving the needle in the right direction. To do that, organizations are starting to take the pulse of their stakeholders more frequently and pragmatically. Pulse surveys are more specific in terms of measuring the behaviours that organizations are aiming for, which may be those they believe will have the biggest impact on performance.

I often compare the measurement process to a health assessment—your annual physical tells you where you're at with your health overall and can help you set goals for the coming year (lose weight, lower blood pressure, and so on), but you need to step on the scale or sit down at the blood pressure machine in the pharmacy on a regular basis to get a sense of how you're progressing toward your goals. That progress isn't going to be linear, and that's okay. What's important is that you're doing the check-ins regularly and that you're celebrating the small changes that drive results, or course correcting when needed.

Transitioning from an annual survey culture to a pulse survey culture requires that leaders shift their mindset. You need to develop a measurement plan that includes both annual or semi-annual surveys and pulse surveys, and you need to get your team into a rhythm so that they know what's being measured and when—but be careful that you're not so rigid that your team doesn't feel empowered to add or remove a survey as needed.

Reliance Home Comfort, a provider of home heating and cooling systems based in Toronto, Ontario, brilliantly transformed its approach to measurement a few years ago. When Sean O'Brien joined the operation as CEO, he engaged Waterstone for an in-depth cultural assessment to get a sense for how Reliance's people—across all locations, functions, and levels—were feeling. He used the cultural assessment to understand the foundational pieces of the corporate culture that would be important to protect and grow, the areas where change was happening organically, and the areas they could focus on to drive culture transformation. "I remember the culture when I joined was friendly, family, service, customer, comfortable—something along those lines," says O'Brien, a 2016 Canada's Most Admired CEO award winner. "Two years later, it was fast-paced, growth-orientated, reward, recognition, friendly."[3]

By focusing on two or three key recommendations that emerged from the cultural assessment, Reliance Home Comfort transformed from a friendly, comfortable place to work into a great high performance place to develop a career. Not everyone liked the change, but it put the organization on a path toward its goals of growth and performance. The next step was to start more frequent check-ins, using pulse surveys, conversations, and social collaboration tools like Yammer to augment annual surveys. This commitment to measurement signalled that the organization was not simply content to grow but was focused on understanding its journey.

"We kept the core things that made us special, and then we elevated the things we needed to get after as an organization. And I'm really proud about what we've done as an organization: keep it simple, try to eliminate hierarchies," says O'Brien. "I like to have my hands on, not as a micromanager, but about evaluating. 'Are we doing the right things? Are the messages that come from HR, are they getting down to Jeff on the truck? Are the messages that come from sales getting all the way out to Scott?' It's really simple, simple things, and it becomes very powerful."[4] The results have been impressive. Between 2015 and 2018, Reliance's market share in the HVAC space grew

5 percent, and its customer satisfaction numbers have gone up steadily; its Net Promoter Score has grown to 69 in 2018 (from 52 in 2015) for sales, and to 59 (from 34 in 2015) for service. The company's revenue has seen a similar upward trend, with a 23.6 percent increase in 2015 over 2014, and consistent growth year-over-year ever since.[5]

Listening

Don't disregard the importance of informal pulses—(virtual) water cooler conversations, town hall meetings, or the small talk that happens at the beginning and end of your meetings. These are excellent opportunities for leaders to listen to what's on the minds of their teams.

Listening is central to the corporate culture at PointClick-Care. In addition to traditional surveys and focus groups, which help the company's leadership collect feedback from a cross-section of teams, they also actively engage in grassroots listening activities to ensure they understand what's on the minds of their team members. Co-founder and CEO Mike Wessinger points to the organization's open concept office as one way they've made leaders accessible, but they also proactively seek out listening opportunities.

"If you're having a conversation with somebody [who is maybe] brand new to your organization, when they say, 'Hey, I really love the culture here,' go, 'Well, what do you love about it? What would you change? What would you keep?'" says Wessinger. "Then just going down to the cafeteria and . . . sitting there, just grabbing a seat and just having a conversation. Try to get as grassroots as possible. I mean, as the CEO, you might intimidate people. I might not always get something other than a packaged answer, but hopefully if you break down those barriers over time, you'll get good, honest responses from people."[6]

The rise of social collaboration tools in the workplace has notably affected our ability to listen. While they're meant to stimulate communication, conversation, and the tracking of discussions rather than to measure culture, these tools and the data they generate are a great resource for leaders looking for new sources of information about employee attitudes. A 2020 article, "The New Analytics of Culture," in *Harvard Business Review* looked at the pervasive "'digital traces' of culture in electronic communications, such as emails, Slack messages, and Glassdoor reviews." By evaluating the way employees communicated with each other, the authors could see culture at work and better understand what was on the minds of various stakeholder groups, without having to formally survey for opinions:

> The explosion of digital trace data such as emails and Slack communications—together with the availability of computational methods that are faster, cheaper, and easier to use—has ushered in a new scientific approach to measuring culture . . . We believe that with appropriate measures to safeguard employee privacy and minimize algorithmic bias it holds great promise as a tool for managers grappling with culture issues in their firms.[7]

Qualitative analytics are proving to be vital for measuring culture and engagement among employee groups. With collaboration tools and technology evolving, and the need for connection among teams growing, this type of data will receive the same (or greater) weight as the quantitative data that has been at the centre of measurement for decades.

Actioning

Just as important as measuring culture and listening is how you follow through on feedback. In fact, communication is as important, if not more important, than actioning feedback, especially in organizations that do more frequent pulses.

If you survey frequently, you will be consistently inundated with data about a variety of topics. Interpreting that information and determining what is actionable and what's important to share but doesn't require action is a key part of a leader's job. It's vital that your team knows you've heard them—whether you communicate back that you've heard them and are doing something about an issue or you say, "Hey, this is something new. We are going to keep listening, and if it continues to be an issue, we will take action." It's important that leaders are receptive to what they're hearing, without being defensive. Don't act out of emotion.

When the COVID-19 pandemic forced Waterstone's team to begin working from home in March 2020, I wanted a way to keep our team connected and so I implemented a daily "huddle" meeting for all staff. These quick morning check-ins were meant as a way to engage with the team, similar to bumping into colleagues in the kitchen while getting our morning coffees and sharing our plans for the day. A few months into working from home, I was told that these huddles were no longer meeting their objectives and that the team wanted to end them. I'd observed declining interest over a number of weeks, and the feedback was supported by several team members. I also knew that our team had numerous other touchpoints that were meeting the initial goal of connection. It was feedback to act on. The daily meetings ended in August 2020, and neither productivity nor collaboration has suffered.

As a culturepreneur, you need to understand where you want to be as an organization and implement the tools and processes to measure your movement toward that goal over time. You need to rethink measurement as an annual activity and see it as an ongoing series of check-ins that keep you on track and identify issues that need to be addressed. And you need to embrace a balance of quantitative and qualitative data to ensure you're getting the most holistic picture possible.

The takeaway:
Measuring culture is about more than just data

- Measurement is about using established quantitative and qualitative methods and enhancing them with technology and digital collaboration tools to ensure that the organization is moving productively toward its goals.

- Employee engagement (how your people are feeling) and corporate culture (what your people are doing and how that drives outcomes) are key metrics for organizations, and tracking both on a regular basis is vital when transforming your culture.

- Social collaboration tools like Slack and Yammer can improve your ability not just to stimulate conversations but also to listen to what's happening within your organization and to informally gain insight into employee attitudes.

- Acting on feedback from measurement surveys is important, especially in organizations doing frequent pulses. But understanding when not to action feedback and instead to keep listening, to distinguish between trends and blips, is equally important.

- Culturepreneurs use the data that they collect as part of their measurement activities to motivate themselves and the team, to inform new targets, and to celebrate successes.

7

CLARITY OF VISION AND LEADERSHIP COMMUNICATION

"The single biggest problem in communication is the illusion that it has taken place."

GEORGE BERNARD SHAW, Irish playwright and literary critic

For the culturepreneur, communication is the thread that ties everything together. Clear communication requires understanding how you work and what lens you (knowingly or unknowingly) use to view the world so that you can effectively communicate your vision to your team. The real challenge for leaders is to leverage our individual strengths, while meeting the communication needs of our teams.

I didn't do a behavioural profile until I was in my early thirties. When I finally completed the assessment and the results were explained to me, I felt liberated. Here was proof that supported my thoughts about what I enjoyed doing and believed I was good at—suddenly I understood why some behaviours came naturally to me and others didn't. I wasn't mechanically inclined, and that's why I was never comfortable with a hammer, not because I simply wasn't good at wielding a hammer. I wanted to share the results of my first profile with everyone. My response was pretty similar to how I imagine it would be to see your reflection for the first time in a pool of water: *This is me. It's who I am.* And it left me wondering why I'd waited so long to explore this type of tool.

In chapter 6, I talked about what I called the "Know Thyself" principle, the idea that to make any meaningful change in an organization, you first have to deeply understand what makes it tick. But knowing thyself goes beyond the organization—as a leader, you also need to know what makes you tick as an individual: your purpose, your strengths, and your weaknesses. To adapt your thinking and embody the five key attributes of a culturepreneurial leader (which I'll discuss in detail in coming chapters), knowing thyself is paramount, especially when it comes to clarity of vision and communication.

Leaders, in many ways, have to be both filters and funnels. We have to filter what's relevant to our team members without trying to shield them. Thanks to the various media channels available today, we all have access to an incredible amount of information, which comes at us from all directions, 24/7. The real challenge here is to simplify the message and communicate with our individual strengths through a variety of media. This is key because the makeup of our teams is so diverse—from digital pioneers, who are comfortable in the digital world but still crave in-person connections, to digital natives, who grew up with digital technology, are confident with digital tools, and may not need in-person connection in the same way as other generations.

Diagnostic tools

The first step is to understand your own communication style. Start with a behavioural profile that articulates your natural tendencies and how others will view them. For example, at Waterstone, we use DISC profiles in both our internal and external recruiting, because our view is that if you don't understand what drives your actions and behaviours, cultivating positive growth is difficult. This simple tool helps us get to know first ourselves and then others by measuring four key qualities:

Dominance. This measures how you typically react to problems.

Influencing. This measures how you relate to people.

Steadiness. This measures how you adapt to pace.

Compliance. This measures how you behave relative to process or procedure.

At Waterstone, we believe that by understanding your own and others' DISC profiles, you will raise your self-awareness and your understanding of others' natural behaviours, improve teamwork and collaboration, make conflict more productive (or avoidable), increase empathy and understanding, and lead more effectively. As an example, you'll see a snapshot of my DISC profile on page 89. It describes a pioneering and determined person who enjoys people and who trusts easily. It reflects the fact that I am extroverted and optimistic, that I prefer a pressure-oriented and changing schedule and work that allows me to follow my own path (which is often not linear or systematic). All of this is good information to have if you're working with me on a project, looking to bring me into a team, or getting ready to pitch an idea to me or my organization.

Another tool we use frequently is the Trust Triangle, which was developed by Frances Frei, UPS Foundation professor of service management at Harvard, and the former senior vice president, leadership and strategy at Uber. The concept is that trust has three drivers: authenticity, logic, and empathy: "People tend to trust you when they believe they are interacting with the real you (authenticity), when they have faith in your judgment and competence (logic), and when they feel that you care about them (empathy). When trust is lost, it can almost always be traced back to a breakdown in one of these three drivers."[1] Frei calls this breakdown a "trust wobble" and notes that if you identify your wobble, you've pinpointed the trust driver most likely to cause you issues.

Empathy is my wobble. To compensate, I have to check in with my audience more than some other leaders—to ask if my people are getting what they need from our meeting or if I've understood what they said and meant. If authenticity is your wobble, it helps to use feelings, to start with saying, "Here's how I'm feeling about this." Another tool to combat an authenticity wobble is to speak only about what you know, which is sometimes hard for leaders because it's not like we know more than anybody else, even if the expectation is that we do. If logic is your wobble, start with your point. Be like a newscaster: "Fourth-quarter financials released today show a 20 percent increase in sales revenue for our company." The release of financials is the headline. Then tell everyone how it's relevant to them. But, as Frei explains, "For most logic wobblers, however, rigor isn't the issue. Much of the time,

Driving	Inspiring	Relaxed	Cautious
Ambitious	Magnetic	Passive	Careful
Pioneering	Enthusiastic	Patient	Exacting
Strong-willed	Persuasive	Possessive	Systematic
Determined	Convincing	Predictable	Accurate
Competitive	Poised	Consistent	Open-minded
Decisive	Optimistic	Steady	Balanced judgment
Venturesome	Trusting	Stable	Diplomatic
Dominance	**Influencing**	**Steadiness**	**Compliance**
Calculating	Reflective	Mobile	Firm
Cooperative	Factual	Active	Independent
Hesitant	Calculating	Restless	Self-willed
Cautious	Skeptical	Impatient	Obstinate
Agreeable	Logical	Pressure-oriented	Unsystematic
Modest	Suspicious	Eager	Uninhibited
Peaceful	Matter-of-fact	Flexible	Arbitrary
Unobtrusive	Incisive	Impulsive	Unbending

Figure 2. Marty Parker's DISC Profile (Profile prepared by Excel Group Development—Building Performance, xlteamwork.com, copyright © 1984–2017, Target Training International, Ltd.)

the problem is the perception of wobbly logic rather than the reality of it. Why does this happen? Because they're not communicating their ideas effectively."[2]

The Trust Triangle framework and other similar tools establish an understanding of how you communicate, so that you can adjust and improve your quality of communication.

Custom communications

I've said it before, and it bears repeating: culturepreneurial leaders need to focus on the individual needs and styles of their team members. You've got to know how to focus on your message and use the medium that best suits your audience—truly understanding how individuals on your team learn and communicate, then adapting your style to connect with them.

A great place to start is by understanding common learning styles:

Visual. These learners respond best to information presented in "maps, spider diagrams, charts, graphs, flow charts, labelled diagrams," and other visual representations of information.

Aural/auditory. These learners prefer to hear information.

Read/write. These learners best process information displayed as words.

Kinesthetic. These learners learn through the experience of doing something and value their own experiences more than the experiences of others.[3]

When you understand how your team members best learn, you can tailor your communications to improve the likelihood that your message will be heard. For example, you may need to provide diagrams for your visual learners, host a town hall or share a podcast for your aural/auditory learners, send a memo for your read/write learners, and include a case study or reference another past effort to connect with your kinesthetic learners. This is asking a lot of leaders, but the results will be incredible.

Michael McCain, whom we talked about in chapter 1, used to write a weekly update for the whole of Maple Leaf Foods.[4] He did town halls and one-on-one conversations, too, but the weekly letter was important from an alignment standpoint, because it focused the team and helped them understand him a bit better. It became a vital tool as the organization went through a large transformation—not only to keep McCain on message but to ensure his team members had one more touchpoint with him that met their communication needs.

Being consistent is important. Figure out not only how to stay true to your messages but also how to communicate them in a way that connects with various stakeholders. Especially now, you need a combination of tools to ensure your message is clear and that it gets across.

Communication in practice

The executive team at Reliance Home Comfort spends a lot of time and effort on communication, and they've learned the value of customizing their efforts to support their message and meet the needs of their various team members.

"We ... realized that as an organization you can talk about things, but humans like to see things, we love to touch things, we love to smell things. And what we did is we spent some time really working on giving back to the organization to support what we're trying to do," explains Sean O'Brien. Early on in his tenure as president and CEO, O'Brien presented to the leaders of the organization. His message was about the value of double-digit growth and some of the intangible things organizations gain when they are in growth mode, such as community investment. "And I remember the audience; they all looked at me like I was crazy," says O'Brien. "Because here's a business that was growing year over year, life was good. And now this guy shows up and he wants to grow it at double-digit rates."[5]

The first month that the company hit double digits—10 percent in a month—O'Brien received a call from their private equity owners. They understood what he was trying to accomplish, they were seeing the results of his efforts, and they were on board with his plans. He'd communicated his plan for business growth to the team, as well as the role that the team would play in achieving the big picture goals, through town hall meetings, the development of an Office of the President that was responsible for replying to all email or phone queries from clients and team members, and by mandating that top leadership, including O'Brien himself, connect in person with team members on the front lines. He'd worked with his team to execute, bringing in new vehicles, new uniforms, new training, and new technology for the frontline team members. And the results followed.

"If you communicate so everyone understands what we do, [where we are going], what we have to execute on, my role in the big picture, my value in the big picture, you're unstoppable."[6]

Clarity of vision starts with understanding your own style and how you want to communicate. For culturepreneurs, that means embracing clarity and focus in your communications. We can't always pull people into an in-person meeting to ensure that our messages reach the team. Instead, we need to use different channels to communicate consistently. Create a focused communication style playing to your strengths while also meeting the communication needs of your team.

The takeaway:
Communication is about more than the message

- Behavioural profiles are useful for raising your awareness of your own style and building a better understanding of the natural behaviours of your team. The results can improve collaboration, increase empathy, and support conflict resolution. Behavioural profiles can help you become a better leader.

- Leaders need to filter relevant information for team members without trying to shield them and to use their own strengths as well a variety of media to ensure that the message is customized to and received by people of all learning styles.

- Culturepreneurial leaders ensure everyone understands what they are doing, where they are going, what they have to execute on, and what their role and value is in the big picture.

PART 3

CULTURE AS STRATEGY

8

WATERSTONE'S CULTUREPRENEUR OPERATING SYSTEM

"When a culture is broken, the cracks show—morale is weakened, but so is profit and performance. That's why culture has to be at the core of any business transformation."

PEGGY JOHNSON, CEO, Magic Leap, former executive vice president of business development, Microsoft

---

You transition to a culturepreneurial process by using it as a business system—planning, developing a strategy, and setting measurable objectives and tactics to get you to the outcomes you desire. At Waterstone, we call this the Culturepreneur Operating System. Let's say you wanted to get from a $50 million business to a $100 million business in three years. Traditional thinking would advise you to sell more stuff, measure your progress against your goal on a regular basis, and adjust the people, processes, and systems as needed.

Waterstone's Culturepreneur Operating System starts with culture. So, when you consider that objective of doubling business in three years, the first question isn't "How do we grow our revenue?" The questions are:

- How do we create a culture that supports the doubling of our business?

- What does that culture look like?

- How do we want it to feel in this culture?

- How do we want people to behave?

- Do we have the right people in the right roles to support that change?

When you put culture at the centre of everything you do, it becomes the first thing you look at when you're determining how to meet your objectives.

Think of it like buying a house. If you need a four-bedroom house, you don't look at every four-bedroom house on the market. You start by asking yourself what your ideal house looks like—style, neighbourhood—and determining your budget. Culturepreneurs start by asking how they want to feel in the house, how they plan to behave in the house, and what will facilitate that behaviour. If you want to do a lot of entertaining, you're looking for an open concept four-bedroom house with a large kitchen and back deck. If you are planning to have one child, maybe you're only really looking for a three-bedroom house, but you want it to be in a neighbourhood with good schools, close to parks, maybe with a pool. You're still working to achieve your objective (home ownership), but now you're doing it through the lens of what makes you unique.

So, how do you do that? If you think in visual terms, imagine culture as competitive advantage at the centre of a wheel,

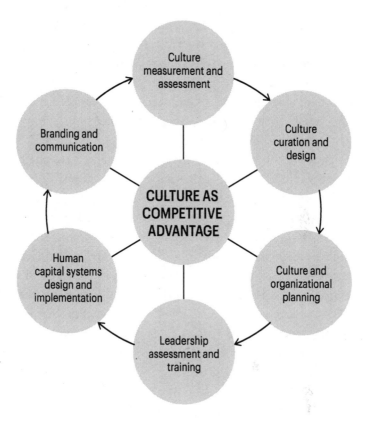

Figure 3. Waterstone's Culturepreneur Operating System

connected by spokes to the key elements of the operating system that work together as a whole, as in the diagram above.

Culture measurement and assessment

You start by understanding your current culture, because before you can know where you're going, you need to know

where you are. This is typically done with a culture and/
or engagement survey, which Waterstone calls a cultural
assessment—it's the best way to identify the behaviours that
are key to your culture and how your company works. I go
into significant detail about cultural assessments in *Culture
Connection*, but in short, a thorough assessment will help you
understand and define your existing culture—your Point A. It
needs to include a period of measurement and assessment,
which should involve a combination of quantitative data
(often an engagement or culture survey that's fairly recent
and includes latitudinal information) and qualitative information on your current state of culture and where leadership
believes the culture is today. I also recommend having qualitative discussions with non-leadership team members (for
example, your top performers across departments or specific team leads), because leadership's view on the subject
of culture can be overly optimistic and/or overly ambitious
and more focused on where they want to go versus where
things are.

There are a number of tools available to help you assess
your culture; the Waterstone ENGAGE program is just one
example. This is an annual employee survey program that
equips organizations with actionable data about their corporate culture, employee engagement, and the level of trust in
their organization. We typically start with one-on-one cultural
assessments to gather qualitative feedback and then customize the survey. We launch the survey to the full employee
group, using the data to develop a customized report that provides insight into a company's current culture and provides
recommendations against areas of strength and opportunity. By combining qualitative and quantitative data, we get

a holistic view of where a company is, so we can help the leadership envision and move toward where they want to be.

Culture curation and design

This step is sometimes called vision, because it's about looking ahead and sensing where you want to go. This is all about planning for the future—your Point B—not deciding how you're going to get there. How do you want the organization to look? To feel? Will the values be any different in the future than they are today? What words would you use to define your culture? What are the key behaviours of your top performers? At Waterstone, we call this process culture curation.

Waterstone's culture is one of a group of hard-working, high performers who are collaborative, true partners to our clients, imaginative, innovative, and trust-based professionals. Knowing that this is how we define our culture allows us to find the people and the causes that fit with our top performers. A solid definition of who we are and who we want to be lets us curate that culture.

One of the tools we often use for culture curation is the Painted Picture, which Brian Scudamore, founder and CEO of O2E Brands, created many years ago.[1] The exercise guides an executive team through a visualization of their culture in the future (typically three years out). We ask what they want to see, feel, and hear about their organization. We ask them to describe the ideal culture and how people will behave. It is enormously powerful and allows for executive teams to jump ahead to the place they want to be.

Culture curation is separate from assessment, and it's not your plan. It's about understanding where you are and framing where you want to be in the next months or years.

To know where you want to go, you have to see it, understand what it looks like, and imagine that place and why it is ideal for your organization.

Culture and organizational planning

Once you know where you are and where you want to be, it's time to start developing your plan. For this, we use something called a From/To plan, so we can chart the path from Point A to Point B. When you look at your cultural assessment and your culture curation together, sometimes the path becomes clear, and sometimes not, but it does help you break down the steps to move your culture toward your goal. At Waterstone, we suggest developing a three-year plan by starting from your goal and working your way back to the present. But how you create your plan is less important than the fact that you're laying out the steps necessary to reach your culture goal.

Think of it like planning a vacation. You know you want to go to Barcelona. You have imagined how Barcelona sounds and smells, and you can see yourself in the city streets, having coffee in a café, a drink in a bar, and enjoying dinner in the Raval district. Now you need to plan out your travel: Will you rent a car, use public transit, or join a tour group? What sites will you visit and which restaurants do you want to eat in? Will you fly direct or stop over in another country to see other sights? There are a myriad of options available to you and no right answer—your plan depends on your individual needs and goals.

Leadership assessment and training

Once you have your plan, it's time to assess what needs to change in order for you move forward with that plan.

The importance of leadership buy-in—senior leadership specifically—to this process cannot be overstated.

For many years, Waterstone has helped organizations assess and curate their culture, and we have provided recommendations for changes and system refinements to achieve their vision. Often, this requires leaders to change their behaviour, and sometimes it requires organizations to change their leaders. Because if you have leaders who don't buy in to the culture, or who are not up to leading in a way that is aligned with the change, then culture change will never occur. The focus from a leadership perspective at this point needs to be change management. In my experience, this often requires an exercise in "why." Why do we need to change? Why do we want to change? What happens if we don't change? And then, of course, how are we going to change? It takes real focus and attention from leaders, as well as a commitment to get there over time.

Change management also means we need to ensure we have the right people with the right skills and training to get us to our goal. And if not, then we need to either develop existing team members or make changes to the team.

Human capital systems design and implementation

Culturepreneurs need to identify and leverage supports that are in place (or that need to be put in place) to unlock the potential of people. That may be compensation; performance management; training systems like change management, onboarding processes, or technology supports; or other key measurements across the business. Whatever you identify as being central to supporting your people in doing their jobs, it needs to be updated and aligned to where you're going as opposed to where you are coming from.

My one caution here is to prioritize—don't try to accomplish everything all at once. It's one of the reasons I always recommend a three-year plan. Check in with your vision and your plan and determine what's vital in year one, what is important but can wait until year two, and what's a longer-lead item that can wait until year three. Determining how you will phase in your changes takes real thought. You won't get it right 100 percent of the time, but you want to set a pace at which you and your team can move forward in a constructive way.

Branding and communication

This may be the final step in Waterstone's Culturepreneur Operating System, but in reality you need to think about communication at the culture and organizational planning stage—as I have mentioned previously, communication is the thread that ties all of this together! Developing a communication plan that outlines what, how, and when you will communicate with your internal and external audiences will ensure that you and your leadership team are ready to champion these changes and support your cultural transformation. Ask yourself:

- Who are our key audiences internally and externally?

- What messages do we want to share? What are the proof points for those messages?

- Do our messages change for internal versus external stakeholders? If yes, how?

- What messages will leaders need to consistently articulate?

- When should we be sharing these messages for the best buy-in? To keep people informed? To encourage participation? To celebrate successes?

- What channels do we want to use to communicate our messages?

- What are the expectations of leadership? What are the expectations of team members?

- What are our calls to action for staff?

- Will these changes need to be reflected in other materials?

- How are we going to make this simple?

Your communication plan should also include some type of recognition so that your team can see, and celebrate, their role in the successes you've had, as well as how far you've come in your broader culture change journey.

And, of course, at each step in the process you are going to want to measure your progress against where you started. Measurement should start at the top, with management—are they changing in the way you have outlined? Pulse surveys are great for these quick check-ins and will give you real-time feedback about how your changes are landing with your team and other key stakeholders. The results are motivating and a recognition of the progress of leaders within the organization.

A culturepreneur must be agile and willing to learn new skills in order to effectively lead a more diverse, dynamic, higher potential workforce than we've ever had before. It means adopting (and championing) a system like Waterstone's Culturepreneur Operating System and the significant change management that comes with that decision. It's a big challenge, but it's one that a culturepreneurial mindset can support.

The takeaway:
A culture operating system supports
successful culture transformation

- A culture operating system is a business system that helps organizations transform their culture and adopt culture-centric processes.

- By putting culture at the centre of strategy, leaders and organizations can work toward their goals through the lens of what makes them unique.

- Waterstone's Culturepreneur Operating System incorporates culture measurement and assessment, culture curation and design, culture and organizational planning, leadership assessment and training, human capital systems design and implementation, and branding and communications.

- Adopting a culture operating system requires an agile leader who is willing to learn new skills and embrace the significant change management that will be required to implement the system.

9

THE NEW
LEADERSHIP MIX

"Change will not come if we wait for some other person or
some other time. We are the ones we've been waiting for. We
are the change that we seek."

BARACK OBAMA, forty-fourth president
of the United States of America

Culture is competitive advantage. It's built by leaders, but
when you break it down, culture is a series of behaviours that
are common to and accepted within an organization. Those
behaviours are aligned to values, which propel high levels of
engagement that in turn gets results.

Historically, leaders developed into their roles based
mainly on their own successes and then on the successes of
the outcomes they drove through others. I've often defined
leadership as followership, because to be a great leader, people must want to follow you. You have to be able to drive
impact through others. But as a result of that followership
mentality, we have tended to work within models where
our people adapted to the leader's style. The paradigm has

shifted, though—today's leaders need to adapt their style to that of their people. This requires a different set of skills, a different approach, and a new energy.

When Waterstone launched the Canada's Most Admired Corporate Cultures program in 2005, it was a way to recognize organizations that had effectively tapped into culture as competitive advantage and that understood how leveraging culture could produce unparalleled performance. The program has grown and evolved from those early days of recognizing ten organizations from across the country. We now recognize up to fifty organizations annually, ten in each of five categories: Emerging (organizations with revenues of $5 million to under $25 million); Growth (organizations with revenues of $25 million to under $100 million); Mid-market (organizations with revenues of $100 million to under $500 million); Enterprise (organization with revenues of $500 million plus); and the Broader Public Sector (government, academia, charities, and not-for-profit organizations).

As part of the awards process, nominated organizations provide a detailed submission that outlines the ways they have linked culture and performance. Every year we get hundreds of submissions; around five years ago, some key themes started to emerge around leadership that were notably different from years past, and yet quite consistent among winning organizations:

Communication and listening. Senior leaders were becoming great communicators and listeners. Their organizations were using multiple communication tools, increasing the ways in which they listened to their various stakeholders, and taking ownership of their communication styles and cycles.

Trust. Leaders were actively building an environment of trust. Team members were encouraged to express themselves and their ideas or opinions with the understanding that they were safe to do so and that they would be free from judgment if and when they spoke up.

Cooperation. Collaboration and cooperation were front and centre. This was resulting in more learning opportunities, better innovation, higher retention rates, and better organizational outcomes.

Purpose. Leaders were connecting the organizational purpose with that of their people. They were leveraging purpose to create teams, roles, and opportunities based on a deep understanding of the individual passions and capabilities of team members.

Recognition. Organizations were adapting the way they recognized success. They understood that celebrating outcomes was no longer enough and were recognizing both individual and team contributions.

Back in 2016, I was speaking at Waterstone's annual Fall Corporate Culture Summit in Vancouver, British Columbia, about the trends we were seeing in the Canada's Most Admired Corporate Cultures submissions. By this point, I had started to talk about these trends as the five key attributes of high performance leaders. After my talk, one of the event attendees approached me and asked if I'd heard of Google's Project Aristotle. It turns out that the trends we'd noticed among our hundreds of award nominees closely mirrored findings from research that Google had done into its own teams.

In 2012, Google launched Project Aristotle to study 180 of its internal teams, higher performing and lower performing teams in engineering and sales, to determine what made an effective team. They conducted hundreds of interviews, looked at data from employee engagement surveys, and introduced an internal study on work and life to determine which variables were related to team success. They found that success was all about how the team worked together and identified five key variables: psychological safety, dependability, structure and clarity, meaning, and impact.[1]

The five key attributes of culturepreneurial leaders

The intersection between Waterstone's findings from the Canada's Most Admired program and Google's Project Aristotle reinforced for me that there was something more to the trend we'd seen. Over time, the words I've used to describe these trends have changed (from "trust" to "psychological safety," for example), and I've come to refer to these as the five key attributes of culturepreneurial leaders: psychological safety, accountability, meaning, impact, and continuous learning. Each element requires leaders to adapt their thinking, leverage their communication skills, and customize their approach to unlock the potential not just of their teams but also of the organization. We are in a leadership renaissance— and it is a game changer. Just as, coming out of the Middle Ages, the Renaissance ushered in a new age of art and thought, today's renaissance is bringing with it a need to customize leadership. We have different kinds of challenges that require new ways of thinking. We are involved in a social movement that is dealing with institutions, thoughts, and limiting beliefs that hold us back. And, of course, we have what I would call the second age of the individual, where everything is challenged and conventions are no longer the same. It requires a new mix of skills for culturepreneurial leaders—it's about adapting our styles to better connect with our team members.

I worked with Waterstone clients to create a pedagogy for training leaders in a new way—a way that focuses on a series of behaviours that drive high performance in organizations—culturepreneurially. What we've seen is that by adopting these attributes to lead in a new, contemporary way that unlocks the potential in teams, leaders can improve results.

Figure 4. Five Key Attributes of Culturepreneurial Leaders

Psychological safety

Google's definition of psychological safety is a terrific one: "Psychological safety refers to an individual's perception of the consequences of taking an interpersonal risk or a belief that a team is safe for risk taking in the face of being seen as ignorant, incompetent, negative, or disruptive. In a team with high psychological safety, teammates feel safe to take risks around their team members. They feel confident that no one on the team will embarrass or punish anyone else for admitting a mistake, asking a question, or offering a new idea."[2] It sounds easy, but relationships built on trust take time. One of the quickest ways to get there is through authenticity and vulnerability. This can be as simple as telling people how you feel or getting to know them, and it requires a mindset of "my team member is a human being, not just a unit of work."

Accountability

Accountability comes down to creating a collaborative and cooperative environment whereby things can get done at a high level with high dependability, but without a command and control style. Consider the example of timelines. When you have high accountability, you can say, "I need this done in the next month," but then hand the who and how of meeting that objective over to the team. Accountability does not mean that there are no tools, processes, or procedures; instead, it's a mind shift away from "Do this by Tuesday at noon" and then following up every day for a progress report to a more autonomous, collaborative model that takes advantage of the strengths of the team.

Meaning

We've talked already about the important role purpose plays in finding and retaining talent. Meaning comes down to aligning an individual's true desire for purpose in their own work with the organization's interests. Culturepreneurial leaders can take this to the next level by finding shared purpose with their team members and making an authentic, personal connection with the individuals on their team. Unlocking the power of such connections is a game changer for leaders.

Impact

People want to be recognized, not just for outcomes but for their contributions. You must find ways to appropriately recognize individual team members, because that matters to people and drives a greater connection and better outcomes.

Continuous learning

We live in a world of great complexity, ambiguity, and fast-paced change that demands a broader set of skills, experiences, perspectives, and open-mindedness than ever before. Continuous learning is about embracing discomfort and agility, and being able to operate with the ambiguity, flexibility, and need for risk-taking that is required to thrive in today's work environment.

These five attributes are the foundation for building high performance culturepreneurial teams and cultures. They are a response to what has been happening societally—with several generations in the workplace, with the shift to hybrid workplaces (where some team members are working in an office and others in remote locations, or where individuals have the option to choose their location based on their day-to-day requirements), and with the increasing importance of self-directed work. From a leadership perspective, the five attributes represent a sea change that requires a new mix of skills and tools, along with a willingness on the part of leaders to think about, understand, and then action leadership differently.

I've said it before but it bears repeating: this new era of leadership is all about adapting our styles to better connect with our team members.

New thinking for new leaders

Why do leaders need to make this shift in style? It comes down to this: the height of a team's performance compared to its potential is directly related to the depth of connection among its members.[3] By way of example, you don't have to look further than your favourite sports team, your local orchestra, or the cast of your favourite movie. It's their timing, their sequencing—their connection to each other—in addition to their individual training and passion for what they do that makes them great. The power is in connection, and that's why this shift is important.

Jan Carlzon, the long-time CEO of Scandinavian Airlines System, often talked about how he focused on soft skills.[4] This seemed like a novel idea when Carlzon's book, *Moments of Truth*, was first published in 1985. Now a community of leaders truly get the importance of soft skills and are willing, in an open sourced environment, to share their knowledge, like Google with its Project Aristotle research and, I would argue, Waterstone's Canada's Most Admired program, which attracts like-minded people who are willing to share what they do.

For the culturepreneur, it comes down to treating people as people, understanding their passions within a broader context, and then doing the right thing. Some of us, who came into leadership roles because we drove outcomes through people, might not be the right fit for the future—unless we learn a new way and adapt to the skills mix required of leadership today.

The takeaway:
Changing the way we lead can unlock
new avenues of performance

- High performance leaders can adapt their style to that of their team members.

- Just like adopting Waterstone's Culturepreneur Operating System supports culture change, adopting the five key attributes of culturepreneurial leaders (psychological safety, accountability, meaning, impact, and continuous learning) can unlock the potential of teams and drive results.

- Connections are vital in a high performance team. Leaders who adopt this new way of leading understand that there's power in connecting with their team and in connecting their team's purpose to that of the organization.

10

BUILDING A
CULTURE OF SAFETY

"Out of your vulnerabilities will come your strength."

SIGMUND FREUD, founder of psychoanalysis

The move from employer-centric to employee-centric thinking has been driven by teams and reflects what's happening in society at large. As I've mentioned before, so much of the workforce was raised to participate in major decisions at home with their families or their friends, and they're used to having a voice. According to a 2019 survey by the National Retail Federation, "over 4 in 5 parents say they involve their children in purchases more than their own parents did with them."[1] This is a natural way of being for many of our team members, and yet many organizations haven't fully adapted to an open, participatory way of working. In my work with Waterstone, I still come across cultures that are very top down or fear-based—where younger team members especially don't feel that they are part of the larger discussions.

Add to that the ways that millennials and Gen Z interact and live in the digital world. Both groups are digital

natives—"'native speakers' of the digital language of computers, video games, and the Internet."[2] As a result, a large cohort
of employees has a different view of safety than perhaps that of
some older team members. There are those who, with social
media in particular, feel they have an open avenue to express
themselves and share their points of view. It gives them a
sense of power and of connection. But no one is immune
to being judged. I think that has exacerbated or facilitated
(depending on which way you want to take it) their sensitiv-
ity to having a safe environment where they feel they can
share, but where they don't want to be judged for that sharing.

Trust and authenticity: The bedrocks of safety

Psychological safety in the workplace comes down to one
question: do people trust their leaders and colleagues to allow
them to be participatory, to express opinions and ideas? If yes,
they will feel a strong sense of safety and, as a result, trust.
With trust in relationships, anything is possible, and with generations of people in the workplace requiring a new level of
trust, that quality becomes a big determinant for building a
high performance culture.

For many of us, myself included, if trust was mentioned
at all in our leadership training, it was in the context of "trust
has to be earned." Generations of leaders have thrived in that
type of environment and countless organizations have found
success with that method. But the trust-earned mindset is not
as productive as it once was. Not only can it unintentionally
drive a culture of fear and uncertainty ("If I do this, will I lose
the trust of my employer? If I lose their trust, will my job be

at risk?"), but it's simply no longer practical given the shifting ways in which we work. During COVID-19, working from home (or adapting to a hybrid work environment) became a necessary and even preferred way of working rather than a perk—and in that type of work environment, a trust-earned mindset is almost counterproductive to performance. As I talked about in chapter 4, people want ownership of their work and the freedom to customize it to their own style and circumstances. None of that happens when leaders micromanage remote workers because of a lack of trust.

Although it represents a significant shift in thinking, especially for leaders of my generation, giving trust can be easy. When you start from a trust-given mindset, you're automatically operating from a place of safety. A trust-given mindset tells your team that you believe in them and in their decisions and ideas; it allows your team to ask questions and test out hypotheses without fear of repercussions. Trust-given environments can be more innovative and productive because people work without fear. The incoming generation of leaders is used to operating in this type of environment. Trust for them is table stakes; for some of us, it's going to require a complete 180 degree turn. That shift starts with turning the mirror on yourself:

· Does your own style promote trust within your team?

· Do you give trust or expect it to be earned?

· Do your team members feel like they can express their ideas and feelings without judgment?

· What would your team members say about you?

There is no replacement for time and shared experience when it comes to building trust (in a work relationship or any other relationship), and we all have opportunities to facilitate trust with our team—being vulnerable ourselves and sharing how we're feeling and/or information about our own lives (as much as we're comfortable). Vulnerability and openness really do set the stage for a trusting and authentic relationship and expand the possibilities for a psychologically safe environment.

Plasticity Labs and Anne Wilson, a social psychologist at Wilfrid Laurier University in Waterloo, Ontario, explored the benefits of authenticity, how workplace culture affects authenticity, and the links between authenticity and workplace well-being. They found that "authentic employees fared better than inauthentic employees, reporting significantly higher job satisfaction and engagement, greater happiness at work, stronger sense of community, more inspiration, and lower job stress. Sharing one's true self at work, then, is related to employees' experience at work: the more of themselves that people shared with others, the better their workplace experience."[3]

Safety comes down to caring about your people. That doesn't mean you have to be close to everyone on your team—some of us are naturally more open while others are more reserved—but you do need to care about them. In its simplest form, this is about being authentic in your words and actions. We saw this in spades at the beginning of the COVID-19 pandemic.

As luck would have it, the pandemic hit at the height of the nomination period for the 2020 Canada's Most Admired Corporate Cultures and Canada's Most Admired CEO awards program. My team and I decided to push forward with the program despite the difficult circumstances facing most, if not all, of the prospective nominees. There was a very real possibility that the program would fall flat in a year during which companies were dealing with mass layoffs and furloughed employees, significant financial losses, and huge uncertainty. What we found instead was that companies were looking for things to celebrate—ways to bring hope and inspiration to their teams and opportunities to highlight the human side of their corporate cultures. We ended up with a record number of nominations in 2020, and each and every written submissions emphasized how they had cared for their people and the trust they gave their teams: implementing work-from-home and flexible work hour policies in record time, hosting regular check-in calls to share experiences and stay connected, hosting regular town hall meetings to keep teams updated on what was happening, coordinating bonus payments earlier than usual to ensure team members had the funds to ride out a lockdown, hiring wellness coaches, developing online programs to support parents trying to coordinate school and work... the list goes on and on. And in every case, they reported back on the dedication and performance that they received in return. These efforts are significant because they came from an authentic desire to help. Three related themes emerged from the 2020 award submissions:

1   There is now an expectation that companies and leaders actively work on their corporate culture.

2   Culture-focused organizations help their people develop themselves both personally and professionally.

3   Psychological safety has become a cornerstone of corporate cultures across the country.

Building a safe work environment

Step 1: Give trust

Building an environment of psychological safety starts with the leader, not with the individuals on the team, and it comes down to caring about those individuals, giving them the trust that they need and deserve, encouraging collaboration, and recognizing their contribution. What that all looks like will depend on the team and the circumstances. To do their best work, some people and teams will need more interaction, some less; some will need more freedom, and some less. Start by asking yourself: what do my team members need in order to feel safe?

Sometimes the answer is going to be more support or more effort on the part of the leader; sometimes it's going to be the opportunity to work without the leader. And that's the ultimate sign of trust, isn't it? Giving your team the time to problem solve or create or innovate on their own. As a team leader, you will still want to engage at some point in the process—whether that's through regular check-ins or at key milestones in a project—and you will want the opportunity to weigh in, ask questions, or ensure the project is on track. But letting the team collaborate and create without you, and giving others the chance to take on a leadership role, is an incredible opportunity and one that concretely demonstrates your trust in your team. It indicates that they are safe to take chances, make mistakes, learn, and eventually succeed.

Step 2: Be open and vulnerable

This can sound scary, especially for those of us who were taught to put on our leadership hat in the office, or for those of us who are more private. But vulnerability can be as simple as telling people how you're feeling in the moment or showing empathy toward others by finding out where they are at in the moment. It definitely doesn't come as naturally to many of us as handing out a meeting agenda and jumping right into what you want to accomplish, but checking in with your team can do wonders to set the tone of a meeting.

One of the tools I often use in Waterstone's Building High Performance Teams and Cultures program is the One Word Open. This tool, developed by Susan Heathfield, a management and organization development consultant and co-owner of TechSmith, is a quick way to read the room before we start the meeting or as we come back from a break. We go around the room and people share with the group one word that describes how they're feeling in the moment—inspired, anxious, grateful, overwhelmed, and so on. The answers connect me to the group and can help build a safe environment. If someone says they're tired, for example, I might not go to them with questions or ask them to participate as much as someone who says they're energized or excited. Tools like the One Word Open establish an environment where people feel safe to say, "I'm here but I'm maybe not at my best today," and where they know that there are no repercussions for that.

Being open and vulnerable requires what I call a humanistic leadership style. This is a little bit like sitting across from your neighbour, family member, or friend. Yes, there is still a line between work and home, between professionalism and familiarity, and there is always the possibility that someone will say, "Boy, they're just too open" or "too familiar." But I think if your words and actions are genuine, more often than not people will see them for what they are—an effort to connect and build trust.

Trust-building tools

- **One Word Open:** in one word, describe how you're feeling in the moment.

- **The Ungame:** answer a series of fun or thoughtful questions about a broad range of topics in this game created by Rhea Zakich in 1972 and available for purchase. (For example, what three things would you want if you were stranded on a desert island?)

- **Hemingway's Six Word Short Story:** in six words or less, write a short story about your life and explain it.

- **Step In:** step forward/in or back/out to indicate your relationship to questions posed by the moderator. (For example, step in if you're left handed.)

- **Lifelines:** draw a chart with one axis showing when life was great and when life was terrible, and the other axis representing years of your life, and then map out the highs and lows to tell your story.

I know that what I'm suggesting here isn't the norm in a lot of workplaces. Focusing on results is. And we're still trying to get to the best possible results: the most direct route to those results is through trust and authentic behaviours on the part of the leader.

Putting your moose on the table

Authenticity is one of the core values at Galvanize, a Vancouver-based builder of award-winning cloud-based security, risk management, compliance, and audit software. For president and CEO Laurie Schultz, it means "being genuinely in the moment and listening to someone and receiving [the message in] the exact way it was delivered. It's stopping the censoring in your head so that you can really learn something from someone's opinion that you didn't otherwise know. That leads into embracing ambiguity because by hearing and learning what you don't know, you're going to be in a position to do something that you've never done."[4] One of the ways that Galvanize promotes open communication is by encouraging team members to "put the moose on the table": addressing issues they feel are awkward or that may be being ignored (the elephant in the room, as it were).

And it's not just a metaphor. There are moose throughout the Galvanize office to keep this value top of mind: stuffed moose in meeting rooms, moose statues in the lobby. It's a visual reminder to the team that not only is authenticity a value, but it's also an expected behaviour. And because of its prominent and open place in the language of the company and in their work environment, it has served to create an atmosphere in which people feel safe to speak up and to share their ideas.

"Being very frequent in how we talk about our values and measuring our values and having symbols like the moose, they really have become a very big part of our culture," says Schultz. "I'll say, until this job, I... never really appreciated the impact of symbols and language like I do today. Having a moose as a metaphor for the value of authenticity has been a really fundamental focal point for our culture."[5]

Galvanize's moose on the table is a great example of creative ways that organizations can reinforce the idea of a psychologically safe environment. I truly believe that we're not going to talk about this much in five or ten years, because it's going to be standard operating practice. But, like any big change, it will start with the workplace environment and the processes to support the change will follow. It's going to require a shift in thinking, and in many cases, it's going to require some leadership training.

The commitment of organizations to developing leaders and team members, to working on their cultures, and to building an incredible workplace environment is at an all-time high. The unprecedented changes brought about by COVID-19 forced us all to re-examine the where and how of work, and many are still playing catch-up to changes that have occurred at record pace. For culturepreneurs, being vulnerable in the face of uncertainty and rapid change, caring about our people, and trusting them to perform will provide a strong foundation for a high performance culture.

The takeaway:
Culturepreneurs build trust to drive performance

- Leaders must move from a trust-earned to a trust-given working style.

- A trust-given culture allows your team the freedom to create, innovate, fail, and succeed in a way that a trust-earned culture cannot.

- Culturepreneurial leaders understand that a psychologically safe environment hinges on them caring about their people and working to authentically connect with team members through both words and actions.

- Adopting a humanistic leadership style can help culturepreneurs build a safe workplace because this style supports trust, authenticity, and vulnerability.

- Using trust-building tools can set the stage for open, productive meetings and build a connection between leaders (department leaders, team leaders, project leaders, and so on) and their teams.

11

FOSTERING ACCOUNTABILITY, MEANING, AND IMPACT

"There's no greater gift than thinking that you had some impact on the world, for the better."

GLORIA STEINEM, American writer, lecturer, political activist, and feminist organizer

The order in which I present the five key attributes of culture-preneurial leaders is important. Only with strong leadership communications as a base can you start to establish psychological safety, where people are free to question the direction and offer up ideas for other ways to reach the desired outcomes. Once you establish a communication-focused, trust-centric culture you can focus on leveraging resources (accountability), connecting with your team and with their purpose (meaning), and recognizing achievements that align with your culture (impact).

Accountability

When I first started talking about the five key attributes of culturepreneurial leaders, I called this attribute collaboration, because it is about how we work together to meet the high standards required to achieve results. Google calls it dependability: "On dependable teams, members reliably complete quality work on time (vs. the opposite—shirking responsibilities)."[1] Whether you think of it as collaboration, dependability, or accountability, this attribute is all about getting things done.

There are great project management tools out there, like RACI, that look at questions such as: Does your team have enough resources? Are team members accountable? Have they been consulted? Have they been informed?[2] And all of that is great, but what's really important is *how* you get the best out of your teams.

Collaboration happens quite naturally if team members have the tools they need to do the job. A leader's job is to help the team with the project framework, information, and resources to get the project done—which includes proper briefings to ensure people have the information and resources they need to work together as a team—whether you are on the project team or not. Team members require the ability to set their own timeframes. That's not to say that as leaders we can't or shouldn't set clear parameters, but it does mean that once the parameters are set, we need to step back and let the team determine how they'll achieve their goals within those parameters.

Culturepreneurs can ask specific kinds of questions to generate collaboration:

- Is the deadline reasonable?

- How can we get this done by the deadline?

- What are reasonable check-in points or progress markers?

- What resources are needed to accomplish this goal?

- What role will each team member play in achieving this goal?

- What is my role on the team?

- How can I help?

Leaders today are often not just leaders; they're player-coaches who can be asked to coach from the sidelines or to hand over complete leadership of the team to someone else and become a player on the field for the duration of a project. In fact, there are often higher degrees of accountability and collaboration if the leader isn't always the team leader and they are instead a contributor being asked to work to the best of their ability as well.

So, accountability means living up to high standards and also giving people the tools to do the same. It's not about removing the processes, deadlines, or objectives, but it may be about altering your style of determining the "hows" of the project. It becomes more of a team-driven process, with the leader providing the resources required for success.

More and more, people have been exposed to working on teams even before they enter an organization—through sport or schooling or other activities. Whether they like or are good at this type of collaboration, they at least have experience with it. Regardless of their tenure in an organization, employees are bringing with them the ability to work on teams, and they have a sense of when to lead, when to follow, when to contribute, and so on.

When I think of accountability, I often think of a restaurant. At dinner service, for each table of guests, at least half a dozen team members are responsible for a smooth dining experience—host/hostess, wait staff, bar staff, chef, kitchen staff, bussers, and so on. Each of them needs to be on their game, and each of them needs to be able to trust that the others know their jobs and will own any problems that arise. If I ask a passing waiter for another glass of wine, whether or not he's the person assigned to my table, he now owns that "problem." In a culture of high accountability, that waiter does what's necessary to resolve the issue—place the order at the bar, add the drink to my bill, ensure the drink is delivered to my table in a timely manner, and/or inform the person looking after my table about the request so that they can step in and complete the transaction. All of this without anyone needing to micromanage the process.

Meaning

I talked a lot about purpose and the important role that purpose plays in recruiting and retaining top talent in chapter 3. Embracing meaning in your leadership is how you draw a link between purpose and performance.

More and more, people in the workforce care deeply about what they do and employees want to know that their work has made a difference. As leaders, we need to really understand what's important to our team and connect that to the larger

Leaders need to connect what's important to the team to the larger purpose of the organization.

purpose of the organization to drive outcomes. Like in any relationship, this takes time.

Understanding what somebody is passionate about is the key to unlocking what they love to do. At Waterstone, we use our Playbook for Success to do this, and there are other great tools that give people the opportunity to share what they love, what they're interested in, their favourite foods, pastimes, and more. Of course, there are certain things about all our jobs that we'd prefer someone else could do, but understanding what team members love to do as a starting point can help you align that person's passions to the organization's goals. It can help you develop an individual's role accordingly, and it can help with finding balance or integration between their work and their life beyond work.

Meaning is about "getting" people and their values, what's important to them, and/or their boundaries. It's about better connecting with your people based on what you know about them—whether that's recognizing someone in a personalized way (for example, a gift card to their favourite restaurant) or going to someone as a resource on a topic they're passionate about (for example, consulting a world traveller when you are planning a trip). From a professional perspective, connecting team members to projects or clients that overlap with their interests might create an excellent opportunity for professional development and support accountability.

Impact

Impact is all about recognizing contribution. It means that we're not only recognizing the wins, but we're also recognizing effort and the learning that is gleaned from that effort—"You may not have succeeded, but we figured out something we didn't know before about the way you work, about what you like about your work, or about the project, and it's going to help us moving forward." Impact is about recognizing the steps along the way, not just the destination.

Impact is also about feedback. People get instant feedback on just about every aspect of their lives, thanks to social media. It's part of the DNA of younger generations, in particular. I grew up in a generation where outcomes were celebrated. Of course, I like to be recognized for what I do, but I don't need a lot of positive feedback. Perhaps that's why I'm not as strong at giving instant feedback as some of my colleagues. But I see others who are great at it and I see how impact can drive positivity in an organization in a way that focusing solely on achievement cannot.

When I think about impact, I recall how easily I could praise my kids for their effort when they were growing up. We celebrated wins, but we also celebrated contribution because every failure led to learning, which allowed our kids to try again and get better, and eventually get that win. It's different in business, of course, but recognizing effort, process, and contribution at work will lead to learning and success in the same way it does in our personal lives.

The value of teams

Even though I'm naturally individualistic, I have always been attracted to team sports more than individual sports. I get value from being on a team, and so despite my natural inclination, I played on teams throughout school and coached teams as an adult. I just enjoy the team atmosphere for the camaraderie, for the learning, and even for the company when assessing a loss. (And, of course, celebrating a win is more fun with others.)

For the next generation of leaders, teamwork will come more naturally. There will be some, like me, who are more naturally individualistic but who can switch to team-based work. But the leadership climate is shifting, and those who find success moving forward will be able to establish environments based on communication, psychological safety, accountability, meaning, and impact. No one is going to get all those attributes right, but we can pay attention and be open to trying and failing; we can be open to adapting.

Leadership begins with knowing your own style and your own passions—and working hard to understand those of the teams and team members you serve.

Culturepreneurial leaders need to be both player and coach, to be ready and willing to coach from the sidelines or to jump in and become a utility player on the field. They also need to foster collaboration and recognize contribution. If you are ready and able to pivot and take on any role on your team, you will be able to effectively provide the opportunities and feedback your team members need to achieve higher levels of performance and to remain connected to your organization.

The takeaway:
Connection and recognition are key

- Leaders need to establish a communications-focused, trust-based culture before they can effectively focus on accountability, meaning, and impact with their teams.

- Accountability isn't just about getting things done; it's about how you do them. This means being a player-coach, ready to direct from the sidelines or jump in and play while someone else on the team calls the shots.

- Meaning is the link between purpose and performance. It requires leaders to understand what's important to their team members and then leverage that knowledge to support an individual's professional development opportunities and team dependability and to ultimately drive performance.

- Impact is about recognizing contribution as well as success. It's also about giving and receiving feedback that will help on future projects.

- Leadership success moving forward will hinge on our ability to embrace the five key attributes of culturepreneurial leaders: psychological safety, accountability, meaning, impact, and continuous learning.

12

CONTINUOUS
LEARNING

"There is no innovation and creativity without failure. Period."
BRENÉ BROWN, American professor,
researcher, and author

Continuous learning is at the heart of what sets a culture-preneurial leader apart from the rest. In fact, you can't begin to be the leader your team and organization needs without a commitment to continuous learning. It's not always easy: learning requires stepping outside your comfort zone, trying new and sometimes uncomfortable things, being curious, and taking risks. It also means getting comfortable with making mistakes and with failing (yes, I said failing). But that is what continuous learning is all about.

Continuous and lifelong learning is one of the practices that the most successful people in the world have in common—from CEOs and entrepreneurs to athletes to artists. Warren Buffett is famously known for reading for five to six hours a day; Bill Gates reportedly reads fifty books a year,[1] and, according to a *Harvard Business Review* article, "Nike founder

Phil Knight so reveres his library that in it you have to take off your shoes and bow."[2] But learning is about more than reading; it is about continuous improvement that will enable you and your team to adapt no matter what is thrown at you. Just as putting culture at the centre of strategy will enable you to leverage it as a competitive advantage, prioritizing continuous learning will help you drive performance and keep you ahead of the pack.

We live in a world of great complexity, ambiguity, and fast-paced change that demands that organizations tap into a broader set of skills, experiences, and perspectives than ever before. It's no wonder a recent *Harvard Business Review* study found that "over the past two decades, the time spent by managers and employees in collaborative activities has ballooned by 50% or more."[3] Because no one person can have all the answers, a group with diverse skills, perspectives, and experiences is needed to solve problems in today's world. But bringing a group of diverse people together isn't enough; that group must actively lean into the unique perspectives of others on the team, challenge assumptions, ask questions, experiment, and try to understand what they do not know. It's the only way to achieve the best possible outcomes for the team and for the organization.

Bersin by Deloitte found that high performance organizations that prioritize learning are 92 percent more likely to innovate, are 58 percent more prepared to meet future demand, have a 34 percent better response to customer needs, and have 37 percent greater employee productivity.[4] The culturepreneur recognizes that learning doesn't just happen in a classroom; learning can and must happen anywhere and at any time if the team is going to excel. They also recognize that it is their role as a leader to foster learning, innovative thinking, and comfort with risk-taking.

Without doubt, the teams and organizations that were able to pivot and adapt quickly to the chaos of the COVID-19 pandemic were already comfortable being uncomfortable, and they were able to operate with the ambiguity, flexibility, risk-taking, and on-the-job learning required to thrive through change. A crisis (or any period of significant change) is not the ideal time to adopt a learning mindset within a team or an organization, but such challenging times do show us that to survive, and more importantly to thrive, we must be willing and able to learn, adapt, and grow.

Table stakes for continuous learning

How can you tell if you are fostering an environment of continuous learning? Start by asking yourself these questions:

- Do I ask questions more than I make statements?

- Do I welcome and seek out different perspectives and experiences?

- Do I encourage team members to take risks by trying new approaches?

- Do I carve out time for my team to innovate and learn together?

- Do I ask for feedback from team members and colleagues?

- Do I challenge assumptions?

- Do I encourage others to challenge assumptions?

- Do I encourage team members to share ideas, no matter how out of the box they may be?

- Do I ensure the team regularly debriefs together to share knowledge, successes, mistakes, and opportunities for improvement?

- Do I coach more than I preach?

- Do I know why learning is important for me and my team?

Culturepreneurs respond, "Yes, of course!" to each of these questions.

Fostering continuous learning

Intention and attention

If learning isn't already a natural part of your team's culture, it is up to you as the leader to set it as a key priority. In Waterstone's Building High Performance Teams and Cultures program, leaders often indicate that they overlook continuous learning, in part because the absence of learning isn't as evident as the absence of other attributes, such as psychological safety, strong communication, or accountability. Leaders are more likely to pay attention to visible issues like poor morale or low productivity, and the absence of learning isn't typically seen as a "clear and present danger" to a team's performance. But it should be. Teams are the vehicle that drive performance and innovation, and as Peter Senge wrote in his book *The Fifth Discipline*: "Team learning is vital because teams, not individuals, are the fundamental learning unit in modern

Learning for the sake
of learning will not drive
better performance,
but learning that is
aligned directly to the
outcomes the team
is striving for will.

organizations. This is where the rubber meets the road; unless teams can learn, the organization cannot learn."[5]

As a leader, you need to declare your intention to focus on continuous learning with your team and link that intention to the team's purpose and to your purpose as a leader. Share your views about the importance of learning and your plan to commit to learning going forward. For example, if you've identified that you need to ask more questions and control your knee-jerk reactions, then share that with your team. If you recognize that not enough time is being spent debriefing and innovating together, then share that observation and work with your team to find a solution. Declaring your intention to focus on learning is important, but it doesn't mean anything if there's no action to back it up.

Challenge assumptions and ask questions

Assumptions can hold teams back from achieving their full potential. Assumptions like "That will never work here," "This is the way it has always been done," "We can't rock the boat," "They'll never go for that," "We don't have time to try something new," and "We have a risk-averse culture" are detrimental to team performance. Whether these assumptions come from an individual's own perspective or from the team's collective experiences, it's important for leaders to notice and then call them out. Left unchecked, unproductive assumptions will stifle creativity, innovation, and learning and will result in a culture of mediocrity and complacency rather than a culture of high performance.

The most powerful way to challenge assumptions is to ask questions. As executive coach Marilee Adams writes in *Change Your Questions, Change Your Life*: "Questions open our minds, our eyes, and our hearts. With our questions we learn, connect, create. We are smarter, more productive, and able to get better results. We shift our orientation from fixed opinions and easy answers to curiosity, thoughtful questions, and open-minded conversations, lighting the way to collaboration, exploration, discovery, and innovation."[6]

Think about how often ideas are passed over in your team meetings because "that'll never work." When you accept that assumption and move on without exploring an idea or the thinking behind an idea, not only do you miss out on a potentially brilliant idea, but you also miss an opportunity for team learning, trust building, and problem solving. Remember, learning isn't always about getting to the right or best decision—it's about building trust, problem solving, and relationship building in a way that fosters team cohesion. It communicates to the group that listening, exploring, and learning with and from one another is a priority.

In meetings and conversations with their teams, culturepreneurs actively encourage dialogue and create opportunities for learning and innovation by asking questions like:

- What if we explored the possibility? What would that look like?

- How could we make it work?

- Why do you feel we can't [fill in the assumption]?

- How can we look at the problem/goal/opportunity differently?

- How does the idea support our team's goal?

- What are you thinking but not saying?

- What don't I/we/you know?

- What can we do differently to achieve better results?

- What questions haven't we asked?

- Who else's perspective should we seek out?

Why not take things a step further and add a learning debrief at the beginning of each quarter, or at another milestone in your project lifecycle? Begin by asking:

- What did you learn in the last quarter that will be important to keep in mind this quarter?

- What teams, people, industries, and so on should we be looking to for inspiration, perspective, and ideas, given our goals?

- What questions are still on the table that have yet to be answered?

- What can we do differently to achieve even better results?

- What could we learn that would make a positive difference to how we achieve our goals?

- Where can we be more innovative and take more risks?

Encourage and support risk-taking

It can be hard for people to embrace risk-taking, mainly because the idea of risk is so closely associated with the fear of making mistakes or of failure. But solving problems requires trial and error, mistakes, and failures in order to get to the best possible outcome. An aversion to risk-taking and a too high comfort level with the status quo means organizations (and individuals) are in danger of becoming stagnant and losing their competitive edge. Culturepreneurial leaders strive to create a culture where people understand what risk-taking means, and where they feel comfortable proposing and taking risks by asking, "How can I approach work, problems, or opportunities differently?" Culturepreneurs also recognize that if they don't encourage their team to experiment, when something unexpected does come up, their team will not be prepared to pivot and adapt.

Risk-taking thrives in an environment rooted in psychological safety and when the change being considered is directly linked to the organization's purpose. One great example of this is offered by Knix. The company's reason for being is to change the way their community and customers feel about themselves. That purpose is front and centre in everything Knix does—both inside and outside the organization—and it served the company well as it was established and began to grow. But in 2016, founder and CEO Joanna Griffiths made what seemed to be a high risk decision: to pivot from operating as a wholesale-focused B2B company to a direct-to-consumer brand. It was more in line with the company's purpose to work directly with its customers and tell its own story than to rely on distributors to deliver on its message and mission.

"[It] is a really intimidating and scary thing to do three years into your startup, or your organization, to raise your hand and kind of admit that you got it wrong, and that you're going to scrap the three years of effort and work that you put in and rebuild," says Griffiths.[7] But what a great decision that turned out to be, especially given the impact that COVID-19 has had on retail businesses globally.

Risk-taking isn't always as high stakes as Griffiths's decision to completely alter the company's model; it can involve small, everyday changes to how work is done. Whether the risk is big or small, it needs to be managed in a way that aligns with your culture. If risk-taking is already ingrained in your culture, then pushing yourself and your team to be even more innovative may be scary but it will be embraced more easily than it would be on a team that is highly risk-averse. If risk-taking and innovative thinking aren't part of your culture, don't jump into the deep end. Instead:

- Define what risk-taking looks like with your team. Invite the team to identify ways in which they can take "smart risks" for the purpose of learning, agility, innovation, and to drive better results and solutions.

- Invite team members to share examples of how they can take more risks. Be prepared to share your own examples of how you will take more risks and how you will support them along the way.

- Work together to identify barriers to risk-taking that exist within the team and to identify ways to minimize those barriers.

- Include time in team meetings for brainstorming and idea generation. Encourage team members to explore ideas, even ones that are not supported by the majority.

- Look for opportunities to try new things and celebrate and acknowledge when team members take a new approach.

Culturepreneurs truly believe that learning is about more than just acquiring knowledge. They see learning as an opportunity to explore ideas, determine what is working and what isn't (and why), challenge the status quo, try new approaches, and actively seek out opportunities to stretch and evolve as individuals, as a team, and as an organization.

The takeaway:
Culturepreneurs create opportunities
for learning and risk-taking

- The teams that thrive through change are those that continuously learn, adapt, and grow. If learning isn't already part of a team's culture, it is up to leaders to set it as a key priority.

- Culturepreneurial leaders know that one of the most powerful tools in their toolkit is to ask questions, and they notice opportunities to challenge assumptions, explore ideas, and create dialogue with questions.

- When left unchecked, unproductive assumptions will stifle creativity, innovation, and learning, which will result in a culture of mediocrity.

- Risk-taking and learning can only occur in an environment rooted in psychological safety and in a team that is meaningfully connected to the organization's purpose.

PART 4

EVOLUTION

13

DIVERSITY AND INCLUSION, BEYOND BUZZWORDS

"When we listen and celebrate what is both common and different, we become wiser, more inclusive, and better as an organization."

PAT WADORS, chief people officer at Procore

When she launched Knix in 2013, Joanna Griffiths saw two main problems in the market: "one from a product standpoint [with] products not being designed for real people, and the second from a marketing standpoint—both of those challenges rooted down to brands that were by their nature not inclusive." Griffiths went on to build a brand that consciously serves people of all ages, races, and sizes, and she cemented that inclusivity as part of the company's values. "I think anything that is a core strength of an organization, that's part of your point of difference, that's at the heart of what it is you're trying to do, it's important to articulate that ... as part of your values," she says.[1]

Discussions around diversity and inclusion (D&I) are nothing new, but they took on a new weight in 2020. When we look back to the 2013 submissions to the Canada's Most Admired Corporate Cultures awards program, we find that 29 percent of organizations were talking about their diversity programs (compared to 50 percent in 2020), and 5 percent were talking about inclusion efforts (compared to 42 percent in 2020). As with all the principles and practices we've been discussing throughout this book, leaders need to approach D&I through an individual rather than an organizational lens. Yes, organizations need to incorporate D&I into their hiring and succession planning, but as leaders we also need to be in tune with how individuals experience working at the organization through a D&I lens, and how inclusion affects their purpose, engagement, and contributions to the team.

I've heard diversity and inclusion defined in various ways over the years. For the purposes of this discussion, let's start with the definitions I use:

Diversity. Diversity is about recognizing and valuing differences. It's about employing people with different stories, different backgrounds or histories, varying experiences and ways of interacting with the world, and divergent ways of thinking. This may mean that people on the team are different genders, different ages, come from different cultural backgrounds, and so on, but it absolutely means people on the team think differently. Embracing those differences brings a more holistic perspective to how and why business gets done.

Inclusion. If diversity is about having a variety of people and perspectives in an organization, inclusion is about how people are able to interact within that organization. It's one thing to be given a job or promoted to a seat at the decision-making table, but if you don't feel safe to contribute or respected as a member of the team, the opportunity means nothing.

Debra Hewson, president and CEO at Odlum Brown Limited, an independent, full-service investment firm in Vancouver, tells a great story about one of the firm's partners, who describes it like this: "Diversity is about being invited to the dance and... inclusion is being asked to dance." Adds Hewson: "We're trying to create an environment where all of our team members feel empowered, and [where] there is diversity in thought everywhere you look... We're trying to celebrate that diversity and that inclusion."[2]

The impact on performance

Sometimes leaders must go out on a limb and say, "We are not as diverse a team as we should be." Or "We have disproportionately weighted our gender mix or our age mix." And that's certainly an important element of any D&I discussion. But we need to go beyond gender, age, colour, or ability—we need to key in on people who think differently as a result of who they are and how they experience the world.

Different experiences and insights that come forward as a result of inclusion impact our decisions and behaviours. Because behaviour is culture and culture is competitive advantage, behaviours that promote D&I become core elements to the success of our organizations. Beyond being the right thing to do, D&I presents an enormous opportunity, if an organization values it. Valuing what we don't know or understand is fundamentally difficult, which means that education has a role to play here.

Sometimes, leaders can't affect diversity within an organization to the extent they want to in a short time—it takes time and commitment to develop—but you can always drive inclusiveness. You can establish an environment of thought and collaboration, one where everyone feels safe and welcome to share ideas. And if you cannot align with a D&I mindset, then the hard truth is that you may no longer be the right leader for the job.

D&I in practice

Embracing diversity is a core value at Rogers Communications Inc., a 2019 Canada's Most Admired Corporate Cultures award winner. In November 2020, the company launched an updated five-year diversity and inclusion strategy, built with feedback from its team and an external race relations expert and grounded in concrete actions to drive progress for its equity-seeking customers, communities, and team members. The company strategy includes goals to increase representation for women and people of colour, including specific goals for Black team members, at the executive level and goals to increase overall representation for persons with disabilities, Indigenous Peoples, and LGBTQ2S+-identifying people. Rogers aims to create a culture of inclusion and belonging with the support of its 25,000 team members, its D&I council, Employee Resource Groups, Black Leadership Council, and leadership team, in order to make Rogers a better place to work for its people and to deliver better as a business.[3]

Diversity is also a core value at Vancouver-based Unbounce, which has put a lot of effort into driving equality and inclusivity in its talent programs. In 2017, after recognizing a lack of women on some of their teams, Unbounce (a 2019 Canada's Most Admired Corporate Cultures award winner) reviewed and overhauled its interview process to combat unconscious bias in their hiring practices. The organization's focused efforts reaped significant benefits. Twelve months before Unbounce's recruitment overhaul, only 17 percent of its new technology hires were women and the organization did not have any women in technical leadership roles. Less than two years after overhauling its recruitment practices, 100 percent of its new director-level hires in technology (three positions in total) were filled by women; 63 percent of all new technical leadership hires and 26 percent of total new technology hires were women.[4]

How high performance tools support D&I

Most leaders, if not all, can advance D&I within organizations just by upgrading their own leadership style. The five key attributes of culturepreneurial leaders come into play when establishing and cementing a culture where D&I are core values:

Psychological safety. This attribute encourages inclusiveness and diversity of thought. Through the development of a safe environment, people become comfortable sharing their ideas, stories, and experiences and step forward to flag concerns or differing viewpoints that feed back into a sense of safety and strengthen the team and the organization.

Accountability. Giving a variety of people the opportunity to take the lead on projects is one way that this attribute can support diversity and inclusion.

Meaning and impact. You can align your efforts to build stronger, higher performing teams with D&I principles when you create an environment where individual purpose is shared with the purpose and values of the organization (meaning), and when you recognize and truly value your team members for their efforts and what they bring to the table as individuals (impact).

Continuous learning. Bringing together a group of people who have different skills, perspectives, and experiences is core to building D&I within an organization. It's also fundamental to a team's ability to share ideas, challenge assumptions, solve problems, and take risks together.

There are so many examples of leaders living values associated with D&I much better than we did a year ago or five years ago, and I think this will continue. But it needs to go further. Most of us need an upgrade of our leadership approach and how we interact with one another. We can all work a lot harder to address these issues—no matter what our industry or our role.

Culturepreneurs should be creating organizational cultures that reflect the communities and the people their companies serve, and this means championing diversity and inclusion on our teams today and among our future leaders. Waterstone's Culturepreneur Operating System provides a framework to help leaders implement the changes we need, but it will only succeed if we continue to educate ourselves and step out of our own comfort zones.

The takeaway:
We're making headway on D&I,
but there's a lot of work to do

- Diversity and inclusion isn't only about giving opportunities to people with a variety of backgrounds, experiences, and ways of thinking. It's also about ensuring that everyone feels comfortable actively participating in activities within the organization.

- Behaviours that promote D&I are core to the success of organizations.

- Adopting the five key attributes of culturepreneurial leaders as part of your leadership style can support D&I efforts.

- There is still a lot of work to be done around D&I at most organizations. While it can take time to move the needle on diversity programs, inclusion efforts can be implemented more quickly with a focus on communication, collaboration, and psychologically safe work environments.

14

THE COMPETITIVE
ADVANTAGE OF SOFT SKILLS

"The functions of intellect are insufficient without courage, love, friendship, compassion, and empathy."

DEAN KOONTZ, American author

I don't know why my Major Atom hockey coach made me team captain. I certainly wasn't our best player. We had many excellent players and I don't know if at ten years old I added any value to the role. But I think I know why the coaches chose me to be a captain while playing football with the Guelph Gryphons at the University of Guelph. Again, I wasn't our star player (or even close to it) but I had a strong work ethic, determination, grit, and a bit of a presence off the field. That work ethic, consistent hustle, and effort made me a voice that my teammates would listen to whether things were going well or not so well. We had many other leaders as well, like Thomas Dimitroff Jr., former executive and Super Bowl champion with the NFL's New England Patriots and more recently the former GM of the Atlanta Falcons, and Mike O'Shea, who became the second leading all-time tackler in the Canadian Football

League (CFL) and coach of the Winnipeg Blue Bombers, winners of the 2019 Grey Cup championship.

At the University of Guelph, O'Shea led by his actions. He was tough but fair, and he defended his teammates—the same qualities he brought to his professional coaching career. As time went on, he became more vocal, and he is one of the great leaders in Canadian sports today. In June 2020, when speaking to football alumni at the University of Guelph, O'Shea was asked what made the difference in his team winning the 2019 Grey Cup. His answer: the love that the players had for each other and how badly they wanted to win for each other created a winning culture.

Dimitroff knew football in a way that many of us didn't. He was a true student of the game and had grown up with football (his father, Thomas Dimitroff Sr., was a former Guelph Gryphons head coach as well as a former coach and executive in both the CFL and NFL). Dimitroff was a passionate player and he excelled at playing to his own strengths on the field. He was the type of leader who knew when to say "Pick it up" and give us all a motivational kick in the behind, or when we needed a hug and some words of encouragement. Dimitroff knew the game, but he really knew people, which is one of the reasons he had so much success in the NFL.

O'Shea, Dimitroff, and I all brought different skills (theirs were high; mine less so) and different leadership traits to the table when we were playing. I credit our coaches—Dan McNally, Pat Tracey, Brian Cluff, and too many others to mention—for recognizing the value in each of those types of traits. They appreciated both the hard skills and the soft skills, honed them in each of us, and took advantage of the behaviours that came with those skills. Tracey always appreciated my work ethic and fearlessness on our special teams, and he made me love that aspect of the game. He saw my behaviour and was able to shine a light on it, first for me and then for others. Later I coached with Tracey and he told me that a good coach understands the value and behavioural attributes of each of their players—and then they figure out how to adapt their own coaching style. It was a great lesson and one that I have taken with me on my leadership journey.

At Waterstone, I hear more and more from clients who want soft skills, or people skills, when they come to us looking to fill a senior leadership role. The thinking is that hard skills, or technical skills, can be taught but a person either does or doesn't have soft skills. According to a 2019 LinkedIn trends study, "92% of talent professionals and hiring managers agree that candidates with strong soft skills are increasingly important. In fact, it could make or break [the hiring of] the perfect candidate as 89% feel that 'bad hires' typically have poor soft skills."[1]

And it makes sense. Technical skills, whether they be in sales, finance, or marketing, drive your ability to execute. You can learn the process and that enables you to achieve concrete results. But with the movement toward a more contribution-based workplace, where collaboration and connection are key, having those human-oriented skills (commonly referred to as emotional intelligence) is vital. And while soft skills can be learned, they tend to be inherent—which means your own personal mix of skills is the secret sauce that, like culture, becomes your personal competitive advantage. Author and business coach Dan Sullivan (co-founder and president of Strategic Coach) calls this your unique ability: "a mindset that honors your natural strengths and all the things you do

that come most effortlessly to you. It's you at your very best—
how you get your greatest results and what people count on
you for."[2]

A quick word about emotional intelligence

Emotional intelligence (often called EQ) is generally defined
as the ability to recognize, understand, and manage emotions
in ourselves and to recognize, understand, and influence
emotions in others.[3] In their 2017 article "Emotional Intelligence Has 12 Elements. Which Do You Need to Work On?"
Daniel Goleman and Richard E. Boyatzis suggest a broader
definition of emotional intelligence—they call it EI—that
includes "four domains: self-awareness, self-management,
social awareness, and relationship management. Nested
within each domain are twelve EI competencies, learned and
learnable capabilities that allow outstanding performance at
work or as a leader."[4]

No one is suggesting that to be an effective culturepreneur,
you need to master each of these areas, or that as a hiring
manager you should seek out candidates that have strong
scores across all EQ, or EI, markers. But, as Goleman and
Boyatzis put it, "to excel, leaders need to develop a balance
of strengths across the suite of EI competencies. When they
do that, excellent business results follow."[5]

The role of soft skills in leadership

The five key attributes of culturepreneurial leaders are
closely aligned with the need to prioritize soft skills in our
recruitment and retention efforts. Clearest among them is

communication—the ability to connect with others, to listen, and to deliver meaningful, customized messages that meet the needs of our individual team members. Right up there, too, is psychological safety—the ability to empathize, to create an environment that allows people to act without fear of judgment, and to collaborate with others in their preferred way. And we can't forget meaning and impact—finding that shared purpose or that opportunity to recognize someone else's efforts and to support them on their own journey. But other skills are important, among them:

Making tough decisions. Leaders have to make some hard calls. Most leaders I speak to tell me the tough decisions never quite leave you. But the ability to make those decisions, and to be okay with mistakes, is important.

Adaptability. In a quickly changing world, adaptability is vital. Leaders who can change course quickly and thoughtfully are a rare (and valuable) commodity.

Aspiration and altruism. I think aspiration, higher intention, and the desire to help others are going to become increasingly important for leaders. Maybe this is better described as wanting, above all else, to recognize and support those on the team who not only want more but also have more to give.

Toronto-based Metrolinx, a Government of Ontario agency that is tasked with improving the coordination and integration of transportation across the Greater Toronto and Hamilton area (and a 2019 Canada's Most Admired Corporate Cultures award winner), provides an excellent example of how leveraging soft skills can drive results. When Phil Verster joined Metrolinx as president and CEO in 2017, he started a tradition of pulling his leadership team into a town hall meeting three times per year (the leadership team would then do similar town halls with their own people).

"In the beginning, it was telling people what was happening, and we transitioned it over three years to be more about listening to what is going on, what is not going on, and what should be going on," says Verster.

He's also introduced what he calls "coffee mornings": informal gatherings where the leaders open up their time for a coffee and a discussion with anyone who shows up. There's no agenda, no set topic of discussion—it's simply a chance for leaders to listen to the questions, concerns, and ideas of anyone within the organization.[6]

Employee engagement has always been strong at Metrolinx (around 70 percent), but as leadership's commitment to listening increased, so did the organization's engagement scores. They jumped to 78 percent, and at the beginning of the COVID-19 pandemic in 2020, they jumped again to 84 percent.

"Engagement and culture are not built by rules," says Verster. "They're built by natural behaviours. It must be second nature for you to listen. And if it's not second nature for you to listen, you're not going to listen."[7]

Soft skills

- Agility/adaptability
- Authenticity/ vulnerability
- Communication/ listening
- Compassion
- Conflict resolution
- Connection with others
- Creativity
- Curiosity
- Decision-making ability
- Determination/grit
- Empathy
- Humility
- Leadership ability
- Listening
- Organization
- Passion
- Problem solving
- Thoughtfulness
- Time management
- Understanding/the ability to learn
- Work ethic/ commitment

The leadership recruitment challenge

The challenge, of course, is how to recruit for soft skills. I've been in the recruitment business for many years, and I still don't have an easy or foolproof answer.

Historically, the answer was to find high performers and trust that they'll make you look like a star no matter what their skills balance. That's not easy—and it's not as rewarding as taking a good performer and helping them become great. It's also not a guaranteed way to identify high performance leaders (as we will explore in chapter 15).

An understanding of (and success with) the technical elements of a job is important, and it's fairly easy to identify and test for technical competency. Given the necessary environment, the resources, the appropriate supports, and assuming you've hired for culture fit, anyone with technical skills that match the role will do just fine. That's why more and more we're seeing clients place a stronger emphasis on soft skills.

In recruiting for leadership roles, testing for soft skills often comes down to identifying behavioural patterns:

- Can they work collaboratively? If yes, how and when do they do so?

- What type of leader are they?

- Are they able to successfully develop others? If so, do they enjoy that?

- How do they make decisions?

- Do they approach their team or their clients with authenticity?

- Are they optimistic?

- Do they have grit?

I'll never forget speaking to the team at Odlum Brown Limited in Vancouver. This was back in 2017 when they were nominated for their second Canada's Most Admired Corporate Cultures award. I'd travelled to Vancouver to do the in-person interview that is part of the awards submission process, and as I waited with members of the Odlum Brown Limited team for their president and CEO, Debra Hewson, to join us, all the team wanted to talk about was Hewson—about how she empowered them, how she has supported them. And I've seen this first-hand. Hewson's vulnerability, openness, and passion for her team make her not only a great leader (and a 2017 Canada's Most Admired CEO award winner) but an exceptional culturepreneur. These qualities are necessary in a leader and tough to learn if they don't come naturally, which is why developing a process to test for them should be on every leader's to-do list.

And then you have to do your homework. Interviews are one important element of the process, but don't underestimate what you can learn through references. At Waterstone, we use something called directed referencing to get a more holistic look at the skills and interests of potential candidates. We don't just talk to the people candidates point us toward; we direct the candidate about who we would like to talk with as well. This allows us to speak to past employers, colleagues, and direct reports who bring a more diverse perspective about the candidate and how they work. It gives us more opportunity to explore those patterns that are so crucial to identifying soft skills in a candidate.

Searching for IQ, EQ, and GQ

Part of PointClickCare's culture revisioning a few years ago was around how to find people who were culture fits and who also had the drive to succeed in their high performance organization. Co-founder and CEO Mike Wessinger says their team knew they were looking for above average talent that was producing above average results, but the question was how would they define above average, and how would they find those people? For PointClickCare, the answer was IQ, EQ, and something they call GQ—grit quotient.

"There's traditionally IQ and you can test for that. I mean, most of the people [who] will come into our offices, with the CVs they have or the schools they've come from, that's a given. They're all smart," says Wessinger. "The second piece is you look at EQ. Do we have people who have a strong EQ that's going to be a fit with our culture?"[8] Wessinger and his team use GQ to filter for people who may not be standouts on IQ or EQ, but who can somehow over-perform when it comes to leading people or driving results.

PointClickCare identified people—not just new hires but existing staff as well—with above average talent as having strong skills in EQ, IQ, or GQ and producing above average results. That meant that some team members needed to be coached up to meet the performance expectations, others needed to be reassigned to departments where they could thrive, and still others either opted out or needed to be coached out of the organization. The integration of EQ and GQ—the soft skills—into PointClickCare's definition of performance and into its recruitment efforts has paid off. "It didn't happen overnight, but you can see that, quarter over quarter, we continue to raise the bar."[9]

As a culturepreneur, you need to focus on soft skills in equal measure to the hard or technical skills required in the roles that you're looking to fill. It means that you need to take the time to honestly evaluate your own soft skills and to work collaboratively with your team to ensure that you're factoring in all of the skills that a candidate brings to the table.

The takeaway:
Test for soft skills by looking
at behavioural patterns

- The movement toward a contribution-based work-place has increased the value of soft skills—sometimes referred to as people skills or EQ—in the workplace.

- Where technical skills can be learned, more human-oriented skills tend to be inherent, making them your own personal competitive advantage.

- The five key attributes of culturepreneurial leaders are closely aligned to soft skills such as listening, empathy, openness, and collaboration.

- There is no easy or foolproof method to test for soft skills. Behavioural profiles and interview questions that focus on behavioural patterns are two common tools, but don't underestimate the value of references for identifying soft skills in candidates.

- Using directed referencing ensures you talk with a targeted and diverse group of people who can give you honest perspectives about the behaviour patterns of your candidates.

15

NEXT-GENERATION LEADERS AND CULTUREPRENEURS

"You go for the best talent available, wherever it is. You fish it out. That's how I've scouted all my career. Doesn't matter where it is—international, domestic, college, anywhere."

MASAI UJIRI, president of the Toronto
Raptors, 2019 World Champions

I was first promoted to a senior leadership role after I'd proven myself to be a competent sales professional and marketing leader. I was confident, good at what I did, hard-working, and ambitious. There have been a lot of extroverts in leadership roles and I fit that bill. I was also willing to learn, to listen to my peers and managers, to do some of the work, and to communicate the more challenging messages. On paper, it made sense.

But once I was in the role, it quickly became clear to me that I wasn't ready. I didn't have the experience or the relationships (yet) that would allow me to help people with their jobs or to remove obstacles for them. I learned fairly quickly that I was not as prepared as I should have been. The people

A leader must have
two main qualities:
followership and impact.

I've talked to who were also promoted at a young age in that era all said the same thing: you learned the job on the job. As young leaders we were studious, we maybe took a management course, or the company invested some time in us. Certainly I had some qualities that other leaders had: good connections within the organization and the industry and an eagerness to learn. But in terms of having the experience in life or even in the role to empathize with other people and what they were dealing with, or the knowledge to help them with challenges in their work? I'm not sure I had that. In retrospect, I needed more time in life and in my previous role.

I tell this story because it highlights the difference between the way things were done in the past and the way we need to identify and develop the next generation of leaders and culturepreneurs. Like many others of my generation, I was put in that leadership role because I fit a profile: I had a strong record of performance, conviction in my abilities, a good work ethic, and I tended to be extroverted in my style, which was often interpreted as having strong communication skills. Thankfully, I also had the ambition to become a leader, and today I'm proud to lead a high performance team at my own high performance organization. But that traditional profile, which worked so well for me, is no longer a completely accurate or thorough gauge for identifying future leaders.

Identification

Historically, leaders were chosen based on a broad set of characteristics: strong character, repeatable pattern of success, hopefully good moral fortitude, some level of confidence and intelligence, and so on. But other skills (and I've talked a lot about those in previous chapters) are required to unlock the potential of people in our modern age. Contemporary leadership is not necessarily for the same type of person who was identified as a leader in the past.

Kirk Simpson, co-founder and CEO of Wave, a Toronto-based firm that designs award-winning financial software for entrepreneurs, has seen this first-hand. When Wave was going through a high growth period, the company was hiring a lot of people and trying to point everyone in the right direction. "But there wasn't a lot of a thought process [as] to what environment are we creating? How are we investing in people?" says Simpson, a 2019 Canada's Most Admired CEO award winner. "We fell prey to something that I think a lot of high growth tech companies fall into, which is... as you think about leadership within a team, you say to yourself, 'Okay, well, they're a great individual contributor, so of course they're going to be a great leader of that team.'"

In fact, Simpson and his team (and countless others) have found that an individual's high performance is not necessarily indicative of their capacity as a high performance leader. "Not everyone is designed [for] or interested in leading teams, or quite frankly, good at it," Simpson explains. "And so, you might not have the best leadership of the team and [now] you've taken your best individual contributor and turned them into a low performer, which is bad for everybody."[1] Wave recognized that some of the people they'd put into leadership positions shouldn't be in them, and it forced the organization to make tough decisions about how to support its people while also ensuring the success of the company.

How do you differentiate between future leaders and those who are going to be champions within the organization in non-leadership roles?

I've often said that to be a leader you need two main attributes: followership and impact. People must want to follow you. Once you have that followership, you must get results. Although you will contribute as an individual, your primary impact will be through your team members. All of this takes place in the context of values, or how things happen in an organization. Culture is the behaviour that extends from an organization's values, and so when you're looking for potential leaders, the questions to ask are:

- Do they exhibit behaviours that reflect the organization's values?

- Do you see proof that they can establish an environment of trust?

- Are they a great communicator?

- Do they understand their own communication style?

Take an interest in those high prospect individuals on your team and help them develop as leaders. More and more, today's leaders (and this will set the stage for tomorrow's leaders as well) are becoming coaches within the context of their organizations. And just as there are all shapes and sizes of coaches, so too will there be all shapes and sizes of leaders—some will have great communication skills or a strong sense of empathy or a style that lends itself well to recognition, but they will be weaker in other leadership attributes. It comes down to whether or not their way of doing things naturally fits the behaviours of the organization's culture, whether they align to the shared purpose and feel that their work makes a difference, and whether they understand this new hybrid work world that requires incredible flexibility. Though you may have all the other leadership attributes, if you can't help people prosper in that world, it's not going to work for you as a leader. And for some of us, that will be a tough transition.

Testing for leadership aptitude

When identifying your next generation of leaders, you want to look for the behaviours that represent your organization's values first. You can do things like behavioural profiles, but the best test is the workplace and their pattern of behaviours in work and in life. Does that mean people need to have been coaches or involved in teaching to make good leaders? Not necessarily, but that would be one indicator that they might enjoy the role.

Another way to test for leadership aptitude is by seeking feedback—asking people for their feelings about a leadership candidate, doing pulses to determine whether this person worked well with their group as a team leader. And we can't forget to ask the most important question: do they even want to be considered for a leadership role? You might discover that some of your top performers aren't interested in that move. Knowing that is vital.

Candidates may opt out of a leadership role for a variety of reasons: they're tired and hesitant about the amount of time and work required to be a good leader; they want to move into leadership but the timing isn't right for them; they love what they are currently doing and have no interest in changing that; they want to explore other interests within the organization, which could require a lateral versus an upward move; and many others.

Leaders need to create an environment where it's safe for our people to opt out of moving up (or opt out for now) and still do well in their career and thrive in their own way. My first boss at Ortho Pharmaceutical, a Johnson & Johnson company, Gary Hough, remained a district sales manager for years. Anyone who worked with him or knew him (and that was everyone in the company) knew he could have been the national sales director at any time. He developed more people than anyone else; he cared about his people; he was on his game—he had all the tools to move up, but he loved what he did, he didn't want to relocate, and he had no interest in going to the head office or to either of the two other company locations. He was the first great example I saw of someone who opted out of climbing the corporate ladder but didn't opt out of leadership.

Development

People are generally more focused on their individual wants and a shared sense of purpose than on climbing the corporate ladder. As leaders, we have a responsibility to identify the skill set, the passion, and the leadership aptitude in people who could serve our organizations in leadership roles well. But beyond identification, it's our responsibility to support their development.

External training programs will always bring in the most contemporary ideas, but more and more organizations are focusing on internal training—supporting the career development of their people and building leadership capacity.

In the 1990s, Longo Brothers Fruit Markets Inc. (Longo's), a family-run grocery chain serving the Greater Toronto and Hamilton areas in Ontario, partnered with Humber College in Toronto to create Longo's College, which has evolved into a manager training program for Longo's associates. It has helped the organization develop high potential team members into department managers, assistant store managers, and store managers. "These [programs] are all about helping people be the best they can be," says Anthony Longo, president and CEO of Longo's and a 2019 Canada's Most Admired CEO award winner. "How do you help people figure out what their gifts are and [figure out how to] highlight those gifts, so that they can be [their best] for their lives and for their families?"[2]

Longo's has also introduced a master coach program to help support managers in becoming the next level of leaders. "One of my favourite questions in coaching is: are the best years ahead of you or behind you?" says Longo. "When I was first asked that by my coach, it stopped me in my tracks, and I had to think about it. Those are the kinds of questions that make you think beyond the moment. And it makes you think, 'What legacy do you want to leave in this world? What are the things that you want to be doing? And what are the action steps you need to take to get there?' And that'll help people be the best they can be and bring out those gifts that they've got."[3]

Another great example is Clio, which has a dedicated internal coach who works with team members. Combined with the organization's ongoing feedback loop (which we discussed in chapter 5), Clio has been able to set up its future leaders for success. "[We ensure our staff has the] resources that they can go to, to increase their bench strength, and go and tackle new challenges," says co-founder and CEO Jack Newton. "Those are some of the ways that we think we're moving forward with, and helping achieve that vision of, being a high performing and human organization."[4]

A word on mentorship

If you've identified someone who has the interest and skill sets to become a leader, and if you have the organizational capacity, then mentoring them is a great opportunity. But remember that mentoring someone is a one-on-one relationship and both parties must want to participate.

A few years ago I was working with a client who was developing a mentorship program where everyone in the organization at the vice president level and up would be required to mentor someone. It was a well-thought-out program, but I wasn't confident it would work and so I asked some hard questions: How did they know everyone would be a good mentor? Had they asked who on the team wanted to be a mentor? Were there other people within the organization who might make better mentors?

For organizations with the capacity, mentoring is a great opportunity both for the mentor and the mentee to learn and grow. And that's an important point: mentoring isn't just about building up the next generation of leaders, it's about developing and expanding the abilities of our current leaders as well—through continuous learning.

Alan Webber, the co-founder of *Fast Company*, has said of reverse mentoring: "[It's] a situation where the old fogies in an organization realize that by the time you're in your forties and fifties, you're not in touch with the future the same way the young [twenty-somethings]. They come with fresh eyes, open minds, and instant links to the technology of our future."[5] (Those of you who have seen *The Intern*, with Anne Hathaway and Robert De Niro, will understand!) Evan Siddall, president and CEO at the Canada Mortgage and Housing Corporation, is a culturepreneur who has taken advantage of the opportunity for reverse mentors. Siddall points to learning how to better leverage social media as one way this type of relationship has been helpful for him: "It's an incredible communication vehicle, and I've used it ... for getting messages out and for promoting what we're trying to do. That's just one example."[6]

Succession planning

Every organization knows how important succession planning is, and now more than ever it needs to be a priority in terms of identifying leaders. Again, we need to get out of the mindset of rewarding high performers with a spot in the line of succession, and into the mindset of identifying culturepreneurial leaders and preparing them for senior roles. That means teaching those who are in the process of succession planning a different way: having a clear, defined list of the attributes and experiences you want in your successor, and then looking for those competencies and experiences.

If it's done really well, succession planning will lead to more people opting out of leadership roles than opting in to them. We need to be more deliberate in the management of high performers who want to be leaders and those who are leaders but may not want a more senior track. It starts with leadership competencies and identifying the kinds of behaviours that you want to see represented in your organization in order to move you toward your desired culture.

Culturepreneurs understand and respect that not everyone is interested in leadership; they support, develop, and encourage those who are—and they identify those who should be. This shift in thinking means taking the time to understand not just the skills but the interests of our team members, so that we can help guide future leaders in the right direction. For some that direction will be up, for others it will be lateral, and for still others it will mean staying where they are happy and performing well.

The takeaway:
Not everyone wants to be (or can be) a leader

- High performance individuals don't always become high performance leaders: some aren't interested in senior leadership, others aren't suited for leadership roles. Don't assume everyone is interested in becoming a senior leader. The most important question to ask is: do you want to be considered for a leadership role?

- Culturepreneurial leaders can be coaches for the next generation of leaders. Take an interest in high potential team members and help them develop their leadership skills.

- Leaders should make it okay for people to opt out of leadership positions, even temporarily. Be deliberate about supporting career development for those who want to take the next step, and for those who want to be leaders but not via the senior leadership track.

- Mentoring is an opportunity for both the mentor and the mentee to gain knowledge and skills—but it only works if both parties are interested and committed to the process.

- In succession planning, leadership roles should be seen less as a reward for performance and more as an opportunity to develop someone with the right mix of attitudes and experiences necessary to do the job. Look for people whose behaviours align with the organization's values, then test their patterns of behaviour and leadership aptitude.

16

PREPARING FOR
THE NEXT EVOLUTION

"Change has to be fundamental to a company's culture, or
there is no way it can survive."

TOBIAS LÜTKE, co-founder and CEO, Shopify

At its core, culturepreneurial leadership and its five key attributes are all about tuning in to yourself and your organization, and then using those tools to connect with your team to drive performance. It's going to take time and a shift in thinking for many leaders—you're going to be great at some pieces of the puzzle right away, but other elements will be a struggle for months or maybe years. Remember, you're on a journey.

But what happens once you've figured out your rhythm and shifted your thinking? What's next?

For leaders looking to take things to the next level, it is as simple as genuinely wanting to help people and executing on that in a positive way. And I want to be clear here: I'm using "leader" not only to mean executives or people who are leading others, but also to mean people who are leading important projects, thought leaders or contribution leaders, and people

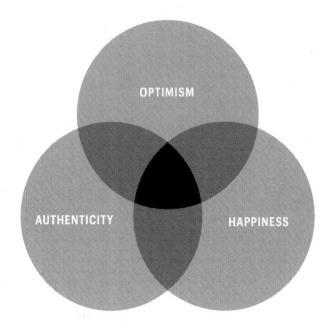

Figure 5. The Culturepreneur Triangle

who are leading working groups and boards. This new mind-set applies to leaders at all levels.

When you come from a place of wanting to help others, your work becomes less about management theory and more about helping others unlock what makes them happy and successful. It's something I call the Culturepreneur Triangle—the sweet spot where optimism, happiness, and authenticity overlap. You guide people to that spot according to the individual: we arrive at the triangle in different ways, and refocusing our thinking in this way allows us to find and connect with people who bring different styles, mindsets, and experiences to the table.

Shawn Achor, CEO at GoodThink Inc., has written and spoken extensively on the benefits of happiness and positivity, saying that "if we change our formula for happiness and success, what we can do is change the way that we can then affect reality."[1] Achor's research has found that 75 percent of job successes are predicted by a person's levels of optimism, social supports, and approach to stress.

Unlocking potential in others, and helping them unlock happiness in their work, is an art. We are going through an unprecedented period during which a large number of leadership talent will be retiring; the youngest baby boomers will reach traditional retirement age by 2029. So we will need to develop not only more leaders but different, culturepreneurial leaders. People will also have to come to leadership roles in new and different ways. Leaders with the skills and knowledge to support their teams to be happy and successful in their work—in addition to knowledge of management theory and organizational development strategy—will become an in-demand commodity. But make no mistake: for many of us, this is going to require significant change, and we're going to have to want to make it.

The age of social enterprise and B Corporations

Corporate social responsibility programs and companies that give back are nothing new; there have always been organizations with incredible programs in place to support causes that resonate with their teams and align with their mission and values. But consumer, client, and employee demand for companies that balance performance with the greater good is steadily increasing. Over the past number of years, we have witnessed, as a Deloitte report puts it, "the growing shift from an internal, enterprise focus to an external, ecosystem one... Organizations on the leading edge of both of these changes embody our concept of the social enterprise: an organization that is alert enough to sense, and responsive enough to accommodate, the gamut of stakeholder expectations and demands."[2] As reported in the *Financial Times*, as recently as 2018, it was estimated that globally "almost half as many people are creating ventures with a primarily social or environmental purpose as those with a solely commercial aim."[3]

Since 2006, we've seen the rise of B Corporations, described by *Triple Pundit* as "businesses that meet the highest standards of verified social and environmental performance, public transparency, and legal accountability to balance profit and purpose. Warby Parker, Danone North America, Patagonia, Natura, Etsy, and Ben & Jerry's are some examples."[4] As of March 2021, there are more than 3,800 certified B Corporations across 150 industries in 74 countries worldwide.[5]

I predict that there will come a day—likely sooner than later—when to remain relevant and competitive at retaining and recruiting talent, organizations will need to be either a social enterprise or a B Corporation. They will need a culture rooted in furthering the social good and culturepreneurs to drive performance of their teams. Leaders who can navigate this path today will be ahead of the game when finding solutions in the future.

Leaders need to
start looking at
performance as
the outcome,
not as the goal.

The evolution of performance

We've talked at length about how trust, passion, connection, and recognition can drive performance. But if you're going to examine (and possibly alter) the drivers of performance within your organization, you also need to revisit the definition of performance. Leaders need to start looking at performance as the outcome, not as the goal. Put another way, performance needs to be viewed through a qualitative lens, not just a quantitative one.

When you define performance only by quantitative markers (volume, efficiency, and so on), you risk having successful, effective performers who are unhappy and disconnected from what they're doing. But when you look at performance through a qualitative lens, when you factor in optimism, happiness, and authenticity and think of performance as an outcome, then your high performers are those who are also happier and more connected to what they're doing—and think of what can be accomplished in an environment where everyone's aligned to what they do! Achor's research found that when people are happy and positive, business outcomes improve: "your brain at positive is 31 percent more productive than your brain at negative, neutral, or stressed."[6]

Recently, I was in a meeting with a potential new client. My goal, of course, was to secure new business, but instead of focusing my pitch on that goal, I shifted my thinking and made it my goal to inspire a high performance culture. New business (I hoped) would be the outcome, but my goal was finding ways for Waterstone to help drive performance within the prospective client's organization. Almost immediately, the company's CEO identified one of their free business offerings that overlapped with the potential needs of the people and talent connections that Waterstone has thanks to our executive search business and the Canada's Most Admired program. Will connecting this company with our contacts definitely result in business for Waterstone? No. And so if my goal was securing new business, the meeting could have been seen as a bust. But my goal was to see where I could help, and together the CEO and I found a clear path for that. Will we get the company's business in the future? Maybe. We'll certainly be on the CEO's radar, and between that and having built up some good corporate karma, I would say the meeting was a success.

Shifting the way leaders view and measure performance is a work in progress. Reducing the role of quantitative measures is going to be a fundamental shift and it's not going to happen quickly. But for culturepreneurs, it's the next big leap. I think the new generations of leaders entering the workforce will get this and embrace it—and if that happens, then we've done our job.

Sharing best practices

I've been a member of either YPO or the Entrepreneurs' Organization (EO) for more than twenty years. To this day, one of the most important benefits I get from my membership is the opportunity to network with other leaders, share best practices, and learn from the experiences we've all had in trying to grow and sustain our organizations and their cultures. I think everyone should be involved in a peer-to-peer network of some sort. Many of these peer groups are geared to CEOs, but I think they need to be available to non-CEO leaders as well, because we learn best from our peers. And when you work in a small group and you build an environment of trust, not unlike what we teach through Waterstone's Building High Performance Teams and Cultures program, there's affinity and relatability that makes it real.

For those who cannot access peer-to-peer networks, just going out and asking questions and having conversations is an incredible tool. If you're not comfortable jumping into a conversation, send out a note and ask for help. I truly believe that 99.9 percent of the world's population is good and wants to help other people succeed. Just be sure to pay it forward!

Once you've harnessed the idea of culturepreneurship and honed the skills behind Waterstone's Culturepreneur Operating System, it can be used for a myriad of purposes—from organizational and people issues to global environmental issues. When we put culture at the centre of strategy, it drives a new way of thinking about all aspects of our business. That opens doors we didn't even know were there, for ourselves and our organizations, and it will ultimately usher in the next evolution of leadership and culture as competitive advantage. Culturepreneurs will lead the way forward.

The takeaway:
The next evolution will be about impact on others

- The Culturepreneur Triangle is found at the inter-section of optimism, happiness, and authenticity. Everyone gets to this place in a unique way, and if we can help people find the connection, we can unlock happiness and success for our team members.

- Corporate social responsibility programs continue to gain importance in finding and retaining talent. There may come a time when, to be competitive, all organizations will need a culture rooted in driving social good.

- Culturepreneurs need to view performance as the outcome, not the goal. By factoring optimism, hap-piness, and authenticity into performance, you can begin to drive performance through shared purpose and connection.

- Peer-to-peer networks are an excellent way to make connections and learn from others who bring diverse backgrounds, experiences, and ways of thinking to the table.

- Culturepreneurs pay it forward.

ACKNOWLEDGEMENTS

The idea behind this book came to me a few years ago when our clients started to use a number of elements of Waterstone's Culturepreneur Operating System with great success. The results were astounding and I knew there was a new world emerging in the form of culture as competitive advantage. I have also lived and witnessed a change in how effective leaders in high performance cultures lead. They are the ultimate examples of self-awareness and adaptation, and they truly value getting to know their team members. This new breed of leaders is changing organizations for the better.

I want to thank all of the clients of Waterstone Human Capital and the nominees and winners of the Canada's Most Admired Corporate Cultures and Canada's Most Admired CEO program for their generosity of spirit, idea exchange, and openness. You are the true culturepreneurs and the innovators behind Waterstone's Culturepreneur Operating System.

Great appreciation and a shout-out to all of the team members and Board of Directors of Waterstone Human Capital—what a team you are and, more importantly, each of you is so special and unique and you make us what we are today and what we will be tomorrow.

Lindsay George was my collaborator on this book. She is, among other things, wonderful and a true rock star. Lindsay ran our marketing team and work, championed the expansion of the Canada's Most Admired program, and worked tirelessly with me almost daily on this book and all through the COVID-19 pandemic. Lindsay, thank you from the bottom of my heart for your commitment to this work. And thanks for stepping out on this journey with me.

To Steve Parker, Don Babick, Mike Cordoba, Mark Healy, Nicole Bendaly, and Matt Burgess for their wisdom, insight, and for pushing me forward to complete this book during the unique times of 2020.

To everyone I missed who invested their time into this book: my apologies. May your futures be bigger than your pasts!

To Kaelen, Braeden, and Blair for believing in me always and giving me another reason to be a better leader. To Jaiden and Corsen—hoping to see you on the other side. I love you all.

Finally, to Tanya, to whom I dedicate this book: here is to our future being bigger than our past—the best is yet to come!

WATERSTONE HUMAN CAPITAL'S PLAYBOOK FOR SUCCESS

Name: Marty Parker

Title: President & CEO

Playbook for Success

20 Loves

1 My beautiful wife, Tanya

2 My kids: Blair, Braeden, Jaiden, Corsen, Kaelen

3 My siblings and parents

4 Close friendships

5 Waterstone: our team and clients

6 Great food and wine

7 Music

8 Great people

9 Sunshine, sunsets, and sunrises

10 The water: oceans, lakes, rivers

11 Winning

12 Coaching

13 Travelling

14 Sports

15 Cooking

16 Great book/movie

17 Fitness and mindfulness

18 Personal growth and development

19 Children/kids/youth

20 Feeling happiness and accomplishment

DISC profile

Descriptors

Driving	Inspiring	Relaxed	Cautious
Ambitious	Magnetic	Passive	Careful
Pioneering	Enthusiastic	Patient	Exacting
Strong-willed	Persuasive	Possessive	Systematic
Determined	Convincing	Predictable	Accurate
Competitive	Poised	Consistent	Open-minded
Decisive	Optimistic	Steady	Balanced judgment
Venturesome	Trusting	Stable	Diplomatic
Dominance	**Influencing**	**Steadiness**	**Compliance**
Calculating	Reflective	Mobile	Firm
Cooperative	Factual	Active	Independent
Hesitant	Calculating	Restless	Self-willed
Cautious	Skeptical	Impatient	Obstinate
Agreeable	Logical	Pressure-oriented	Unsystematic
Modest	Suspicious	Eager	Uninhibited
Peaceful	Matter-of-fact	Flexible	Arbitrary
Unobtrusive	Incisive	Impulsive	Unbending

Motivators

1	Aesthetic	IND
2	Individualistic	STR
3	Social	SIT
4	Theoretical	SIT
5	Traditional	IND
6	Utilitarian	STR

IND: Indifferent

SIT: Situational

STR: Strong

Professional goals

3-year plan

- Diversify and grow Waterstone in culture talent management
- Become the best leader I can of high performance teams and cultures

1-year plan

- Grow our team, business, and culture
- Make the transition to leader and builder of people
- Grow, find, and develop the right people to scale the business

6-month plan

- New Waterstone Culture Institute leader recruited and onboarded
- New people and culture leader trained and onboarded
- One acquisition complete—others identified

Personal goals

3-year plan

- More time to enjoy my wife and family
- Exceptional health in the top 5 percent of my age
- Travel to ten additional new destinations

1-year plan

- Extremely fit: 180–185 lbs, top 5 percent
- Support the transitions and lives of my wife and children

6-month plan

- Build a deep and loving daily relationship with my wife
- Foster a supportive and growing relationship with my kids
- Expand my mindfulness training

Development and coaching

Development needs

- Listen actively—ongoing development channels

Coaching needs

- Fitness and mindfulness: an ongoing journey—Greg Wells
- How to unlock the potential of highest performers—various

Best day

A great day at work is:

Coaching, winning, growing, and building with an engaged and high performance team and clients.

A great day at home is:

Peace, health, love with Tanya, the kids, and our close friends.

Favourites

Food:	Greek/Italian (pizza)
Drink:	Water/wine
Snack:	Berries and nuts
Candy:	Swedish Berries
Sport:	Hockey, football, golf
Colour:	Blue
Hobby:	Golf and personal growth
Restaurant:	Capra's/Rogues/Craft

Favourite quote

"The last of the human freedoms—to choose one's attitude in any given set of circumstances."

VIKTOR FRANKL

Superpower/unique attributes

At work:	Coaching and inspiring
At home:	Laughing and supporting

RESOURCES

Over the years, I have been inspired by and come to rely on many books, websites, and podcasts. I've pulled together a few of my favourites—and I couldn't help including my own previous book, which is somewhat self-serving, but I honestly think it's a great guide for helping to develop high performance cultures.

Books

Achor, Shawn. *The Happiness Advantage: The Seven Principles of Positive Psychology That Fuel Success and Performance at Work.* New York: Crown Business, 2010.

Adizes, Ichak. *Managing Corporate Lifecycles.* Upper Saddle River, NJ: Prentice Hall Press, 1999.

Collins, Jim, and Jerry I. Porras. *Built to Last: Successful Habits of Visionary Companies.* New York: Harper Business, 1994.

Connors, Roger, Tom Smith, and Craig Hickman. *The Oz Principle: Getting Results Through Individual and Organizational Accountability.* New York: Penguin Group, 2004.

Covey, Stephen R. *The 7 Habits of Highly Effective People* (30th anniversary edition). New York: Simon & Schuster, 2020.

Drucker, Peter. *The Effective Executive: The Definitive Guide to Getting the Right Things Done.* Boston, MA: Harper Business, 2006.

Duckworth, Angela. *Grit: The Power of Passion and Perseverance*. New York: Scribner, 2016.

Gordon, Jon. *The Energy Bus: 10 Rules to Fuel Your Life, Work, and Team with Positive Energy*. Hoboken, NJ: John Wiley & Sons, 2007.

Jackson, Phil, and Hugh Delehanty. *Eleven Rings: The Soul of Success*. New York: Penguin Books, 2014.

Kaplan, Barry, and Jeffrey Manchester. *The Power of Vulnerability: How to Create a Team of Leaders by Shifting Inward*. Austin, TX: Greenleaf Book Group Press, 2018.

Maister, David H. *True Professionalism: The Courage to Care About Your People, Your Clients, and Your Career*. New York: Free Press, 2000.

Montminy, Zelana. *21 Days to Resilience: How to Transcend the Daily Grind, Deal with the Tough Stuff, and Discover Your Strongest Self*. New York: HarperCollins, 2016.

Parker, Marty. *Culture Connection: How Developing a Winning Culture Will Give Your Organization a Competitive Advantage*. Toronto: McGraw-Hill, 2012.

Pontefract, Dan. *Flat Army: Creating a Connected and Engaged Organization*. Vancouver: Figure 1 Publishing, 2013.

Sandberg, Sheryl, with Nell Scovell. *Lean In: Women, Work, and the Will to Lead*. New York: Alfred A. Knopf, 2013.

Schmidt, Eric, Jonathan Rosenberg, and Alan Eagle. *Trillion Dollar Coach: The Leadership Playbook of Silicon Valley's Bill Campbell*. New York: HarperCollins, 2019.

Sharp, Isadore. *Four Seasons: The Story of a Business Philosophy*. New York: Penguin Group, 2009.

Sinek, Simon. *Start with Why: How Great Leaders Inspire Everyone to Take Action*. New York: Penguin Group, 2011.

Stein, Steven J., and Howard E. Book. *The EQ Edge: Emotional Intelligence and Your Success*. Mississauga, ON: Jossey-Bass, 2000.

Podcasts

- *Building High Performance Cultures* (anchor.fm/waterstone-human-capital)

- *The Dr. Greg Wells Podcast* (drgregwells.com/podcast)

- *The John Maxwell Leadership Podcast* (johnmaxwellleadership podcast.com)

- *Leading on Purpose* (voiceamerica.com/show/3971/leading-on-purpose)

- *SmartLess* (smartless.simplecast.com)

- *The Tony Robbins Podcast* (tonyrobbins.libsyn.com)

NOTES

Introduction

1 Marty Parker's DISC Profile, Excel Group Development—Building Performance, xlteamwork.com, copyright © 1984–2017, Target Training International, Ltd.

2 Marty Parker, *Culture Connection: How Developing a Winning Culture Will Give Your Organization a Competitive Advantage* (Toronto: McGraw-Hill, 2012), 21.

Chapter 1: A Brief History of Corporate Culture

Epigraph: Confucius quotation, "Past and Future Sayings and Quotes," Wise Sayings, wiseoldsayings.com/past-and-future-quotes/#ixzz6YKL5NFOY.

1 Marty Parker and Michael McCain, "Episode 18: Owning Your Culture," August 19, 2020, in *Building High Performance Cultures*, podcast, 47:14, youtu.be/ZherCxmBu14.

2 See "Early Postwar Developments: Domestic Affairs," *Encyclopedia Britannica*, britannica.com/place/Canada/Early-postwar-developments; and Andrea Rees Davies and Brenda D. Frink, "The Origins of the Ideal Worker: The Separation of Work and Home in the United States from the Market Revolution to 1950," *Work and Occupations* 41, no. 1 (2014), doi.org/10.1177/0730888413515893.

3 *Merriam-Webster*, s.v., "the American dream," (noun phrase), accessed December 6, 2020, merriam-webster.com/dictionary/the%20American%20dream.

4   Lizabeth Cohen, "A Consumers' Republic: The Politics of Mass Consumption in Postwar America," *Journal of Consumer Research* 31, no. 1 (2004), doi.org/10.1086/383439.

5   Edgar H. Schein and Peter A. Schein, "A New Era for Culture, Change, and Leadership," MIT *Sloan Management Review*, June 5, 2019, sloanreview.mit.edu/article/a-new-era-for-culture-change-and-leadership.

6   "About," Drucker Institute, accessed November 21, 2020, drucker.institute/perspective/about-peter-drucker.

7   Gail L. Perry, "Management Theory of Robert Waterman," Business.com, March 17, 2011, business.com/articles/management-theory-of-robert-waterman.

8   "About," Drucker Institute.

9   John Kotter, "Does Corporate Culture Drive Financial Performance?" *Forbes*, February 10, 2011, forbes.com/sites/johnkotter/2011/02/10/does-corporate-culture-drive-financial-performance/?sh=2d3d78327e9e.

10   Ed Michaels, Helen Handfield-Jones, and Beth Axelrod, *The War for Talent* (Boston, MA: Harvard Business School Press, 2001).

Chapter 2: The Era of Culturepreneurship

Epigraph: Nick Santaniello, "The 50 Most Inspirational Company Culture Quotes of All-Time," *Northpass*, July 26, 2017, northpass.com/blog/the-50-most-inspirational-company-culture-quotes-of-all-time.

1   Kevin Nogle, "Football 101: What Is a West Coast Offense?" *The Phinsider*, February 13, 2014, thephinsider.com/2014/2/13/5406774/football-101-what-is-a-west-coast-offense.

2   Adrian Dater, "The '95 Devils, 20 Years Later: How a Team and Its Infamous Trap Changed the NHL," BleacherReport.com, June 7, 2015, bleacherreport.com/articles/2481173-the-95-devils-20-years-later-how-a-team-and-its-infamous-trap-changed-the-nhl.

3 Marty Parker and Mike Wessinger, "Episode 12: Performance-Driven Cultures," *Building High Performance Cultures*, July 8, 2020, podcast, 22:37, youtu.be/59Z0wV4qlH4.

4 Parker and Wessinger, "Episode 12."

5 Parker and Wessinger, "Episode 12."

6 Rob Reed, "The Kat Cole Story: Unlikely Success at the Intersection of Hooters and Cinnabon," *Forbes*, August 26, 2020, forbes.com/sites/robreed/2020/08/26/the-kat-cole-story-unlikely-success-at-the-intersection-of-hooters-and-cinnabon/?sh=3c34fab21a84.

7 Email correspondence with David Ossip, February 2021. See also Marty Parker and David Ossip, "Episode 21: The Role of Leaders in Transforming Culture," *Building High Performance Cultures*, September 16, 2020, podcast, 31:26, youtu.be/m1YysIY6nrM.

8 Email correspondence with David Ossip.

9 Email correspondence with David Ossip.

10 See Katie Roof, "Ceridian Up 42% Following Payroll Software IPO," *TechCrunch*, April 26, 2018, tcrn.ch/2KdfeOp; and "Ceridian HCM Holding Inc (CDAY)," Yahoo! Finance, accessed December 8, 2020, finance.yahoo.com/quote/CDAY/.

Chapter 3: Purpose Is Your New Mission

Epigraph: Amit Chowdhry, "Lessons Learned from 4 Steve Jobs Quotes," *Forbes*, October 5, 2013, forbes.com/sites/amitchowdhry/2013/10/05/lessons-learned-from-4-steve-jobs-quotes/#1a2e35d74f69.

1 Simon Sinek, "The Science of WHY," LinkedIn Pulse, November 16, 2017, linkedin.com/pulse/science-why-simon-sinek.

2 Marty Parker and Alim Somani, "Episode 14: The Link Between Values, Behaviours and Culture," *Building High Performance Cultures*, July 29, 2020, podcast, 41:42, youtu.be/NfH8QoHW-Og.

3 Parker and Somani, "Episode 14."

4 Parker and Somani, "Episode 14."

5 Marty Parker and Joanna Griffiths, "Episode 30: Building a Mission-Led Organization," *Building High Performance Cultures*, January 13, 2021, podcast, 32:10, youtube.com/watch?v=YL1Z rovi3rQ.

6 Nathan Chan and Joanna Griffiths, "328: Building a $50M Underwear Empire Off $20K: Joanna Griffiths KNIX," *Foundr*, October 15, 2020, podcast, 51:41, foundr.com/joanna-griffiths-knixwear.

7 Parker and Griffiths, "Episode 30."

8 Marty Parker and Mohamad Fakih, "Episode 7: Purpose-Driven Culture," *Building High Performance Cultures*, June 3, 2020, podcast, 42:04, youtu.be/9vf937qWlc4.

9 Parker and Fakih, "Episode 7."

10 Mohamad Fakih, Canada's Most Admired CEO award submission, 2019.

11 "UNHCR Canada and Paramount Fine Foods CEO Mohamad Fakih to Raise Funds for Rohingya Refugees," UNHCR Canada press release, May 16, 2018, unhcr.ca/news/mohamad-fakih-raise-funds-rohingya-refugees.

12 "Lebanese-Canadian Entrepreneur Mohamad Fakih Joins the Humanitarian Coalition in Beirut for Relief Efforts," Cision press release, August 20, 2020, newswire.ca/news-releases/ -r-e-p-e-a-t-lebanese-canadian-entrepreneur-mohamad-fakih-joins-the-humanitarian-coalition-in-beirut-for-relief-efforts-- 835218788.html.

13 Parker and Fakih, "Episode 7."

14 Ed Michaels, Helen Handfield-Jones, and Beth Axelrod, excerpt from *The War for Talent*, Working Knowledge, Harvard Business School, October 29, 2001, hbswk.hbs.edu/archive/ war-for-talent.

Chapter 4: The Rise of Bespoke Leadership

Epigraph: Pink quotation, BrainyQuote, accessed September 17, 2020, brainyquote.com/quotes/pink_406666.

1 Zechuan Deng, René Morissette, and Derek Messacar, "Running the Economy Remotely: Potential for Working from Home During and After COVID-19," Statistics Canada, May 28, 2020, www150.statcan.gc.ca/n1/pub/45-28-0001/2020001/article/00026-eng.htm.

2 Daniel H. Pink, *Free Agent Nation: The Future of Working for Yourself* (New York: Business Plus, 2001), 25.

3 Nick van Dam, ed., *Elevating Learning & Development: Insights and Practical Guidance from the Field* (McKinsey & Company, 2018), 3, mckinsey.com/business-functions/organization/our-insights/elevating-learning-and-development-insights-and-practical-guidance-from-the-field.

4 As cited in "Freelancers Predicted to Become the U.S. Workforce Majority Within a Decade, with Nearly 50% of Millennial Workers Already Freelancing, Annual 'Freelancing in America' Study Finds," Upwork press release, October 17, 2017, upwork.com/press/releases/freelancing-in-america-2017.

5 Marty Parker and John Anderson, "Episode 8: The Role of Culture in Recruitment and Retention," *Building High Performance Cultures*, June 10, 2020, podcast, 22:20, youtu.be/hN7QqNkgCjc.

Chapter 5: Balancing People and Performance

Epigraph: Heike Young, "9 Thought-Provoking Quotes About Work-Life Balance," Medium.com/@Salesforce, July 8, 2015, medium.com/@salesforce/9-thought-provoking-quotes-about-work-life-balance-64673dea0747.

1 "Our History," Mr. Lube, accessed September 28, 2020, mrlube.com/About-Mr-Lube/History-of-Mr--Lube.aspx.

2 "58% of Canadian Workers Are Stressed on a Daily Basis: Survey," Benefits Canada, February 6, 2017, benefitscanada.com/news/58-of-canadian-workers-are-stressed-on-a-daily-basis-survey-93454.

3 Marty Parker and Dr. Greg Wells, "Episode 1: Building High Performance Cultures: Dr. Greg Wells of Wells Performance," *Building High Performance Cultures*, April 22, 2020, podcast, 43:25, youtu.be/ZVgrEID2rbc.

4 Cal Newport, *Deep Work: Rules for Focused Success in a Distracted World* (New York: Grand Central Publishing, 2016), 3, 6.

5 Newport, *Deep Work*, 224.

6 Marty Parker and Jack Newton, "Episode 20: Building a Deliberately Developmental Culture," *Building High Performance Cultures*, September 9, 2020, podcast, 28:18, youtu.be/UUF e5PpSrLM.

7 Parker and Newton, "Episode 20."

8 Parker and Newton, "Episode 20."

9 "Workplace Mental Health Playbook for Business Leaders," CAMH, accessed September 29, 2020, camh.ca/en/health-info/workplace-mental-health-playbook-for-business-leaders.

Chapter 6: The Why and How of Measuring Culture

Epigraph: Nick Santaniello, "The 50 Most Inspirational Company Culture Quotes of All-Time," *Northpass*, July 26, 2017, northpass.com/blog/the-50-most-inspirational-company-culture-quotes-of-all-time.

1 Parker, *Culture Connection*, 2–3.

2 Parker, *Culture Connection*, 92.

3 Marty Parker and Sean O'Brien, "Episode 4: Leadership's Role in Culture Change," *Building High Performance Cultures*, May 13, 2020, podcast, 39:33, youtu.be/sj4_zt4EE_4.

4 Parker and O'Brien, "Episode 4."

5   Reliance Home Comfort, Canada's Most Admired Corporate
    Cultures award submission, 2019.
6   Parker and Wessinger, "Episode 12."
7   Matthew Corritore, Amir Goldberg, and Sameer B. Srivastava,
    "The New Analytics of Culture," *Harvard Business Review*,
    January–February 2020, hbr.org/2020/01/the-new-analytics-
    of-culture.

Chapter 7: Clarity of Vision and Leadership Communication

Epigraph: George Bernard Shaw quotation, BrainyQuote, brainy.
    quote.com/topics/communication-quotes.
1   Frances X. Frei and Anne Morriss, "Begin with Trust,"
    Harvard Business Review, May–June 2020, hbr.org/2020/05/
    begin-with-trust.
2   Frei and Morriss, "Begin with Trust."
3   "The VARK Modalities," VARK, accessed October 21, 2020,
    vark-learn.com/introduction-to-vark/the-vark-modalities.
4   Parker, *Culture Connection*, 55.
5   Parker and O'Brien, "Episode 4."
6   Parker and O'Brien, "Episode 4."

Chapter 8: Waterstone's Culturepreneur Operating System

Epigraph: Peggy Johnson quotation, BrainyQuote, accessed January
    14, 2021, brainyquote.com/quotes/peggy_johnson_886880.
1   Brian Scudamore, "This Visualization Technique Helped Me
    Build a $100M Business," *Inc.*, October 21, 2015, inc.com/
    empact/this-visualization-technique-helped-me-build-a-
    100m-business.html.

Chapter 9: The New Leadership Mix

Epigraph: Barack Obama quotation, BrainyQuote, accessed October 11, 2020, brainyquote.com/search_results?q=change.

1   "Guide: Understand Team Effectiveness," re:Work, accessed October 12, 2020, rework.withgoogle.com/print/guides/57213 12655835136.
2   "Guide," re:Work.
3   Kevin Eikenberry and Jeff Manchester, "The Power of Vulnerability with Jeff Manchester," *The Remarkable Leadership Podcast*, March 21, 2018, podcast, 24:46, youtu.be/U6LBJ2iXP08.
4   Harvard Business School, "Scandinavian Airlines System," video prepared by John P. Kotter, copyright 1989 by the President and Fellows of Harvard College.

Chapter 10: Building a Culture of Safety

Epigraph: Nick Johnson, "45 Inspiring Quotes About Business Growth—and Tips for Success," Salesforce, December 11, 2020, salesforce.com/blog/2019/01/inspirational-business-quotes-2019.html.

1   *Keeping Up with Gen Z*, National Retail Federation, Fall 2019, cdn.nrf.com/sites/default/files/2019-10/NRF%20Consumer%20View%20Fall%202019.pdf.
2   Marc Prensky, "Digital Natives, Digital Immigrants," *On the Horizon* 9, no. 5 (October 2001), marcprensky.com/writing/Prensky%20-%20Digital%20Natives,%20Digital%20Immigrants%20-%20Part1.pdf.
3   As cited in Vanessa Buote,"Most Employees Feel Authentic at Work, but It Can Take a While," *Harvard Business Review*, May 11, 2016, hbr.org/2016/05/most-employees-feel-authentic-at-work-but-it-can-take-a-while.
4   Marty Parker and Laurie Schultz, "Episode 19: Getting the People and Culture Formula Right," *Building High Performance*

Cultures, August 26, 2020, podcast, 28:15, youtu.be/h2he1V
Q1591.

5 Parker and Schultz, "Episode 19."

Chapter 11: Fostering Accountability, Meaning, and Impact

Epigraph: Gloria Steinem quotation, BrainyQuote, accessed
October 12, 2020, brainyquote.com/search_results?q=impact.

1 "Guide," re:Work.

2 John Leo Weber, "RACI Matrix Template," Project Manager,
May 1, 2020, projectmanager.com/blog/how-to-make-a-raci-
chart-for-a-project-with-example.

Chapter 12: Continuous Learning

Epigraph: Brené Brown quotation, BrainyQuote, accessed January
17, 2021, brainyquote.com/quotes/brene_brown_553057.

1 Michael Simmons, "Bill Gates, Warren Buffett, and Oprah All
Use the 5-Hour Rule. Here's How This Powerful Habit Works,"
Business Insider, February 25, 2020, businessinsider.com/
bill-gates-warren-buffet-and-oprah-all-use-the-5-hour-rule-
2017-7#1-read-1.

2 John Coleman, "For Those Who Want to Lead, Read," *Harvard
Business Review*, August 15, 2012, hbr.org/2012/08/for-those-
who-want-to-lead-rea.

3 Rob Cross, Reb Rebele, and Adam Grant, "Collaborative
Overload," *Harvard Business Review*, January–February 2016,
hbr.org/2016/01/collaborative-overload.

4 "Leading in Learning: Building Capabilities to Deliver on Your
Business Strategy," Bersin by Deloitte, accessed January 16,
2021, www2.deloitte.com/content/dam/Deloitte/global/
Documents/HumanCapital/gx-cons-hc-learning-solutions-
placemat.pdf.

5   Peter M. Senge, *The Fifth Discipline: The Art & Practice of the Learning Organization*, rev. ed. (New York: Currency, 2006), 10.

6   Marilee Adams, *Change Your Questions, Change Your Life: 12 Powerful Tools for Leadership, Coaching, and Life*, 3rd ed. (San Francisco, CA: Berrett-Koehler, 2016), 8.

7   Parker and Griffiths, "Episode 30."

Chapter 13: Diversity and Inclusion, Beyond Buzzwords

Epigraph: Shannon Howard, "5 Diversity and Inclusion Quotes for the Workplace," The Predictive Index, accessed October 30, 2020, predictiveindex.com/blog/5-diversity-and-inclusion-quotes-for-the-workplace.

1   Parker and Griffiths, "Episode 30."

2   Marty Parker and Debra Hewson, "Episode 11: Creating a Culture of Trust and Empowerment," *Building High Performance Cultures*, June 29, 2020, podcast, 33:40, youtu.be/tTwm9eYOVAE.

3   Rogers Communications Inc., Canada's Most Admired Corporate Cultures award submission, 2019.

4   Unbounce, Canada's Most Admired Corporate Cultures award submission, 2019.

Chapter 14: The Competitive Advantage of Soft Skills

Epigraph: Dean Koontz quotation, Goodreads, accessed October 27, 2020, goodreads.com/quotes/94552-some-people-think-only-intellect-counts-knowing-how-to-solve.

1   As cited in "LinkedIn Releases 2019 Global Talent Trends Report," LinkedIn press release, January 28, 2019, news.linkedin.com/2019/January/linkedin-releases-2019-global-talent-trends-report.

2 "Dan Sullivan's Best Career Advice: 10 Secrets to Success for Today's Entrepreneur," *Multiplier Mindset Blog*, Strategic Coach, accessed February 28, 2021, resources.strategiccoach.com/the-multiplier-mindset-blog/dan-sullivan-s-best-career-advice-10-secrets-to-success-for-today-s-entrepreneur.

3 "The Meaning of Emotional Intelligence," Institute for Health and Human Potential, accessed December 6, 2020, ihhp.com/meaning-of-emotional-intelligence.

4 Daniel Goleman and Richard E. Boyatzis, "Emotional Intelligence Has 12 Elements. Which Do You Need to Work On?" *Harvard Business Review*, February 6, 2017, hbr.org/2017/02/emotional-intelligence-has-12-elements-which-do-you-need-to-work-on.

5 Goleman and Boyatzis, "Emotional Intelligence Has 12 Elements."

6 Marty Parker and Phil Verster, "Episode 26: Building Trust Within Your Corporate Culture," *Building High Performance Cultures*, November 4, 2020, podcast, 36:01, youtu.be/T3gVtTMt0Yg.

7 Parker and Verster, "Episode 26."

8 Parker and Wessinger, "Episode 12."

9 Parker and Wessinger, "Episode 12."

Chapter 15: Next-Generation Leaders and Culturepreneurs

Epigraph: Masai Ujiri quotation, BrainyQuote, accessed October 16, 2020, brainyquote.com/authors/masai-ujiri-quotes_2.

1 Marty Parker, Kirk Simpson, and Ashira Gobrin, "Episode 3: Culture During Times of Growth and Change," *Building High Performance Cultures*, May 6, 2020, podcast, 39:16, youtu.be/pugTlENNcSU.

2 Marty Parker and Anthony Longo, "Episode 6: Culture and the Family-Founded Organization," *Building High Performance Cultures*, May 27, 2020, podcast, 22:37, youtu.be/9dOa_wszwbY.

3   Parker and Longo, "Episode 6."
4   Parker and Newton, "Episode 20."
5   Lisa Quast and Kristi Hedges, "Reverse Mentoring: What It Is and Why It Is Beneficial," *Forbes*, January 23, 2011, forbes.com/ sites/work-in-progress/2011/01/03/reverse-mentoring-what-is-it-and-why-is-it-beneficial/?sh=c9a8a8921cc0.
6   Marty Parker and Evan Siddall, "Episode 22: Building Leadership and Leveraging Purpose," *Building High Performance Cultures*, September 23, 2020, podcast, 22:42, youtu.be/ cUEzNcUPY24.

Chapter 16: Preparing for the Next Evolution

Epigraph: Tobias Lütke quotation, BrainyQuote, accessed November 5, 2020, brainyquote.com/authors/tobias-lutke-quotes.
1   Shawn Achor, "The Happy Secret to Better Work," TEDxBloomington, May 2011, video, 12:04, ted.com/talks/ shawn_achor_the_happy_secret_to_better_work.
2   Deloitte Insights, *The Rise of the Social Enterprise: 2018 Deloitte Human Capital Trends*, 2018, www2.deloitte.com/content/ dam/insights/us/articles/HCTrends2018/2018-HCTrends_ Rise-of-the-social-enterprise.pdf.
3   Brian Groom, "A Third of Start-Ups Aim for Social Good," *Financial Times*, June 14, 2018, ft.com/content/d8b6d9fa-4eb8-11e8-ac41-759eee1efb74.
4   Abha Malpani, "The Outlook for Social Enterprises in 2019 and Beyond," *Triple Pundit*, January 22, 2019, triplepundit.com/ story/2019/outlook-social-enterprises-2019-and-beyond/ 81931.
5   "A Global Community of Leaders," Certified B Corporation, accessed March 1, 2021, bcorporation.net.
6   Achor, "The Happy Secret to Better Work."

INDEX

ABOUT THE AUTHOR

Marty Parker is founder and chief executive officer of Waterstone Human Capital.
Founded in 2003, Waterstone is a leading cultural talent management firm that
offers retained executive search special-
izing in recruiting for fit, culture change
and transformation services, leadership
development, succession planning, cul-
tural and engagement measurement, and advisory consulting
for entrepreneurial-minded, high-growth organizations across
North America.

In 2005, Marty founded Canada's Most Admired Corporate Cultures, an annual program that recognizes best-in-
class Canadian organizations for having a culture that has
helped them enhance performance and sustain a competitive advantage. In 2014, the program expanded to include
Canada's Most Admired CEO.

Marty is considered a global leader and expert on human
capital and corporate culture. He is a frequent commentator
and keynote speaker on issues surrounding leadership and
organizational culture. He is the author of *Culture Connection:
How Developing a Winning Culture Will Give Your Organization*

a Competitive Advantage (McGraw-Hill, 2012) and *The Culturepreneur: How High Performance Leaders Craft Culture as Competitive Advantage* (Page Two, 2021). He has provided expert commentary on the impact and importance of corporate culture and human capital for CNBC, the *National Post*, *Canadian Business*, and *Profit*, and he has appeared on *Canada AM*, BNN, and CP24. He also is the host of *Building High Performance Cultures*, a vlog and podcast where he interviews leaders who use culture to drive competitive advantage.

Marty is a very active member of Young Presidents' Organization (YPO), in the Great Lakes Ontario and Miami–Fort Lauderdale chapters. He is a member of the Canadian Region executive, former chapter chair, learning chair, network chair, membership chair, and forum chair.

Marty holds a bachelor of arts with honours, as well as a master of science degree from the University of Guelph. He and his wife, Tanya, live in Mississauga, Ontario, and Delray Beach, Florida, and they are the parents of five children. A serial entrepreneur, Marty loves sports, coaching, fitness, food and wine, reading, and personal and professional development.

TELL US YOUR CULTUREPRENEUR STORY

Share a story about your culturepreneurial journey or tell us about how you or someone you know puts culture at the centre of their organizational strategy and makes culture their competitive advantage!

Go to waterstonehc.com/inspiringculturestories.

We will post your story as a way of sharing inspiration and best practices and to encourage others to become culturepreneurs.

For every story submitted, Waterstone will donate $10 to our Future Leaders fund.

GET

THERE

FASTER

THE NO-NONSENSE,
NO-FLUFF GUIDE TO
THE CAREER YOU WANT

By: Christine DiDonato

Published by Traveling Swallow Press

ISBN: 978-1-7345038-9-0
e-ISBN: 978-1-7345038-0-7

TABLE OF CONTENTS

SPECIAL INVITATION

I'm overjoyed that thousands of professionals have taken advantage of my career resources on LinkedIn Learning and CareerRev.com. Together we've built a community of passionate and curious people who want to expand their opportunities and accelerate the time it takes to achieve their goals. Most importantly, they want to channel their talents into work that makes a difference and enables them to live their best lives.

Below are additional resources I'd like to offer you to support you on your career journey.

Exclusive Access to our Assessment

I'd like to offer you discount access to the most popular assessment from The AccelerateME Program.

1. Go to AccelerateME.com/feedback-assessment

2. Complete the form provided

3. Upon submission you will receive an email with a discount code to the *AccelerateME Career Feedback Assessment.*

Thank you so much for trusting me with your time and questions. I look forward to connecting and hearing about your success!

THIS IS FOR YOU

Have you ever felt stuck in your career, not knowing if you're in the right job or not sure where to go next or how to get there?

If you answered yes to any of those questions, you're not alone. Recent studies show that only 25% of today's employees feel confident enough to navigate their career path.

Whether you're ready for a promotion, considering a job change, trying to turn your internship into a full-time job, transitioning from college to career, or want to validate if you're on the right path, I designed this book for you.

My name is Christine DiDonato, and I'm on a mission to empower young professionals to take charge of their careers. I launched Career Revolution, Inc., and developed AwesomeBoss. com to help a new generation of talent navigate today's often confusing and ever-changing workplaces.

During the last 20 years, I've lived through many workplace transitions in a variety of roles. As a passionate young professional, I earned a vice president title before the age of 35. I have bumbled through awkward job interviews and sat on the other side of the table while hiring. I've worked in small and large companies alike in an assortment of industries, from financial services to technology to entertainment.

I've also been a big consumer of career advice and tools—of which I know there is no shortage. There's so much that it's difficult to know what to read and watch. It's even more challenging to understand what advice is helpful or not. Lately, I've become frustrated with the number of opinions being given by people who make a living advising without any real experience to offer.

I have a unique perspective to share with young professionals. It wasn't that long ago that I was one myself. So, I know how it feels. I've also been a manager and understand their perspectives and difficulties.

Most importantly, as a former human resources executive and consultant for Fortune 100 and 500 companies, I've been in many closed-door meetings where decisions are made about raises and promotions.

In these meetings, I started to notice a trend. When I asked managers why younger team members weren't selected for many of the growth opportunities, the managers would tell me all the reasons the employees fell short. They would talk about poor communication skills and work ethic, entitlement, and an inability to get their ideas across—to name a few. As if that wasn't bad enough, many managers would confess that they never provided this feedback directly to the employee!

My immediate reaction was, "How can you expect these young professionals to have a meaningful career if they don't know what they're doing wrong or even right?"

As a leadership coach, I quickly learned that many of today's managers are just as lost as the people they're trying to lead. To survive, managers must stay agile, do more with fewer resources, and be awesome coaches. The reality is that most don't have enough time, and sometimes experience, to give individual contributors fruitful feedback and engage in helpful career conversations. In fact, many managers have shared with me that no one has ever engaged them in conversations about their own careers.

I finally realized that although today's companies need young professionals' talent and most managers want them to succeed, they aren't always equipped with the resources or skills to make it happen in a way—or at a pace—that meets the individual's needs.

So, I decided to do something about it and share my insider knowledge with today's emerging professionals.

This book will give you access to the closed-door-conversations that impact your career. With this unique knowledge, you can channel your energy and focus on the right development at the right time.

I'll guide you through the five-step career acceleration formula from The AccelerateME™ Program, which many of today's most sought after employers use to develop the youngest segment of their workforce.

To ensure your learning is as relevant as possible, I've handpicked activities, shortcuts, and stories from other up and coming professionals.

THIS IS NOT A BOOK FOR PASSIVE LEARNING

This book is all about you. Each chapter contains a series of challenges, self-discovery experiences, and activities. Throughout it, you will be asked to reflect, complete assignments, and develop tools to grow your career. Have a pen and paper on hand to complete each challenge. We find it helpful to keep a journal to record all your responses and insights in one place, as they will build upon each other. That's why I've created the "Get There Faster Workbook" that compliments this book. It includes each activity and challenge discussed in this book, along with space to record responses as well as bonus activities. Challenge yourself and take advantage of this time to focus on you and your career development.

In the chapters ahead, you will be guided through a self-discovery process to help you:

- Identify work activities and job roles at which you will most excel

- Select companies and teams that align with your personal values

- Focus your learning and development on only activities right for your unique needs

- See hidden opportunities for growth where others might not
- Be seen as having high potential, therefore, yielding the best roles and rewards
- Identify where you want to go next and know how to get there.

This book is dedicated to helping you, a new generation of emerging leaders, be in the driver's seat of your career. I want to help you make decisions that are authentic to your values and get to where you want to go faster!

Are you ready to accelerate your career? Keep reading.

Here's to your success!

Christine Di Donato

SECTION ONE:

WHAT'S YOUR PROBLEM?

IT'S NOT YOU, IT'S THEM

I'd like to introduce you to Anna.

Anna is a twenty-something college grad and feels optimistic about the future and figuring out who she is. She's exploring romantic partners, learning to budget and pay her bills with an entry-level job, and trying to navigate her career to find the type of work that's fulfilling—all typical rights-of-passage that her parents may have also experienced.

Anna, however, is experiencing some unique challenges. While she landed a job right out of college, it's more entry-level and underuses the skills and knowledge she developed while pursuing her degree. It also pays far less than she expected, especially because she must pay off her student loan debt, which is at least double that of her parent's generation. These financial realities, coupled with skyrocketing rents in her city, forced Anna to move back home with her parents. She spends almost two hours a day commuting to work, which means she spends less time taking care of herself and developing her relationships. Anna still feels hopeful about her future, but she doesn't know how to navigate her present.

ANNA IS NOT ALONE

Today's young professionals, a generation that spans those just entering the workforce to individuals in their mid to late thirties, face challenges that previous generations did not experience. This population includes Millennials, who are roughly 23 to 38 years old, and Gen Z, people born after 1997. Although most research to date has centered around Millennials, the first wave of Gen Z is now graduating college, entering the workforce, and sharing many of the same experiences.

A 2016 Gallup Study concluded that Millennials have not been able to forge better paths for themselves than the generations before them. It continues to elaborate that, "while it is every parent's dream to have their children lead a better life than their own, not all of today's Millennials are positioned for such success." In the simplest terms, the cost of living has increased more dramatically than wages. This stagnation of earning and buying power holds back new generations as they try to make their way in the world.

The Washington Post ran an interesting article at the end of 2019 titled, "The Staggering Millennial Wealth Deficit, in One Chart." It outlined the share of the United States' wealth held by each generation. Individuals who were 35 years old in 1990 held about 21% of the nation's wealth. However, people who will be 35 years old in 2023 will hold only about 3%.

HOW THIS AFFECTS YOU

Let's start with what you spent to get your first job and what that job pays. Recent college grads carry on average $28,000 of debt, of which $19,000 is student loan debt. Compare that to Gen Xers, those who are now between 40 and 53 years old, who had an average balance of $12,800 at the same age. This increase in debt wouldn't be as big of an obstacle if you made commensurately more money than previous generations.

Instead, the Pew Research Center reported that your paycheck today only has the same purchasing power as it did almost 40 years ago! In 1973, a $4.03-an-hour job had the same purchasing power of a $23.68-an-hour job today. The problem?

The U.S. federal minimum wage in 2020 is \$12.00! That means you must earn about double the minimum wage to live at the same standards that your parents did at your age.

I created a fun chart to demonstrate what this really looks like in terms of daily life. For demonstration purposes, let's assume you're 30 years old today and your parents were 30 years old in 1990. Below is what the same expenses cost today, in the "2020 Actual Column" and what they should cost based on standard inflation.

	1990	WHAT IT SHOULD COST BASED ON STANDARD INFLATION	2020 ACTUAL COST
1-Year at Harvard	\$17,100	\$33,651	\$44,990
Average Student Loan Debt Monthly payment – post graduation	\$82	\$162	\$393
1-month rent (national average)	\$571	\$1,124	\$1,476
Average Home Price (national average)	\$79,100	\$155,663	\$226,800
Gas	\$1.12	\$2.20	\$2.90
Movie Ticket	\$4.23	\$8.32	\$9.16

To make matters worse, today's young professionals are navigating their careers in one of the most confusing times ever, and the tried and true career advice that worked for previous generations just doesn't apply. The "follow the rules, keep your head down, and eventually you'll get to where you want to go" mantra was established when workplace norms were very different. Stability, predictability, and loyalty are at the foundation of that mentality.

Today's world and workplaces are described using the acronym VUCA—Volatile, Uncertain, Complex, and Ambiguous. If you take a small step back and look at the world we live in today, it's not difficult to understand how people of all ages look at their life and their careers differently than before.

There will always be generational differences. However, the degree of change you've experienced compared to what your parents experienced at your age is unprecedented. Fashion trends aside, entering into the workplace in the '80s and '90s was vastly different. The financial inequities are just half of the story. The workplace itself is very different today than it was only twenty or thirty years ago.

LET'S VISIT 1985—YOUR PARENT'S WORKPLACE

Picture the workplace in 1985—fluorescent lighting, fax machines, and yellow ceiling tiles. Your parents came into work between eight or nine in the morning and stopped by the break room to get a cup of coffee. Remember, Starbucks didn't scale outside of Seattle until the late '80s. This meant that they had to put a quarter into a machine that dispensed mediocre brown liquid, or if they were really lucky, their company offered free coffee in Styrofoam cups from a single coffee pot.

Heading to their cubicle, or perhaps a shared office space, they sat down and opened a hard copy version of their calendar and to-do list. They might have had a stand-alone computer, but networked systems didn't exist on a large scale yet, which meant … no email, Slack, internet, or social media! Emails didn't pile up, and they couldn't communicate after work hours unless they picked up a phone. If they were really important, they got a beeper.

After attending a few meetings, writing and receiving memos, sending faxes, taking a full hour lunch break, your parents would depart the office about 5:30 p.m. And, here's the kicker, no one could get a hold of them unless they called their home phone line. Back then, it was not uncommon to "accidentally" take the phone off the hook, so that callers would hear a busy tone. They couldn't leave a message on the answering machine, which sat on the counter and recorded messages using small cassette tapes.

During ten to twenty years of repeating the same day for the same company, your parents could expect to receive regular raises and promotions from their company. They knew that there were opportunities to advance their career in their company. By the time they retired, they could expect a pension and a financial safety net waiting for them.

FAST FORWARD TO 2020

Now, let's take a look at your life in 2020. It's 6:30 a.m., and you hear a ping from your smartphone, which is sitting on your nightstand. You can't help but reach over and try to discern the email characters through your hazy morning view. A panic races through you. Your boss requests a last-minute change to the presentation you're giving at today's all-hands meeting. You pop out of bed and log into your laptop to make a few edits and send the new document.

You commute about 45 minutes in traffic to the office. Passing by the office coffee bar, you order a half-caf, soy latte, that the resident Barista knows you like about 120 degrees. While waiting for your coffee, you answer a few texts, get FOMO from seeing an influencer's vacay pics on Instagram, and post an inspirational quote your BFF sent to you this morning.

Your next stop is an impromptu meeting with a team member in a collaborative space where you review the changes to your presentation. A few more tweaks and you're ready for the all-hands meeting downstairs. Two hours later, you walk out of the meeting with several new to-do's, of which you can do a few while multitasking in your working lunch meeting this afternoon.

After about eight hours of back-to-back meetings, you wrap up your day by catching up on emails, seeing who's checked you out on LinkedIn and comment on a few funny posts on social media. Hopefully, you can make it to a 6:30 p.m. yoga class before sitting in traffic to commute back home.

You repeat this day, growing wearier each time you do. After a few months at the job, you still feel uncertain if you'll even be with the same company in a year. You don't know if there are opportunities for you to further your career and increase your earning power. And don't even mention retirement—there's no clear path to that either.

THEN v. NOW

As you can see, your parent's workspace, pace, and work-life balance looked drastically different than yours. Less technology made for a slower-paced work environment. Expectations for quick turn-around deliverables were exponentially less than today. Without social media, your parents couldn't connect with their friends or family instantly, which created more boundaries between work and home life.

In 2020, you have more technology, more connectivity, more convenience, and more choices than your parents could dream of or have. But, with it comes more pressure, more expectations, more ambiguity, and more decision fatigue and paralysis. It's a trade-off, and sometimes it's easy to feel like you got the short end of the deal.

STOP LISTENING TO YOUR PARENTS

OK, that sounds a little harsh. However, you may have to filter their career advice through the reality of the world you experience. Perhaps they've told you about John. John's career story, or some version of it, has been told over and over to today's emerging professionals when they ask for advice. Chances are your parents have introduced you to such a role-model.

John joined his current company right out of college. He got his job by dropping by the office unexpectedly one day and asking if there were any openings. Magically, there were, and he was hired on the spot. He worked hard, and each year received a fair salary increase during his annual performance review. The longer he stayed with the company, the bigger his bonuses became as well. After five years in the same role, he was selected to join an exclusive training program to prepare him for potential management roles, all while being mentored by an executive team member.

Allow me to give you a few more details that your parents may have forgotten. John graduated from college in four years with far less student loan debt than you have. His first salary was enough to pay his loans and rent an apartment close to work. His company covered close to 100% of his healthcare costs and paid into a pension for him.

How nice for John.

What your parents don't realize is that John's career path has become an urban legend of years past.

Instead, let's go back to our friend Anna.

Anna applied to five colleges and was accepted to two of them. Then, she realized she needed to take student loans earlier than expected to pay the tuition and expenses.

Due to high tuition costs and competition to get into classes, it took Anna five years to graduate. Anna completed three internships that paid minimum wage before landing a full-time opportunity. Although Anna was excited to receive a job offer for a full-time role, she was shocked at the low salary. Given her debt and the inflated cost of living to be within a comfortable commuting distance to work, it wasn't enough to make ends meet. So, she moved back home to save money on rent.

After six months on the job, Anna started to get into a groove, only to learn that her team would be merging with another team with different leadership. At the same time, she began questioning the meaning of her work, and if she was on the right track to develop her career. She tried to get time with her new manager to discuss her development, but the meetings kept getting rescheduled or double-booked.

After one year of working on what felt like meaningless tasks, she decided to leave the company for a new opportunity. She needed to make more money and living with her parents was wearing on her sanity and seriously hampering her social life and romantic relationships. With the move, she negotiated a small salary increase. But she faced the same challenges at the new job as the old job. As a result, Anna will move companies every two to three years, building a variety of valuable skills in the process. All the while, she will feel unsure of her career's direction. She just knows she wants to do purposeful work and earn more financial freedom to live her best life.

Anna's story is a more typical experience of today's young professionals. How would John survive today? What would he need to do differently to respond to this changing and challenging environment?

THE WORKPLACE IS STRUGGLING TO ADAPT

You are living in a dramatically changing workplace. We can categorize these changes into three groups of major shifts, which are essential to understand as they impact your ability to navigate your career path.

SHIFT #1: THE WORKFORCE IS GETTING YOUNGER

By the year 2025, experts predict that 75% of the global workforce will be made of Millennials—those who are roughly 23 to 38 years old today. A large population of Gen Z, those born after 1997, will graduate college in 2020 and have already begun to enter the workplace.

If you identify as a Millennial, I'm guessing I don't have to remind you of how many stereotypes are out there about what you like and dislike, and what you think and feel. If you identify as Gen Z, there's also no shortage of research being published about your needs and wants. Millennials have been associated with growing up in a new era of on-demand technology and services. Gen Z reports piggyback on Millennial data, citing this generation's reliance on technology and demand for instant-everything as a critical trait impacting the way they work.

Whether or not you agree with some or none of that research, one thing is for sure: Organizations are struggling to find the magic formula to retain you. The Gallup organization reports that while overall employee engagement scores are on the rise, less than a third of Millennial employees are engaged at work. It's predicted that Gen Z will follow those trends. Other studies predict that more than 45% of the youngest segment of the workforce will leave their organizations within the next year.

Companies know this and continue to try all kinds of strategies to keep you happy and productive, from promoting health and wellness activities to providing creative benefits and flexible work arrangements, to offering education reimbursement, free meals, pimped out office spaces, and everything in between. They know they NEED to keep you and that retaining you helps their bottom line, so they will try almost anything it takes.

Yet, despite all of these efforts, I consistently hear from younger employees that they're simply not happy with the career growth potential at their current employer.

SHIFT #2: ORGANIZATIONAL STRUCTURES ARE CONTINUALLY CHANGING

To keep up with the pace of change in the world, many companies sped up decision making to execute more quickly. This resulted in flatter organizational structures and into fewer layers of management, leaving the remaining managers with more direct reports.

The average span of control, the number of people one is responsible for managing, has more than doubled for a CEO in the last twenty-five years. This trend extends into all levels of management. Gallup research reports that more than 84% of employees are matrixed to some extent. In other words, instead of an employee reporting to just one manager, they have dual reporting relationships. You might report to a team manager as well as a project manager. This means that management structures are more complex. Today's managers have nine direct reports on average and can have more than eleven in larger organizations. Ultimately, your manager has more direct reports than they did in the past and less time for you and your unique needs.

Team structures also shifted throughout the years based on changing priorities and shifting goals and resources. Having worked and led in Fortune 500 and 100 companies for more than a decade, I noticed a growing trend where employees could have more than three managers in any given year.

All of these trends reduce the amount of time a manager can spend coaching and developing each employee. It's why even getting on your manager's calendar can feel like a challenge in and of itself.

SHIFT #3: THE RISE OF VIRTUAL TEAMS

The third shift that continues to impact the way we work is the increase of virtual teams. As technology has enabled the world to be more connected, companies no longer need every employee to be working in the same place at the same time. In fact, Gallup reported that 43% of individuals work remotely in some capacity, and that number is increasing every year.

Work doesn't always happen at work anymore. Even office workers got a taste of this reality when being asked to work from home in response to the COVID-19 pandemic. While the debate continues on how productive remote teams are compared to their office counterparts, the trend to reduce costs and take advantage of talent around the world continues.

While many remote workers report having fewer chances of being interrupted while focusing on real work, they also have a more difficult time bonding with co-workers. So, if you work remotely or have a boss who does, you may have a better chance of producing quality work but will have less of an opportunity to get in front of key decision-makers. As a result, remote workers must be very deliberate about how they communicate and manage relationships.

THE SHIFT FLOWS DOWNSTREAM

I don't expect these changes to slow down anytime soon. The organizations we work in understand that to survive, they must continuously adapt to their environment.

However, sometimes these shifts and the ripples they create aren't obvious and create ambiguity in the workplace. This is especially true when it comes to navigating your career. As I continue to work with emerging professionals, I hear them voice some of the same frustrations:

- Being asked to take on more responsibility without a promotion or pay increase
- Frequently switching teams and perhaps reporting to multiple managers
- Not getting consistent feedback and coaching
- Struggling to see a clear path forward in their career
- Managers who don't know how to guide or support their career path

WITH CHANGE COMES OPPORTUNITY

Automation has changed how we do almost everything. Have you ever asked your grandparents or older relatives about the jobs they had at your age? What about your parents? It wouldn't be a surprise to learn that those jobs might not exist anymore.

I love hearing my mom tell stories of her days as a switchboard operator. Without watching "Mad Men" or "The Marvelous Mrs. Maisel," I don't think I'd even know what the job entailed. My dad had a newspaper route, a job that is also becoming extinct as more of us consume our media digitally.

Think about jobs that exist right now that are being done by robots rather than humans. McKinsey reported that 45% of our current jobs could be automated. Drivers, cashiers, and office administrators are just a few that are predicted to dwindle in the years to come due to automation.

At the same time, technological advances have also created new jobs that didn't exist twenty or even ten years ago. Many of us may be in a job now that didn't exist for previous generations. Think about social media managers, app developers, Lyft drivers, podcast producers, genetic lawyers, and the list goes on.

All these rapid changes make it difficult to map out a ten-year career plan because it's almost impossible to know what opportunities will be available in ten years or even in five years. The times of a predictable career ladder are fading.

FORGET THE CAREER LADDER—GET READY FOR THE CLIMBING WALL

A 21st-century career is best defined by a series of developmental experiences, each offering a person the opportunity to acquire new skills and perspectives.

Today's career paths are more like a rock wall. Careers aren't just upward, linear climbs. Instead, they include sideways moves in addition to upward movements. Sometimes you even have to step backward to adjust your path upward. Each person will take a different route up the wall, depending on their viewpoint, skill level, strengths, skills, and desires.

Although the time of defined career ladders is quickly fading, there are new career opportunities that didn't exist in the past. They can sometimes be more difficult to see, but if you know what to look for, they present exciting opportunities for your career.

YOUR FIRST TEN YEARS IS CRITICAL

Using the earnings data of more than five million people, The Federal Reserve Bank of New York concluded that the bulk of pay increases an individual will receive throughout an entire career will come in the first 10 years of work. Pay increases slow in the following decades. Knowing this only confirms that the faster a young professional can figure out where they're headed and take actions to get there, the better off they will be for years to come.

A new world requires a new approach to career development. You can't rely on the rules of the past. You can't dutifully move up the rungs of a ladder—you need to learn how to scale a climbing wall.

So how do you do it? How do you make a difference and enjoy the journey? The next chapter outlines my method of navigating your career, which addresses the real needs and challenges of those who strive for purpose, financial freedom, and success in today's workplace.

Keep reading to learn how to accelerate your success today so you can have a purposeful, authentic, and rewarding career for years to come.

THE CAREER ACCELERATION FORMULA

HOW PROMOTABLE ARE YOU?

If I gathered all of your co-workers in a room without you and asked them to describe your capabilities, talents, and skills, what would they say? Do you think their statements would be an accurate assessment of you? Would you agree with their opinions?

Essentially, this question directly connects to how promotable you are. It's the last question in Career Revolution's *AccelerateME*™ Feedback Assessment, and it yields a "Marketability" grade. The participant, AKA you, first answers the question:

"People who work with me or have worked with me would highly recommend me for a new opportunity."

A = Without a doubt

B = Most likely

C = Depends on the opportunity

D = Most likely no

Then the participant selects between three and eight respondents to answer this question about them. Respondents are asked to answer the question anonymously:

"I would put my personal reputation on the line to recommend this person for future opportunities."

A = Without a doubt

B = Most likely

C = Depends on the opportunity

D = Most likely no

This answer to this question really sums up how promotable you truly are. It's the same question asked in formal job references, as well as informal ones—the confidential calls made by recruiters and hiring managers to people in their network who have worked with you in the past.

How would you answer this question? How do you think those in your network would, anonymously, answer it about you?

Our assessment data reveals that the average participant rates themselves one grade higher than their respondents. In other words, if they rated themselves a "B, most likely," then the average score of their respondent group would be a "C, depends on the opportunity."

This is a big eye-opener for many young professionals. It's a critical piece of information to use to focus your development efforts.

TAKE BACK YOUR POWER

After sitting in years of closed-door management meetings, I've learned that career opportunities are often defined by how others perceive us—what value they think we bring, how easy they think we are to work with, and their perception of our overall potential. To grow our career in a direction that feels authentic to what success looks like for us, we need the people who have the power to promote us, implement our ideas, fund our businesses and use our services to believe in our abilities and potential.

That may sound discouraging at first. You may think, "Why should I try anything new if I can't control my own career?" The opposite is actually true. You can control how others perceive you and your abilities using the Career Acceleration formula. This formula, when practiced, will speed up progress in your current path and help you make critical career decisions and focus your efforts on activities that will help you.

WHERE DID THE FORMULA COME FROM?

The early career workforce is one of the more studied and observed groups out there. Most of the surveys and studies conducted speak to similar trends in the wants and needs of Millennials and, recently, Gen Z employees. The ones I find most helpful to young professionals navigating their careers in today's confusing workplaces are those that speak to perception.

After reviewing and conducting numerous studies and focus groups related to young professionals and the organizations they work for, I've found the following perceptions to be most prevalent.

Organizations **seek to employ YOU** because they perceive that you:

- Are not afraid to take risks
- Think outside of the box
- Are technology savvy
- Are entrepreneurial
- Look to peers as role models
- Want to help others in difficulty
- Embrace diversity

- Commit to community and service
- Welcome change
- Strive for continuous growth and education
- Want your work to reflect positive contributions to society
- Are independent and can work with little supervision
- Can find effortless or straightforward ways of doing things
- Possess an openness to give feedback

Organizations are **challenged by YOU** because they perceive that you:

- Lack financial literacy
- Struggle with interpersonal communication skills
- Struggle with effective work habits such as time, priority and workload management
- See work-life-balance as a way out of working hard
- Expect promotion without having earned it
- Rely too heavily on technology to get your job done
- Lack respect for older workers or those in formal leadership roles
- Challenge already established and tested policies and procedures
- Crave too much outside stimulation during work time
- Are not loyal to the organization
- Define yourself with material items
- Ask "what can you do for me?" before asking what you can do for them

You may not take ownership of all of the perceptions listed. What's most important is not if you agree with these perceptions, but that you understand they exist. The first time I presented these lists to a group of young professionals, I was prepared to stir up some heated discussion. I was the one who ended up surprised. The group told me they agreed with several perceptions from the lists, both positive and negative.

PERCEPTION IS REALITY

What other people think of you is not who you really are. However, perception is the reality of the person who perceives it.

If you perceive someone to be dishonest or untrustworthy, then you will take action to avoid trusting them and how that person sees you will not change how you act toward them. The same is true for the lists above. Your manager or organization will take actions that support their perception. While you cannot control how someone sees you, you can influence their perceptions by changing your behaviors and actions.

WHERE DO THESE PERCEPTIONS COME FROM?

While leading the Talent Development function for a Fortune 100 company, I experienced firsthand these perceptions about young professionals, both negative and positive. Whether it was managers complaining about their latest hire's work ethic, recruiters swapping stories of recent college grads asking for abnormally high salaries for entry-level jobs, or executives ordering ping pong tables to be installed in break rooms to appease a perceived need among young professionals for "fun" at work, I realized that the perception problem was growing.

Employee data also led me to believe that we had a big challenge ahead of us. Our team worked countless hours and spent thousands of dollars to attract and hire the best young professionals we could find, only to see more than 65% of them quit within their first year. For those who stayed, they reported their frustrations via our employee opinion survey. Each year we saw declining scores from those employees younger than thirty-five years old in areas concerning purpose, values, and career opportunities. There was indeed a statistical difference between age groups in the organization.

Once I was aware of these trends, I started hearing other organizations report the same types of data and anecdotes. The voluntary attrition of young professionals has increased over the last five years for most organizations. This is a growing problem for companies who strive to become more stable. Of course, this might work in your favor—more about that later.

PERCEPTION IS A TWO-WAY STREET

Just hearing the complaints and frustrations from hiring managers was only half of the equation. Interestingly enough, organizational leaders and managers are not the only ones experiencing workplace frustrations. Young professionals also expressed feelings of confusion and disillusionment when asked about their first job or two.

While many young professionals entered the job market with optimistic visions of rapid growth and on-going development, they have experienced the opposite. Feelings of disappointment, frustration, helplessness, and sometimes crushing defeat seem to be more prevalent than the excitement, optimism, and vision with which they began their careers.

In my company's research, we found that the perception challenges coming from both sides actually stems from misalignment in what each group believes about productivity, potential, and success at work.

Career Revolution was able to capture those differences in beliefs and create the *Career Mindset Model*. The model speaks to differing beliefs regarding critical and sometimes contentious workplace topics, such as how long it takes to get promoted, what work-life balance looks like, whose ideas get heard, and what types of behaviors get rewarded.

This model helps organizations, people managers, and young professionals identify their beliefs in seven key areas and then determine if those beliefs are helping or hurting their ability to achieve their career goals. We'll dive into this model in more detail when we discuss uncovering blind spots.

BE A PART OF THE CONVERSATION, NOT A VICTIM OF IT

I mentioned earlier the closed-door conversations that happen where decisions are made about who gets rewarded and given the best opportunities. The information I'm sharing in this book gives you a glimpse into those conversations to help you understand how hiring managers perceive your strengths and challenges even before they know you as the wonderful and talented human being that I'm sure you are.

With those insights, you can be a part of those conversations before they happen. To help you do that, I created the *AccelerateME*™ Career Acceleration Formula. This formula will help you answer the following five sets of questions:

- **Step 1: Energizers**

   What types of work activities come most naturally to me and are most energizing? What do I do better than most?

- **Step 2: Values**

   What do I value most in my life right now and in the next couple of years? How do I make career decisions that support my personal values?

- **Step 3: Vision**

  What does success look like for me? What are the elements of success that will make me happy? What can I do in the next 12 months to move me closer to that vision?

- **Step 4: Blind spots**

  What could be holding me back or getting in my way from achieving my career vision? How do others perceive my capability and potential?

- **Step 5: Conversations**

  How do I gain support from my manager to take the next step in my career? How do I structure and initiate career conversations that move me forward?

This formula is the foundation of the *AccelerateME*™ Career Development Program. This program is offered at some of today's most successful organizations. I wrote this book as a way to give the same learning opportunity to all emerging professionals, regardless of where you work or which stage of your journey you're in.

By rolling up your sleeves and taking the challenges in each step of the formula, you will be in the driver's seat of your career. No more wondering where you should go next. No more guessing what activities will yield the best reward. No more waiting for others to recognize your hard work.

Are you ready to take charge of your career? Start with Step 1, discovering your Energizers.

SECTION TWO:

5 STEPS TO ACCELERATE YOUR CAREER

STEP 1:

DISCOVER YOUR ENERGIZERS

In this chapter, you will:

- ❑ Recognize activities that come naturally to you.
- ❑ Identify your primary and secondary Energy Zones at work.
- ❑ Assess how often you leverage your natural strengths in your current job.
- ❑ Learn to make career decisions based on what most energizes you.

When was the last time you felt like you were confident and adding real value? When you produced awesome results with what seemed like little effort?

Numerous studies reveal that people who play to their natural strengths regularly are more productive and happier than those who don't. This is especially true in our careers. Imagine a job that you actually enjoy, where you feel like the work you do is valuable and can be your authentic self.

The first step to a career like that is knowing what energizes you. Then, you can apply that knowledge to learning how to play in your zone of energy daily and make decisions that put you on an authentic and fulfilling career path.

Energizers are things we are naturally good at. They are actions or activities that give us energy.

Drainers, as you would imagine, are just the opposite. These are the activities that take energy away from us. In other words, if you had to spend a lot of time doing them, they would require more energy and effort, and you would feel less joy.

I've found that it's easy to identify your drainers. Energizers, on the other hand, can be a little trickier. This is especially true when it comes to work activities.

You know you're using an energizer when you are in a flow state—when you get absorbed in a task or activity and lose track of time. It's like the old saying: "Time flies when you're having fun." When you realize that also can apply to work, you start to understand how to accelerate your career path.

This is a widely taught concept, and one you will see in almost every modern career development book. What's important isn't what model or words you use to identify your Energizers, but that you are clear about what they are and how you're using or not using them right now.

When I'm coaching emerging professionals, I often start by asking, "What most energizes you?" More often than not, the response I get is a laundry list of everything the person is bad at. That question seems to trigger thoughts of what drains us.

MEET BEN

This was especially true for Ben. Ben was a 26-year-old family friend who graduated from college with an accounting degree. After working for a few years with a small accounting firm, Ben was having trouble passing the CPA exam. This held him back from getting a promotion with a guaranteed pay raise.

Ben's parents were frustrated after having supported him financially while he incurred substantial student loan debt. So, they asked me to meet with him to see if I could help get him back on track.

When I met with Ben, he expressed the same concern. He felt as though he was never going to pass the exam. He told me he was frustrated and felt stuck in his career.

After hearing of Ben's challenges, I asked him what most energized him in his current job. He shared he had made a few friends and that his manager and other company partners were supportive and offered a lot of encouragement that he would pass the exam. Then, Ben quickly began speaking about the things that he didn't like. He had very few peers his own age to socialize with, he had to work alone on most projects and tasks, and he had little opportunity to interact directly with clients. He left each day drained and hopeless.

Knowing that Ben got top grades, had studied hard for his CPA exam, and was a smart person, I still didn't understand why he couldn't pass the exam. To better understand how to help Ben, I asked him to participate in the challenges listed in this chapter to identify his natural strengths—what energized him most.

Through that process, Ben discovered that he was most energized when he was working on a team and collaborating. He was most motivated when he could coach others and help them achieve their goals. I would classify Ben's natural strengths as relationship-based Energizers. He also acknowledged that he made occasional mistakes when his work required a lot of detail orientation. Therefore, he was drained by making something perfect but had learned a strong skill set in using Excel.

Essentially, Ben had chosen a field that would often require him to work alone, focused on data, and not people, and he was also working in a company that didn't provide many opportunities to play to his strengths. This was a double drainer! Then, Ben shared that he wasn't sure he even liked accounting, even though he had developed strong skills in it. That was no surprise now that I knew his Energizers and drainers.

I also began to understand why he wasn't passing his CPA exam. When we set goals for ourselves based on what others expect of us or what we think we should be energized by, it's much more difficult to achieve those goals. It can feel as if we're being forced to eat that one vegetable we hated as a child but had to sit at the table until we cleaned our plate. The longer we sit there, the more unappetizing it becomes.

Once Ben had these insights, we had a much more powerful conversation. If the goal was for Ben to navigate a career path that enabled him to feel energized daily, then we had to look at the problem differently. Instead of solving for how Ben could pass the CPA exam, I asked Ben to take a step back and ask a different question. I challenged Ben to decide what his next career move would be if he looked through the lens of Energizers.

Ben's energy immediately shifted, and he appeared excited at what might be possible for him. I presented him with a couple of options to think about related to his career path.

Let's come back to Ben's options after you've identified your own Energizers.

WHAT ARE YOUR ENERGIZERS?

Energizers are what make you feel energized! It's important to differentiate Energizers from other aspects of yourself, such as your academic achievements or learned skills. We can be good at tasks and activities that don't energize us because we've learned a skill. However, if we build a career path on just that—and I know many people who have—we can wake up one day and realize we're miserable.

By starting with what energizes you and guiding your career through that lens, you will achieve success and enjoy the journey. A great shortcut to discovering your natural Energizers is to take a validated strengths-based assessment. One of the most popular and widely used is The Clifton Strengthsfinder. Based on a forty-year study by The Gallup Organization, this assessment identifies your natural talents using a model of 34 strengths. The Gallup Organization teaches that the chances that another person will have the same top five strengths as you are one in 33 million. So, your grandmother was telling you the truth: You are indeed special.

All kidding aside, you gain valuable insight when you realize that you can be your best and most powerful self when you learn to play to your strengths instead of focusing on your weaknesses. It can be a hard concept for our brains to digest, though. The corporate performance model has been built on pointing out the one or two things that drain us and then creating a development plan on improving those things.

I remember the day the light bulb went on for me. I started to think about all of the performance reviews I received through the first several years of my career. If I laid them all out in front of me, I could see that the things I did well were the same—just with different names and dates. And the things I needed to work on, my weaknesses, were also the same year after year.

By taking validated assessments and completing the challenges in this chapter, I've learned that I'm energized by activities such as brainstorming, problem-solving, and helping others be successful. These are all things that my managers have also provided examples of in every performance appraisal I've ever had. I've also learned that I'm drained by activities that require a strong attention to detail and those that have me working alone for long periods. As you can imagine, the act of sitting alone and writing a book has been a challenge. Whereas the time I spent listening to the experiences of young professionals, mentoring and coaching is energizing. Given my natural Energizers and drainers, I'm already stressed about how I can write a whole book that has no spelling and grammatical errors in it!

I can still feel the fear and anticipation of heading into a performance review, knowing that although my successes would be celebrated, I'd be asked to focus on fixing my drainers even though I had been focusing on them year after year. I've suffered years of professional development plans focused on making me more detail-oriented. I'm here to admit that no matter my efforts, I will never be as detail-oriented as someone who is naturally energized by it.

What I finally learned after years of reading and training is that you can find far greater success by leveraging your natural strengths versus focusing on developing a core weakness. Now, this doesn't mean simply ignore or avoid your drainers. It's important to know what they are. However, when you're trying to improve a work situation or improve your work results, you have a better chance of doing so by tapping into one of your strengths.

Once I understood that I could achieve more by using what energized me to get work done, my life changed. In fact, it's the reason I have my own company today.

Many people start to assess their Energizers by taking a strengths-based assessment. Even if you have taken one, I urge you to do these energizer challenges to validate your results and then learn how to apply it to your career choices.

Although research reveals that our strengths are stable over a lifetime, our top strengths can shift over time. During the first years of our careers, we don't always have a job that lets us play to our strengths every day. This can create a situation where you don't feel like you can be your true self.

The following challenges will help you identify what your natural Energizers are today and how you can better apply them at work and make important career decisions.

ENERGIZER CHALLENGE #1

Remember when time flew

Think about a time at work in the last 30 days when you were in your zone—that place where time flies and you feel productive with what seems like little effort.

What were you doing? How did you feel?

If you're having trouble identifying such a moment, I recommend closing your eyes and thinking about a recent time you felt happy. A time when you weren't checking the time or thinking about what you were going to do next. Think about a moment when you were working on something or with someone when what you were doing or talking about came easy, naturally. What was happening at that moment? What were you doing? Where were you? What was the environment like?

If you ask this question to a group of your friends, you will find a variety of answers. For some, it would be brainstorming new ideas with a team, coaching someone, or meeting new people. For others, it might be fixing a broken process, planning an event, or designing a new model.

Activities that energize one person may drain another. Thank goodness for that, or we'd all be the same, and that would be boring. We are all unique, and all bring something different to the table. This gives us something special to offer to the workplace and our careers. But we have to know what it is to start focusing our careers on what energizes us.

ENERGIZER CHALLENGE #2

Feel The Love

Another way to discover your Energizers is to seek insights from people who know you well.

Have you ever asked those closest to you what makes you so special? I realize that sounds like a weird egotistical thing to do. But to identify your Energizers, it can be a powerful and gratifying activity.

Think of two or three people who know you well. Tell them you're trying to articulate your natural Energizers and would like their feedback.

Ask them:

"What qualities do you most admire in me?"

"What do I do better than most?"

It might feel awkward at first to ask such questions, but you will be pleasantly surprised by their answers. I bet if you think of those you know well, you could easily answer those questions about them.

How did they respond? Were you surprised by the responses you received? Did they validate what you already knew?

Record any themes you heard. They will be helpful to have on hand as you complete the remaining challenges.

ENERGIZER CHALLENGE #3

Identify your primary Energy Zone

You can also think about your Energizers in terms of Energy Zones. By identifying activities that share common themes, you can identify a zone that gives you the most energy.

Based on the challenges you completed thus far, which of the following zones are you most energized by? What about least energized by? Rank each zone by placing a 1, 2, or 3 in the box to indicate the zone you are most to least energized by.

THE *THINKING ZONE*

The Thinking Zone is all about feeling energized by activities related to how you process and make sense of information.

THE *THINKING ZONE* ENERGIZERS

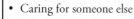

- Generating new ideas
- Collecting and storing information
- Imagining the future
- Using logic and reason to solve problems
- Finding connections, patterns, and themes
- Searching for reasons or causes
- Creating a hypothesis
- Paying attention to details
- Crafting a strategy

THE *DOING ZONE*

The Doing Zone is about feeling energized by execution-focused activities. These are action-focused and speak to the amount of instruction or oversight one needs before they are comfortable taking action.

THE *DOING ZONE* ENERGIZERS

- Completing tasks
- Implementing repeatable processes
- Committing to a decision
- Doing things efficiently
- Meeting deadlines
- Taking initiative
- Delivering results
- Adapting to unfamiliar situations
- Operating under clear direction
- Following procedures

THE *RELATING ZONE*

The Relating Zone is all about getting energy from activities that involve interacting with people. It also speaks to getting energy from being able to see things from another's perspective and have compassion.

THE *RELATING ZONE* ENERGIZERS

- Caring for someone else
- Influencing and persuading
- Motivating
- Networking
- Developing a connection with people
- Collaborating
- Coaching and mentoring
- Understanding where someone is coming from
- Identifying unique qualities in others
- Mediating an argument

WHAT IF YOU FEEL STRONGLY ABOUT MORE THAN ONE ENERGY ZONE?

Most people will naturally identify with one zone over others. However, sometimes you will find that two resonate with you. While it's not outrageous to be attracted to more than one zone, we generally tend to be most energized by one more than the other. Remember, the question wasn't what you like to do, but rather the types of activities that make time fly.

Of course, we are complex beings with a variety of experiences and can be energized at any given time by different activities. This is why I encourage people to rank the zones rather than select just one. Another way of looking at this challenge is to consider if you had to live in one zone every day, which one would you choose?

ARE ENERGY ZONES SUITED FOR SPECIFIC JOBS?

A natural question, and one I get asked often, is whether or not certain Energy Zones are best suited for specific jobs. In other words, can you determine if you're in the wrong job simply by the primary Energy Zone you selected? Indeed, different job profiles align best with different Energy Zones. However, what makes someone successful at any job is self-awareness and a variety of other factors, such as learned skills, motivation, and attitude. You can use your new knowledge of Energizers to pivot in your career, whether by making adjustments within your current job or a big transition to another role or company altogether.

Let's take a look at a coaching session I did with Lindsay. Lindsay was a 28-year-old sales professional questioning her career path and thinking of exploring another field. When I asked Lindsay why she was contemplating such a big move, she shared with me that she was struggling to meet her tough quarterly goals. She also said the frequent travel and volume of clients she had to manage had become exhausting. While working with Lindsay to identify her natural Energizers, we discovered that she got a lot of energy from getting to know her clients personally. She also told me that she had a competitive nature and got bored with repetitive tasks. Lindsay confessed that she wasn't very detail-oriented and got flustered when presenting the many technical details of the product she was selling.

We then compared the core elements of her sales job with the types of activities that she enjoyed most. We discovered that Lindsay actually thrived in most of her job responsibilities. Then, the light bulb went on for Lindsay. She realized that the product she was selling was at the core of her challenges. This differentiation helped Lindsay understand that switching career paths entirely wasn't the best move. Instead, Lindsay decided to explore sales roles that focused on services instead of products. She also explored ways to get support on the more technical details of her current product.

By thinking of her career and what energized and drained her, Lindsay understood the root of her challenges. Once she did that, she could focus her career decisions with that knowledge.

ENERGIZER CHALLENGE #4

Determine how you can further work in your Energy Zone

Now that you can articulate your natural Energizers, let's apply them to your current career situation. Think about a typical work week and the activities you spend most of your time doing. Sometimes, it helps to keep a time log and record what you did each hour throughout the day.

Looking at those activities, on a scale of 1-10 (1 = Never and 10 = Most of the time), rate how often you play in your primary Energy Zone in your current job. Then, identify the opportunities you have in your current job to work in your primary and secondary Energy Zones.

Keep in mind that it's rare for anyone at any point in their career to rate themselves a 10, and if they do, it's often not sustainable. Most people who can play in their top Energy Zones every day still have to do activities that drain them from time to time. It's almost impossible to avoid some of those drainers.

However, if you rated yourself lower than a 6, you have an opportunity to make some pivots. What additional types of work activities might you also want to explore to apply your natural Energizers further?

Another way to answer this question is to interview people you admire or who you think may share some of your Energizers. You can ask them what type of personal or professional experiences they've had that most energized them.

Here are some examples of activities emerging professionals have shared with us related to activities in each Energy Zone.

THE *THINKING ZONE* ACTIVITIES	THE *DOING ZONE* ACTIVITIES	THE *RELATING ZONE* ACTIVITIES
• Join a project team working on an innovation • Craft a new strategy to solve an old problem • Host a brainstorming session with co-workers interested in a similar topic • Audit new software to test for issues	• Build a project plan, including milestones and key dependencies • Manage a project from start to finish • Implement a more efficient process • Design a system to align individual goals and hold people accountable	• Be the spokesperson for your team that defends an idea or result • Join a cross-functional team • Mentor a more junior member of the organization or someone new to the company • Create a new system of recognition to celebrate individual and team wins

Once you've identified your primary Energy Zone and how you are or could be using your Energizers at work, you've laid the foundation to set yourself on a positive path.

HOW DO YOU MAKE DECISIONS BASED ON ENERGIZERS?

Remember Ben? I presented some options for Ben to think about based on his career challenge and the Energizers he identified.

The first was staying in accounting and working for a larger company that could provide the type of relationship-building opportunities Ben needed. Given his accounting knowledge, expertise in Excel, and investment in an accounting degree, Ben could explore finding a company and team culture where he would thrive. This would buy him time until he could work his way up to a role and where he could manage and motivate others—his natural strengths. If Ben chose this option, he would be acknowledging that the accounting work might continue to drain him at times, but that it was only temporary. This might motivate him to pass the exam finally.

The second was to explore other fields where the work he would do would play to his natural strengths more regularly. The ideal scenario would be to find a career that would value his accounting skills and provide him opportunities to expand his expertise and focus on relationships more than data.

I've stayed in contact with Ben over the last few years as he took this new and unexpected direction in his career. I'll share details of his journey throughout the book, but I am happy to report that Ben successfully made the transition into a role outside of accounting. After taking some time to do the same reflection, Ben expressed an interest in a different field altogether—human resources. After following the steps in the remaining chapters,

Ben did indeed get hired into an HR role in a top entertainment company in Los Angeles and has left accounting altogether.

I sometimes try and imagine where Ben would be if he hadn't made that important pivot based on his new knowledge of his Energizers. He could still be in accounting, feeling drained each day and not knowing how to get unstuck.

Now, this decision may not be right for everyone in Ben's situation. However, he determined it was right for him based on all of the reflections and assignments he did. After you complete all five steps in the formula, you will be able to determine your next steps and have a plan to move in the direction you want to go.

Identifying what energizes you will lay a foundation for an authentic and successful career path. Energizers serve as a foundation for navigating our careers. The goal is to create opportunities for us to play to our strengths, which is where we will most shine.

Now that you've identified your Energizers, the next step is to take a look at what you value most in life.

SHORTCUTS

HOW TO DISCOVER YOUR ENERGIZERS

CHALLENGE #1	**Remember when time flew:** When were you in your zone in the last 30 days?
CHALLENGE #2	**Feel The Love:** Ask your trusted friends, "What qualities do you most admire in me?" or "What do I do better than most?"
CHALLENGE #3	**Identify your primary Energy Zone:** What are the activities that most energize you in the thinking, doing, or relating Energy Zones?
CHALLENGE #4	**Determine how can you further work in your Energy Zone:** What opportunities do you have in your current job to work in your primary and secondary Energy Zones? What additional types of work activities might you also want to explore to apply your natural Energizers further?

STEP 2:

LIVE YOUR PERSONAL VALUES

In this chapter, you will:

- ❑ Identify what you value most in your life right now.
- ❑ Assess how well your life aligns with your personal values.
- ❑ Establish what values are missing from your current work situation.
- ❑ Find opportunities to live your top values more fully.

"I want to be my own boss."

"I want to have a beach body."

"I want to have an amazing marriage."

These are just a few of the ideas and dreams many of us share when asked what we most want.

As an entrepreneur, people often tell me they want to create a new product or run their own business. I've been on the receiving end of comments such as, "You are so lucky you get to do what you love every day," and "It must be so nice to set your own direction."

The first few years after leaving my corporate job, I agreed with these kinds of sentiments. I really was lucky and really appreciated my freedom. Actually, it was awesome.

On many occasions, young professionals would ask me to mentor them, coach them, or simply spend some time with them to learn about how I started my company and turned a profit in the first year.

As I shared my story with others, I realized that my transition from a high-paying corporate job to entrepreneurship didn't happen overnight. And, it most definitely involved a lot of risks, sacrifice, and hard work. Once I decided to start my business, it took me more than a year to save money to have a financial cushion. I spent countless hours talking to experts and just about anyone who would listen. I wanted to learn as much as I could about what I would need to have a real shot at success.

Through these conversations, I really understood the power of personal values. I see now that I was living my values. I valued freedom, creativity, and challenge more than stability. I know this because of the decisions I made, how I used my time, and where I spent—or didn't spend—my money.

Once this light bulb went on for me, I started asking aspiring young professionals what they would sacrifice to achieve their dream of entrepreneurship. Could they see themselves not taking a vacation for a couple of years? How about not upgrading their phone each year? Could they avoid purchasing new clothes for months on end? Would they be willing to give up the security of a regular paycheck for the unpredictability of creating their own income?

Through these questions, I tried to help them become aware of their personal values—what they cared about most in life. To achieve our goals, our decisions and actions must align with our values.

We all have more than one personal value, and we can live more than one of them at a time. Often, a close inspection of our behaviors will show us what we value.

For example, health and fitness is a great and simple example of misalignment in my personal values. When I talk about getting in shape, I must sound like a broken record to friends and family—and that's true in my head too! While I enjoy some activities such as Pilates, spin, or long walks with friends, I value other aspects of my life more. If, for example, I'm on my way to a spin class and a friend calls asking if I'm free for an impromptu lunch while they are unexpectedly in town, then bye-bye spin class. This is a test of my values. Almost every time a situation such as this arises, I will choose to meet my friend, often without hesitation.

When I'm out with one of my really fit friends, I think about how strict and rigid their life seems to be. How can they pass up happy hour cocktails, or not eat a slice of my birthday cake in the name of staying on their routine? My thoughts show I clearly don't value fitness as much as the person making the sacrifices.

Through these experiences, I've learned that I value relationships and friendships more than fitness. I think fitness is important, but, as shown by my consistent actions, not as important as relationships and sometimes having fun. Being honest about what I value helps me understand why I'll never achieve my fitness goals the same way someone else who truly values health and fitness will.

VALUES AND CAREER DECISIONS

To start identifying your personal values, think about the last big decision you had to make. It could have been choosing between two job offers, moving to a new city, or even breaking up with your significant other.

Fast forward to today. What were the consequences of that decision? In other words, how did things turn out? Are you happy about the choices you made? Do you feel satisfied? Or do you feel dissatisfied?

Consider what was happening at that time in your life. Think of all of the various factors that went into your final decision. Making decisions is part of life. However, whether or not we're happy with the outcomes is unique to the process we go through when making them.

I recently met a young woman on an airplane who shared with me that she was moving across the United States for a new job. She explained that she was a west coast native and that her family was sad she was moving so far away. I couldn't help but ask how she came to make this big decision.

She shared that she felt stuck in her previous job. She joined a company right out of college and realized after two years that she didn't care for the work and didn't feel like part of a team. However, she received a sizable raise and bonus after her first year, which made her stay.

Then, a few months before she decided to relocate, a recruiter urged her to apply for a job in Boston. At first, the thought of being so far away sounded crazy. However, once she learned more about the company, she became intrigued. She did some research and saw how highly rated the company and leadership team was on sites like Glassdoor. She also found someone from her graduating class on LinkedIn who currently worked there. While interviewing with the hiring manager, she became excited about his vision and believed in what the company was doing. Most importantly, her role would have a lot more influence on strategic decisions.

My new airplane friend evaluated this opportunity through the lens of her personal values. Although her family was very important to her, she wasn't married and didn't have any children. At this time in her life, she was really motivated by being a part of something bigger. She made a career decision aligned with her values.

The decisions we're most happy with are those we make based on what's most important to us—our values. Those that we're most dissatisfied with are often those we make that do not support our values. This applies both to day-to-day decisions and to more significant life choices.

I've coached many people who, after taking the Values Challenges outlined in this chapter, realized that the reason they're so unhappy in their current career is that they're not being true to what they really want.

It's not uncommon to fantasize about working for a popular brand, having a prestigious job title, or earning a big salary. Sometimes, we get caught up in the outward appearance of a role or company, and we forget to ask ourselves what personal needs these goals will fulfill.

When we align our goals with what we care about most and what will fulfill us most, it is reflected in the decisions we make and whether we feel good about them or dissatisfied with them later.

MEET FRANK

Let me share an example. After teaching a management course, one of the participants, Frank, asked to meet one-on-one to get some advice on a career challenge he was having.

Frank was a 30-year-old, first-time manager in an online Marketing company. He told me he wanted to get to the next level of management but didn't see an opportunity to make that happen soon. The company, although a very popular and respected brand, only had about 400 employees. Unless his manager left, Frank didn't see how he could move into a higher-level role. Therefore, he had begun to talk to other companies that might have such a role for him. He ultimately wanted to know if it was time to leave the company and take on a larger leadership role elsewhere.

I quickly learned that Frank excelled at his managerial role. He was energized by coaching and developing others and loved leading his team. He seemed meant to be a manager and a leader.

Next, I asked Frank about his top personal values. Frank told me that he'd never stopped to think about what he valued. So, I gave him an assignment.

Using Career Revolution's *My Personal Values Card Deck*, I asked Frank to select the five values that were most important to him today and in the next couple of years.

Frank and I met a week later to continue our discussion. Before I share Frank's response, let's take some time to explore what your personal values are.

WHAT ARE YOUR PERSONAL VALUES?

What do you value most in your life right now? What do you think you might value for the next few years? Sometimes, the best way to answer these questions is to evaluate what's not working in your life and career right now.

VALUES CHALLENGE #1

Establish what's missing

Think about your current work situation. What have been your biggest frustrations? Have you ever felt like something was missing? Are you looking for more personal fulfillment? A more stable environment? More opportunities to advance? Or perhaps more money or benefits to support a growing family?

I find the most honest way to do this activity is to write down everything that comes to mind. Don't worry about how you're going to solve it quite yet. It's also your one opportunity to complain. By getting it out of your head and on to a piece of paper, you can acknowledge how you've been feeling, even if only in moments. This will help you complete the remaining challenges.

VALUES CHALLENGE #2

Identify your top values

The next step is to identify what you value most. I've translated Career Revolution's *My Personal Values Card Deck*, which includes 34 distinct values, into values categories, shown in the chart below. The goal of this challenge is to hone in on what's truly most important to you.

Access to the online *AccelerateME*™ Values Assessment can be found in the "Get There Faster Workbook."

Read each value category and corresponding definition. Then, rank the level of importance each one has in your life from 1, least important, to 5, most important. If you don't see what you're looking for, use the "Other" category to write it in.

VALUE CATEGORY		RANKING (1-5)
Security & Stability	• Pay, benefits, and job stability.	
Freedom & Mobility	• Flexibility with time or even freedom from schedules. • Amount of movement you might prefer or freedom from repetition.	
Self-Improvement & Self-Fulfillment	• Learning, development, personal growth, or contributing to a larger purpose. • Health and Fitness	
People & Relationships	• The type of culture you want to work in, the amount of teamwork you prefer, workplace friendships, or the desire to manage others. • Helping others.	
Authority & Power	• Job title, prestige, and influence over people or outcomes.	
Other: _____	Define: _____	

VALUES CHALLENGE #3

Put your money (and time) where your mouth is

Now that you have an idea of what your personal values are, you can ask yourself if the way you spend your money and time aligns with your values.

A great way to answer this question is to look at your calendar and bank statements. If examined by an outsider, would they know what's important to you? Would they see your most highly rated values reflected? What do you make time for? What do you spend money on?

BANK STATEMENT

Print your last bank and credit card statements. Next to each transaction, write the name of the value category you believe it reflects.

For example, if you see a charge for a new book, label it "Self-Fulfillment" because you bought it to learn or be entertained. If you transferred 5% of your paycheck into a savings account, you might label it "Security & Stability."

After reviewing each transaction, determine what percentage of your total transactions support the top two values categories you identified or the top five individual values if you used the online assessment or card deck.

CALENDAR

What did you do this week? How did you spend your time?

You can answer these questions by auditing the last month of your calendar. If you only keep a professional calendar, you may want to add personal items to get a holistic picture.

Now, review each hour and label which value you believe it supported. For example, if you had dinner with a friend, you would label it "People & Relationships." Or if you initiated a career conversation with your manager, you might label it "Self-Improvement" or "Authority & Power" if the discussion focused on asking for a promotion or opportunity to influence higher-ups.

VALUES CHALLENGE #4

Create a values-based commitment

How well are you living your values? Which ones are in alignment with how you spend your time and money? Which ones are not?

For any that you aren't living as much as you'd like, you have an opportunity to make some changes. This challenge will guide you through a process of bringing awareness to potential misalignments and identifying actions to bridge gaps.

1. Select one value category that you want to live more fully.

2. Describe the specific value within this category that your life is most lacking.

3. Describe what that would look like for you to live that value more fully. What would you need to change?

4. What opportunities are within your control to make those adjustments?

5. Pick one or two actions you are willing to take to create more alignment between this value and how you practice it.

This activity always makes me think of one of my program participants from a U.S. government agency, Sarita. Sarita was new to the workforce and was recently hired after completing a senior internship. She shared with the class that she didn't think about her values or had ever articulated them when she accepted her new job. Through the process, she realized that she valued helping people and having authority and power. She also identified that these were two values she wasn't living as much as she'd like. Although she liked her new role, she was an individual contributor and was often on the receiving end of most tasks rather than given the authority to lead others.

Sarita outlined what it would look like if she were helping others and leading more. She determined she would be working with other people to listen to their needs and sharing her own experiences. She would be mentoring and coaching and potentially be the go-to person for others.

With a little help from her table group, she came up with a couple of ideas for potential opportunities she could take advantage of or even create with the right support, including:

- Finding an organization to volunteer outside of work

- Volunteering to take new interns to lunch. She had just graduated from the company intern program and could have empathy.

- Asking her manager to mentor an intern formally.

If Sarita were to take on any one of these opportunities, she would more fully be living her values.

Another example that comes to mind is Marco, a program participant from a tech company in Minneapolis. He had been with the organization for two years, and in that time worked long hours and no longer participated in sports like he used to before he started his full-time job.

In this activity, he identified self-improvement, specifically health and fitness, as his top value, but rated it low in terms of how fully he was currently living it. He wasn't sure how to change this, as he had a substantial workload and didn't want to have to quit to get his fitness routine back on track.

By going through this activity, Marco identified a few small adjustments he could make, including:

- Joining a local soccer league and commit to a weekly practice evening and one weekend day.

- Getting up one hour early three times a week to run.

- Finding a trusted co-worker with the same value to schedule fitness activities together and hold each other accountable.

The trick with this activity is to think of ways to live your values more fully, but only pick one or two small adjustments or experiments to start with. Little shifts can make a big difference.

VALUES CHANGE AS YOU DO

Values will change throughout your life. For example, some people may value having variety and change early in their careers. Then after settling down and having a family, stability and financial security may take higher priority. Often, people find that their values have shifted, but they're still making career decisions based on an outdated definition of success or view of their values.

That brings us back to Frank. Frank and I reconvened a week later to discuss the values card activity I gave him. After sorting through 34 values and a little deliberation, Frank said that he identified the following as his top five values:

- Financial Freedom: Possessing wealth or the means to have life essentials and luxuries
- Health and Fitness: An active lifestyle that allows time to maintain good exercise and nutrition.
- Leadership: Leading others through direction, influence, and inspiration.
- Relationships: Developing close personal relationships with people as a result of work.
- Family: Being able to maintain and support close relationships.

I thought Frank's current job situation might not be aligned with some of his personal values. So, I asked him to describe how well he was living or not living each value.

Frank shared that he had a new baby at home and was happy that he could be home for dinner and bedtime most nights. He said he runs in the morning before work and has access to a company gym for strength training. The company provided a nutritious lunch a couple of times a week and many fun social engagements where he could enjoy the company of co-workers.

He also shared that he had been promoted just eight months earlier into his current job—his first management role. This enabled him to buy a new home for his family close to the office, reducing his commute to just 15 minutes, a rare benefit in his city.

Slightly perplexed, I told Frank that it sounded like his personal values were being met in a significant way. In fact, most people I work with always have one or two that aren't being supported by their current life situation. From my perspective, Frank should have considered himself lucky.

I then asked Frank the million-dollar question, "Why do you want to leave the company?" Frank responded with where he started the conversion, "I don't see an opportunity to get to the next level here."

My next question was, "Why do you feel you need to get to the 'next level' right now?"

Frank just stared at me and didn't provide an immediate response. In fact, he appeared a little frustrated by my question. I explained that I wanted him to identify the driving force behind his desire for a career move right now. After a bit of back and forth, a light bulb went on for him. He told me that when he first started his career, his goal was to get promoted as fast as possible and manage a large department or division. Many of his friends, especially those who didn't have children, were being promoted into senior management roles.

I took Frank back to the top five values he identified and asked him if he chose them because they were authentically what was most important to him. He replied, "Yes."

Then I asked Frank if he thought these values had shifted over the last couple of years, which he agreed they had.

I asked Frank to play out a scenario with me. If he were to leave his current job and go to another company, what would be the chances it would be as close to his new home? If he managed a larger team in a larger company, would there be other locations he would have to travel to? More employees also often equal more meetings, and more meetings equate to longer work hours, especially in your first year of a new job. The likelihood of Frank being home on time for dinner most nights and having time to work out started to fade.

Frank then realized that the career move he was seeking actually didn't support his values. In fact, a move now to another company might actually diminish his ability to live them as fully as he currently was.

If you're not honest about what you value most, an authentic and fulfilling career will be difficult to achieve.

BE TRUE TO YOURSELF

If you're currently unhappy in your career, you may not be being true to what you really want.

For example, some people realize that they work for a company or are in a role that offers them excellent compensation, but they don't feel like they're contributing to a larger purpose. Without identifying their values, they made career decisions based on job titles and bonus opportunities. While these can be significant benefits, if one of your core values conflicts with your career choices, you may still feel unfulfilled and frustrated.

It's also important to understand that it's problematic to meet all of your needs throughout your entire career. Sometimes you have to make trade-offs to grow.

I recommend revisiting the values challenges in this chapter at least once a year to help you reevaluate what's most important to you. I do it every January to set myself up for success in the new year. It forces me to think about the types of decisions I might make and how I want to prioritize my time and relationships.

You can also reuse these challenges if you are struggling at work and want to remind yourself of what's most important to you and make adjustments as needed.

Now that you know what energizes you and what you value most, you're ready to create a compelling career vision.

SHORTCUTS

HOW TO LIVE YOUR PERSONAL VALUES

CHALLENGE #1	**Establish what's missing:** Think about your current work situation. What have been your biggest frustrations?
CHALLENGE #2	**Identify Your Top Values:** What is most important to you today and in the near future. Prioritize each of the five values categories.
CHALLENGE #3	**Put your money (and time) where your mouth is:** Examine your bank statements and calendar to see if how you spend your money and time aligns to the top values you identified.
CHALLENGE #4	**Create a values-based commitment:** Select one value you want to live more fully. What would have to be adjusted for you to live that value more fully?

STEP 3:

ENVISION YOUR FUTURE

In this chapter, you will:
- ❑ Define the elements that inspire your success and happiness.
- ❑ Create a five-year career vision statement.
- ❑ Create a one-year career goal that aligns with your broader vision.
- ❑ Learn a creative method to increase personal accountability in achieving your goal.

"Where do you want to be in five years?"

"What are your career goals?"

Have you ever been asked these questions in an interview? For most, these questions can be intimidating.

As an interviewer, in most cases, I remember receiving one of two responses. I either got the deer-in-the-headlights response or what I call the visions-of-grandeur response. In the first scenario, the young interviewee wouldn't have an answer and would squirm in their seat and turn red. Or, they would simply say, "I don't know." On the other end of the spectrum, I recall several young professionals, especially those fresh out of college, tell me about their plans to be the next Mark Zuckerberg or, my favorite response, "I will have your job."

Now, don't get me wrong, I would never want to discourage someone from pursuing their dreams, no matter how big they are. However, more often than not, the career aspirations in response to this question didn't appear to have any thought behind them. Sometimes it seemed as though the interviewee, instead of having a real vision, simply made something up that sounded ambitious.

A career vision is a big-picture view of what you want to achieve and how you see yourself in the future. It's about what you aspire to, and it ultimately serves as your North Star as you make career decisions.

If you ask a five-year-old, "What do you want to be when you grow up?" in a matter of seconds, you'll hear a variety of imaginative, aspirational, and sometimes outlandish, career choices. From firefighters to chefs to doctors to superheroes, the child often gives their top picks with zeal, passion, and enthusiasm. So, what do YOU want to be when you grow up? This was a much easier question to answer when you were a child. It's much more complex now!

WHY YOU NEED A CLEAR VISION

You may have heard the saying, "If you don't make a decision, then someone else will make it for you." Nothing could be more real than when it comes to your career.

Your career vision encapsulates your view of success according to your personal values and Energizers. It draws a path to create meaning in your work and directs your actions as you move towards your career purpose.

You may have many passions and find it's difficult to have one specific path. The goal of a career vision is to think of the elements of success that are most important to you. Your vision may shift over time as you have new experiences and gain new knowledge. However, it's essential to establish your North Star as you see it today so you can guide yourself in a direction.

Remember Ben? Without creating an intentional career vision, he was making decisions based on other people's views of success. He could only see choices that ultimately wouldn't lead him to the type of fulfillment he really wanted. Once he was aware of his Energizers and defined his values, he could establish a vision of success that was right for him.

Since everyone's strengths, values, and desires are unique, your career vision will also be one-of-a-kind. Creating a career vision doesn't mean committing to a ten-year plan but rather focusing on important decisions that are highly relevant today.

To help you form this vision, I've provided a few challenges to prompt your thinking and put yourself into a future state. These challenges will help you get out of thinking about the details of today and let you daydream a little. They will also help you transform many of the aspirations and ideas floating around in your head into a clear career vision you use to set your next immediate career goal.

Let's start with the first challenge.

VISION CHALLENGE #1

Design your perfect career

Try answering at least one of the questions below. I find that one to two of them will produce an immediate thought or gut instinct for most, while one or two questions might leave you stumped.

As with all vision-related activities, the key is to withhold judgment about the likelihood you can commit to the things that come to mind. Don't worry about taking action on your responses. This challenge is all about opening up your mind and checking in with your future self.

1. What type of work would you want to do if all of your bills were paid, and money was not a factor in your career decisions?

2. Who are the people you most admire? Is there anything about who they are or what they've done that you want for your own life?

3. Do you feel as though you have a gift or a special talent? How might you share this gift or talent in a way that will fulfill you?

Another great way to take on this challenge is to find a friend and ask each other these questions.

Once you've answered a question or two, think about your responses. Do they validate ideas you've been tossing around for a while? Or is this the first time you've said them out loud? Either way, you now have a more heightened awareness of what your career vision might be.

VISION CHALLENGE #2

Create your five-year vision of career success

Let's take it a step further by visualizing the perfect day. Use the prompts below to guide you through a visualization exercise to design your future. Instead of thinking about ten or twenty years from now, I find it helpful to think about a timeframe a little less ambiguous. Imagine that you just woke up five years from today on a workday. Now, answer these questions:

- How did you wake up?
- What time is it?
- Where are you?

- Is anyone next to you?
- What is your morning routine?
- What do you eat for breakfast?
- What clothes do you put on?
- Where is your workplace?
- How do you get there?
- Who are your colleagues?
- Do you have direct reports?
- What are your team members like?
- What does your workspace look like?
- What type of work activities are you engaged in?
- What types of interactions are you having?
- How do you wrap up your day?
- At what time are you finished for the day?
- How do you feel leaving work?
- What do you do now?
- Where do you go for dinner?
- Who do you eat with?
- What's your evening routine?
- Do you have any free time?
- What do you do before going to bed?
- What time do you fall asleep?
- What are you most grateful for today?

Now, think about the week ahead while still using the five-years in the future timeframe. Answer the following questions:

- How are the days to come different or similar to today?
- Does your work differ?
- Is each day somewhat the same?
- How will you spend the weekend?
- How much free time do you have?
- How do you spend it?

Zoom out and think about the next month of your life, five years into the future. Now, answer these questions:

- What do you hope to achieve in the next month?
- How much of your time will be spent working?
- How much time will you spend with your friends or family?
- Do you have any passion projects?
- What types of interactions do you expect to have?
- What will have to be accomplished for you to feel successful and happy?

Now that you have a vision for your perfect day, week, and month, take a moment to see what you can extract to help you craft a vision. What themes do you see? How much of what you envisioned aligned to the values that you identified in the previous chapter? What about your Energizers?

How would you summarize your vision? Take a moment to craft a few sentences that highlight your vision. Write the statements in the present tense, even though they reflect your ideal future self.

There's no one way to encapsulate a career vision. Some people draw a picture, some write a personal mission-like statement while others make career vision boards. The method doesn't matter. Get clear on your vision and document it in a way that works for your brain.

Here are three examples of how to document your vision. Simply pick one that feels most authentic to you.

CREATE A PERSONAL VISION STATEMENT

You can use the following formula to help.

I am a _____ who _____ to/by _____.

Here are a couple of examples. I'll start with mine.

"I am a respected author and speaker who helps young professionals live their best lives by providing coaching and sharing knowledge."

Here are a few others from young professionals who have been through this activity.

- "I am a leading scientist who conducts cutting-edge research to help improve the lives of children around the country."
- "I am a creative force who helps improve businesses and lives by solving problems with a positive attitude that spreads to everyone around me."
- "I am a restaurant general manager, who provides excellent food and service to customers by being a fair and inspirational leader to my staff."
- "I am a sales ninja who consistently exceeds expectations and creates financial security for my family."
- "I am a software developer who creates innovative solutions that makes people's lives easier."
- "I am the head of the strategy office for an innovative brand."

DRAW A CAREER COVER STORY

Welcome to the future. Pretend today is five years from today, and you are featured on the cover of a publication for your career achievements. Draw your career cover story by answering the following questions.

- What's the name of the publication?
- What are the headlines?
- What quotes are included?
- What accomplishments are you being recognized for?
- What does your picture look like?
- What are the highlights of the story?

CREATE A CAREER VISION BOARD

A vision board is an interactive and imaginative visual tool that paints a picture of your future. It's a great activity for visual learners and those with a creative spirit.

You can create a physical board using magazine clippings or go digital and create a virtual board using Pinterest, or a vision board app such as DreamItAlive or Vision Board. What's most important is that you continuously look at it. I remember an episode of the Ellen show in 2012 when she revealed her vision board and a goal of being on the cover of Oprah's "O Magazine." She said, "You've got to have a dream. Put it out into the universe, and it will come to you." The science behind it is based on the law-of-attraction.

THE LAW OF ATTRACTION

Simply put, the Law of Attraction is the ability to materialize whatever is in our thoughts into reality. The theory states that if you focus on negative possibilities and ideas, you will, in turn, experience adverse outcomes and situations. Whereas, if you focus on positive thoughts and focus your energy on bringing them to life, then you will find a way to attract favorable circumstances and outcomes and into your life. Of course, this isn't magic. Rather, the Law of Attraction teaches us that our thoughts are powerful. If we focus on possibilities and positive outcomes, then our brain believes good things are happening. Therefore, we feel positive and start to see opportunities.

PUTTING IT ALL TOGETHER

Regardless of the method you used to document your vision, what do you notice about what you created? How does your vision compare to your current life? What aspects seem easy to achieve, and which seem more challenging?

The next vision challenge is designed to help you move your vision into reality by identifying what you can do in the next year to move you closer to your 5-year vision.

VISION CHALLENGE #3

Commit to a one-year milestone

The only thing standing between you and making your career vision a reality is translating it into a series of tangible goals. Think deliberately about the actions you would need to take to make your career vision a reality. For example, if your vision is to start your own business, you would need to secure funding or save a specific amount of money, create a prototype, and create a business plan.

Given your unique vision, think about what you could do in the next year. What will success look like one year from today? What needs to be in place for your career vision to become a reality? What significant milestones will you need to achieve? Take a moment to jot down everything that comes to mind.

Now that you've considered some achievements that would move you closer to your career vision, let's solidify a one-year milestone by completing the sentence below.

By the end of the next 12 months, I will feel successful if...

Picture yourself sitting next to a friend one year from today. You are telling your friend what an amazing year it was for your career. What achievements do you picture yourself telling your friend about? How you respond to that question is your one-year milestone!

This activity isn't about holding yourself accountable to an out-of-reach or inauthentic pipe dream. Instead, it's about defining success for yourself in a way that gives you direction and focus.

MICHELLE'S STORY

Sometimes it helps to see an example. Let's look at one from Michelle, a 33-year-old project manager I recently coached. Her career vision was one of the examples I provided in the last section: "I am the head of the strategy office for an innovative brand."

She knew that to achieve that vision, she would need to be promoted into a management role. She then brainstormed how she could position herself to be considered for a promotion into management.

To be promoted, she would need to be considered "promotable." For that to happen, she would need to be seen as a top performer in the department. Therefore, she identified that she needed to improve her performance rating to the highest level possible on the company's performance scale.

Michelle then thought about what would help her achieve a higher performance rating. It would entail managing higher-visibility projects to gain more exposure to her skills as well as improving her credibility as a team member and influencer.

So, when Michelle decided on what her one-year milestone would be, she said: "By the end of the next 12 months, I will feel successful if I'm leading a high-visibility project that earns me an 'exceeds expectations' on my next annual performance review."

Michelle focused on how to be seen as more promotable, rather than how to head the department. She worked her way back from her goal to find the actions that would support her ultimate career vision.

WORK BACKWARD

The easiest way to set career goals is to work backward as Michelle did. Michelle started knowing she would need to be promoted to a manager role and then kept asking the question, "What would need to happen for that goal to be achieved?"

This methodology will help you create a set of related goals for which you can put timeframes. Before you know it, you're well on your way to your larger vision.

Here are some additional one-year milestones successful young professionals have shared with me:

- Improve my performance rating from a "meets expectations" to "exceeds expectations"
- Become a certified mentor to gain coaching skills
- Move from the sales to Marketing teams within my organization
- Take on a direct report
- Get promoted to the next level in my organization
- Become a first-time manager
- Complete a year of graduate school
- Create a prototype to test my side hustle idea
- Increase my sales numbers by 25%
- Earn a certification in project management

So, what's your 1-year milestone?

Start with your big-picture vision or at least elements of it. Do you see yourself in a leadership role? Doing work that helps others or the environment? Do you envision working for yourself or being part of building something new? Ask yourself, "What would have to be true for my vision to be a reality?" Once you have a list of those items, ask yourself, "What can I do this year that will move me closer to that vision?" Lastly, ask yourself what you can achieve in the next 12 months that will move you a step closer to your vision?

IS YOUR VISION STILL FOGGY?

On occasion, one of my program participants will tell me that they don't have a clear vision. They sometimes feel lost and frustrated when they see their peers light up during these visioning activities.

So, what do you do if you still don't have a clear vision? Sometimes the most powerful one-year milestone is about gaining clarity. Therefore, you might consider a goal such as, "By the end of the next 12 months, I will feel successful if I have a clear career vision for the future."

Ben is an excellent example of this. Recognizing that he didn't want to continue pursuing a career in accounting was in itself a big decision. To ask him to turn around and have a clear five-year vision immediately was too much. In fact, he may have just been guessing at that stage.

To make sure Ben had a clear direction, I challenged him to articulate what success would look like one year from now. If we were to meet one year from that day and he would share his success, what did he picture himself saying?

Ben simply said, "I will be in a new job that allows me to play in my primary Energy Zone and to see career opportunities I'm currently not exposed to."

As you can see, this is a very different goal than what he started with. If you remember, when I first met with Ben, his immediate vision was to pass the CPA exam and get a higher paying job in the field of accounting.

By articulating this shift, Ben took an entirely different set of actions. I recently caught up with Ben to see how things were going. Ben successfully transitioned into a human resources support role and took it as an opportunity to learn everything he could about the various roles in HR. Through this experience, he learned that he had a passion for Talent Acquisition and is now exploring his next step as a recruiter.

If your vision is similar to Ben's, you could ask yourself what you would need to gain that type of clarity. You might consider some actions such as engaging with a professional career coach, finding an experienced mentor, or even taking a career development course, just to name a few.

Most importantly, you should be in the driver's seat of your decisions and finding your vision. If not, you are giving your power away.

VISIONS ARE FLEXIBLE

Since the world and workplace continue to change, and we continue to flex, learn, and grow, your career vision will do the same. Throughout those transitions and ambiguity, you must gain clarity regarding what success looks like for you. Then, and only then, can you know where to aim.

Creating a career vision can be both exciting and daunting at the same time. I've found that many emerging professionals have expectations about what should be happening in the next year of their careers but have no idea why. This is an important step in the process and one that can require more time and thought.

When I was at a critical career junction and thinking of leaving my corporate job, a colleague shared a fun activity to help me shift from the here and now to thinking about the near future. She told me to write a letter to myself one year in the future. The goal of this activity is to imagine the future one year from now—but the catch is that you do so by writing about it as if it has already happened.

VISION CHALLENGE #4

Write a one-year letter to yourself

Date a letter with today's date but one year later. For example, if today is July 2020, date the letter July 2021.

Then write what you achieved over the last year that brought you to today. Speak to the things you did, the people you met, and even the challenges you overcame. It's like taking a time machine to a year from now.

Having done this activity year after year, I've found that I could go back to my story and further refine it as new things came to my mind. What I realized is that the more I put focused energy envisioning the future, the more detailed that vision becomes.

The clearer we are on what we want as well as on how we achieved it, the greater chance we have in taking action—not just any action, but rather purposeful action. The goal is to create a career vision that's unique to you, and that you can take action to achieve.

Remember, we're living in an ever-changing world, so our goals can flex as needed. The objective is to give yourself clarity on what's most important. This will help you focus your energies on what will most accelerate your career growth.

SHORTCUTS

HOW TO ENVISION YOUR FUTURE

CHALLENGE #1	**Design your perfect career:** What type of work would you want to do if all of your bills were paid, and money was not a factor in your career decisions?
CHALLENGE #2	**Create your 5-year vision of career success:** • Create a personal vision statement. • Pretend today is five years from today, and you are featured on the cover of a publication for your career achievements. • Create a career vision board.
CHALLENGE #3	**Commit to a one-year milestone:** Set a one-year career goal that connects to your vision by completing the sentence, "One year from today, I will….
CHALLENGE #4	**Write a one-year letter to yourself:** Write a letter to yourself one year from the future.

STEP 4:

UNCOVER YOUR BLIND SPOTS

In this chapter, you will:

- ❑ Identify when your Energizers may be in overdrive.
- ❑ Uncover how promotable you are in the eyes of others.
- ❑ Address the blind spots that could derail your career potential.
- ❑ Assess yourself against the *AccelerateME*™ *Mindset Model* of early career success.

I vividly remember the summer before my sixteenth birthday when my dad taught me to drive. Learning to drive is one of the most exciting and anxiety-inducing experiences of being a teenager. I waited all year, anticipating the freedom I would have to go when and where I wanted.

I studied the driver's manual and practiced getting comfortable driving in parking lots and around my neighborhood. Finally, it was time for the big leagues—the highway! As I approached my very first onramp, my dad encouraged me to step on the gas.

When I quickly sped up to merge into the first lane, I heard a loud and extended honk and saw a car swerve around me! My dad screamed, "You need to check your blind spots! You almost hit that car!"

I was shaken to my core and didn't give the highway another try until months later. Needless to say, when I did, I was super careful to look over my shoulder before changing lanes.

A similar dynamic happens with our careers. We don't think about looking over our shoulder for potential obstacles because we are so focused on driving our career forward. It's not until we crash, or almost crash, that we become conscious of looking in the mirror to get a better view.

Have you been passed up for a promotion you believed you deserved? Maybe you thought you interviewed well, but you didn't get the job. Or, you may feel like your work is going unnoticed, or you're not rewarded for your contributions. If so, you may have a career blind spot that may be holding you back.

A blind spot is a behavior that others notice but that you don't. Everyone has blind spots. Yes, even you and me. Research tells us that about 90% of us have at least one blind spot. They can be hard to see in ourselves, even if we can easily see them in others. Blind spots can be big or small, positive or negative, but if not addressed, they can derail your career potential.

WHAT ARE THE ORIGINS OF OUR BLIND SPOTS?

In the LinkedIn Learning course *"Leadership Blind Spots,"* author and leadership expert, Sara Canaday says blind spots happen "when our intentions and perceptions don't match." She further explains this as "a disconnect between what we believe we're projecting and how others actually experience us."

In the workplace, we rely on others, especially our managers, to give us cues along the way to ensure we're on the right path.

The problem is that most managers aren't skilled at or comfortable with giving developmental feedback. Research from Lominger, a well-established leader in talent development consulting, reports that management competencies such as "developing others" and "confronting direct reports" are among the lowest-rated when their employees evaluate managers.

Therefore, it's possible to go through your career without anyone telling you about a glaring blind spot that's preventing you from achieving your goals. In fact, I hear from many young professionals that they rarely get feedback from their manager and assume that no news is good news. That may be the case, but it may also not be.

The challenges in this chapter will help you discover your blind spots and address them. This enables you to be seen as having high potential and will create more opportunities and career possibilities for you.

BLIND SPOTS CAN DERAIL YOUR CAREER

Whenever I'm teaching about blind spots, a particular intern I employed always comes to mind. I've hired several interns over the years and have continued to be impressed with their passion for learning and desire to do meaningful work. This one, however, was a different case.

One year, someone in my professional network connected me to a graduate student looking for a summer internship in my field. He diligently followed up with me and provided impressive examples of his knowledge and experiences relevant to my business. Most of all, he demonstrated excitement and enthusiasm for the opportunity to work with me. I was impressed and did something I never do—I hired him without checking his references. Given that he was a referral from my network, and had a lot of relevant experience, I paid him almost double the rate of a typical internship.

Based on the experiences he spoke of in our interview and his confidence, I took a risk, and in his first week, I invited him to help me with an event I was doing with PlayStation, one of my longest-standing and cherished clients.

His first assignment was to design and facilitate the warm-up activity for the client event, a team-building exercise. Without hesitation, he came to our first meeting prepared with an activity and a strategy for how we would lead it. I was so happy with this meeting. I patted myself on the back for taking the right risk and hiring him. I gave him some kudos and asked him to make a few important and immediate changes based on my history and in-depth knowledge of this client's needs. He agreed. We ended our meeting by confirming the time he would arrive at the event and help me set up.

It was the day of the big event. Twenty minutes after his designated arrival time that morning, and he still hadn't arrived. I started to worry, wondering if I gave him the wrong address or perhaps worse, he had been in an accident. Thirty minutes after he was supposed to arrive, he rushed into the event space, looking disheveled with wrinkled pants and messy hair. He told me he was sorry that he was late, but he cut himself shaving. "That's a first," I thought to myself.

Since the client was already there and we had a job to do, I just smiled and asked him to get set up for his activity. He then went to the breakfast table to enjoy a coffee and muffin and introduce himself to the client team members.

I recall moving from annoyance to perplexity. "What is this guy thinking?" I thought. "He's having a jolly old time engaging with the client while I set the room up—work I hired him to do!" After a few deep breaths, I started the session and introduced him to the group. He went through his activity and, to my surprise, did not make the changes I had asked. Although he displayed the same confidence I saw in his interview, he facilitated the activity in a way that didn't align with the content for the rest of the day.

As if this wasn't bad enough, during the remainder of the session, he would interject while I was speaking to add in his two cents. I wouldn't have minded if he had any real leadership experience or had anything to contribute that was relevant for this client. Judging from the awkward looks, I could tell my client wasn't happy.

I was so taken aback by the day's events. I really had to think about how to give this feedback. Where would I even begin?

As we debriefed after the event, I asked him how he thought everything went. I asked him to share with me what he thought he did well, what he learned, and what he would change if he could do it all over. He told me that he had an awesome day. He loved working with such a prestigious client and felt completely energized.

"If given a chance, what would you do differently the next time?" I asked. "Nothing," he replied.

I then gave him feedback about his tardiness and misalignment of content. It seemed to go in one ear and out the other. He just smiled and told me he felt he was meant to do this work and that he really helped the executive client and her team. I tried explaining again how his behavior came across to me and possibly to the client. But, he didn't appear to see that his confidence, although good in some instances, was making him blind in others.

Given his lack of self-awareness, I decided I wouldn't give him any client-facing work for the remainder of our time together. I never had another conversation with him about my perception. I sometimes think back to that experience and feel bad that I didn't try a little harder to help him see his blind spots. Ultimately, his hubris and lack of introspection made me hesitant to invest any more time or energy in him. I'm not proud that I gave up on him so soon. I hope by sharing this story, you can gain an insight into how moments like these can create hidden career roadblocks.

Despite my attempt to help him see the blind spot I saw, and obvious decision to not put him in front of any more clients, I received several calls, after he graduated, from prospective employers for which he used me as a reference—of course, without telling me! As you might imagine, the response I gave to the job reference calls wasn't glowing. Of course, I spoke to the benefits of his confidence, but also to where he needed development. Imagine how differently these reference calls could have been. Imagine what new opportunities could have opened up for him if he had been more open to uncovering his blind spots.

Let's play this out. If he had listened to my feedback, I would have given him a second chance. If he incorporated the feedback or been open to more coaching, I would have continued to provide him with client-facing work. If he had more client-facing work, he would have been qualified for more prominent and higher-paying roles when he graduated. Most of all, I would have given more positive evaluations when he used me as a reference for those opportunities.

In the book "The Right—and Wrong—Stuff: How Brilliant Careers Are Made and Unmade," author Carter Cast speaks to common blind spots that can create roadblocks in our careers. One of his key findings is that it's often excessive pride or ego—not lack of talent—that causes people to fail.

In the case of my summer hire, he was so focused on himself and the prestige of working with big-name clients and executives, that he didn't listen. As Cast points out in his book, my former intern is not alone in his cluelessness. The odds are that we've all received direct feedback or subtle signs of our blind spots. However, some of us miss them.

OUR BLIND SPOT IS RECOGNIZING BLIND SPOTS

If blind spots were easy to identify, we wouldn't use the word "blind." The reason we refer to them as blind spots is because most of us are entirely unaware of them until we take intentional action to discover them. We are biased in our own perspective. So, the shortest path to uncover them is to get feedback from others.

We actually get feedback every day all day long. It may be direct verbal feedback, like someone telling us what they thought of our presentation. It can also be non-verbal feedback, like how people's body language or facial expressions change when we ask them for something.

It takes excellent emotional intelligence and self-awareness to read the nonverbal feedback we receive all of the time. I've found that some people have that gift, while others simply don't, and the majority of us fall somewhere in between.

Regardless of how good you are reading others, the best way to uncover a blind spot is to ask for direct feedback. The thought of this can bring on a lot of varying emotions. It is common to experience defensiveness, curiosity, shame, or even flattery or excitement. I have found that young professionals get especially anxious at this step in the process.

FACING THE FEAR OF FEEDBACK

When I work with groups of young professionals, and we begin the process of identifying their blind spots, many participants share that this is the first time they've received this kind of feedback, and it's an eye-opener. Many express their initial apprehension and even anxiety about asking for an assessment from a boss or peer. However, after completing the challenges in this chapter, they often share that their results were better than expected.

Here are some of the "light-bulb" moments they've shared:

- "Getting feedback was scary and made me anxious, but seeing the good and the bad was actually helpful. Now I know what to focus on to really grow my career. Thank God, I learned that sooner than later."

- "I'm more powerful than I thought. I didn't realize how positively others saw me."

- "I got feedback that I'm negative and get frustrated when things don't go my way. I didn't realize I came across that way until now."

- "Now that I see my feedback in front of me, it's making it easier to know what specifically to focus on. I only need to make a few little tweaks."

- "This is the first time I've gotten this kind of feedback. I have a couple of blind spots I was not aware of. I guess it's better to know now so I can do something about it."

- "I was freaked out at first, not knowing how others would evaluate me. I was happy to see that it was only one area that there was a gap. Now I can stop guessing and just focus on that one thing. Easy!"

The challenges I've designed are to help you uncover your blind spots. Move through them one at a time at a pace that is comfortable for you. I encourage you to push yourself slightly outside of your comfort zone. This is a crucial step in your journey and one that can be rewarded with significant breakthroughs that will lead you to your next big career move.

IDENTIFYING BLIND SPOTS

When teaching people to identify blind spots, I often ask them to think of someone they work with or have worked with, who has a glaring blind spot. It doesn't take long for someone to pop in their head.

I hear stories of bosses who everyone disliked, know-it-all co-workers, and rigid team members. It's easy to identify blind spots in others, just as I did with my intern.

Give it a try. Close your eyes and think of your worst manager or most annoying co-worker. What made them so difficult or unlikeable? Do you think they were aware of how they were perceived? Perhaps they were aware but didn't know what to do about it.

Some of our blind spots are referred to as positive blind spots—something we aren't aware we do well. In these cases, the blind spot may be a lack of confidence. Can you think of anyone who is perceived as more capable than they think they are? Maybe that's you!

At the beginning of the book, I asked you to picture me gathering all of your co-workers in a room without you there. Picture me asking them to describe your capabilities and attributes. What do you think they would say? Do you think their statements would be an accurate assessment of you? Would you agree with their opinions?

The only way to really know is to get direct feedback. A great first step is to do some reflection. I find the easiest way to start is to think about Energizers in overdrive, which is your first challenge.

BLIND SPOT CHALLENGE #1

Discover your Energizers in overdrive

Think about your primary Energy Zone from Step 1. These may be qualities or skills that come so naturally to us that we can't see when we're overusing them. Sometimes we use our strengths in the wrong situation or overuse them and create problems for ourselves and others. I refer to these situations as Energizers in overdrive.

Below are the most common blind spots for each Energy Zone. Check off the ones that might apply to you.

THE THINKING ZONE

☑ Getting so focused on details that you can't see the bigger picture.

☐ Missing a deadline while trying to make something perfect.

☑ Continuing to ask questions when the team has made a decision and is ready to move forward.

☐ Generating an excess of ideas, most of which are unusable.

☐ Questioning the "why" behind a decision to the point of appearing difficult.

☐ Creating solutions that are un-executable.

☐ Identifying connections that don't exist.

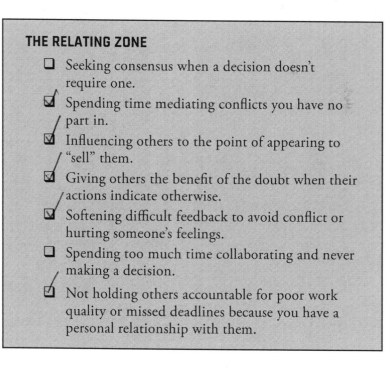

THE DOING ZONE

- ❑ Getting so focused on processes and procedures that you appear rigid.
- ❑ Overtalking in meetings to get to execution.
- ❑ Re-engineering processes that don't need it.
- ☑ Becoming so committed to a decision or direction that you can't pivot when needed.
- ☑ Leading when it's not appropriate.
- ❑ Stepping on other's toes.
- ☑ Micromanaging projects or people.
- ☑ Ignoring a team member's feedback and opinions because it may change the direction of a project or decision.

THE RELATING ZONE

- ❑ Seeking consensus when a decision doesn't require one.
- ☑ Spending time mediating conflicts you have no part in.
- ☑ Influencing others to the point of appearing to "sell" them.
- ☑ Giving others the benefit of the doubt when their actions indicate otherwise.
- ☑ Softening difficult feedback to avoid conflict or hurting someone's feelings.
- ❑ Spending too much time collaborating and never making a decision.
- ☑ Not holding others accountable for poor work quality or missed deadlines because you have a personal relationship with them.

What did you discover? Did any of the blind spots related to Energizers in overdrive resonate with you?

Before we move to a challenge that will help you validate your selections, it's essential to identify how you want to be seen by others.

BLIND SPOT CHALLENGE #2

Draft your ideal reputation

What is your ideal reputation? How do you want to be perceived? Use the questions below as a guide to outlining the reputation you want to have.

- What do you want to be known for?
- How do people benefit from working with you?
- How do you want to make others feel?
- How do you want people to describe you to others?

Most people, even later in their career, never stop to think about these types of questions. It essentially boils down to a personal value proposition. Successful products or services demonstrate to the buyer what they will get and why it's better than the competition. The same is true for your career. What do you bring to the table, and why is working with you a benefit to others? Before you can articulate that, you first need to define your personal value proposition.

Now, think about a product with great Marketing, but poor or mixed customer reviews. Would you feel good about making that purchase? Or would you shop around to see who has a better reputation?

The same is true for your career. Once you've defined what you want your reputation to be, look for signs that support or disagree with it. A good way to do this is to reflect on the feedback you've already received.

BLIND SPOT CHALLENGE #3

Consider past feedback

Think back on the past twelve months of your career, Maybe you received a performance review, verbal feedback from a manager or team members offered you some observations. Now, ask yourself the following questions about those assessments:

- What feedback have you received over the last year that supports the ideal reputation you identified in the previous challenge?

- Where might you have gaps?

- What feedback have you received that differs from your ideal reputation?

- Does this feedback differ from group to group?

- Do you think you're perceived the same from higher-ups and peers?

That last question is important. I remember hiring a direct report whom I considered a star player. He was the highest-paid team member, and one of the best at self-managing his deadlines. I continuously received feedback from his internal client groups that he was a pleasure to work with and consistently exceeded expectations. He seemed easy to get along with people and made my job easier.

However, a few months into his tenure, I started to notice an odd dynamic on the team. When we would present at a team meeting, no other team members would talk—not the norm for this boisterous group. They just kept making eye contact with each other. It was like they were speaking to each other without talking. This made me curious, so I started to pay more attention to their day-to-day interactions. I noticed that other valuable team members would avoid volunteering for projects if he was on that team. When I would carefully dig for information in one-on-one meetings, they would change the subject.

I finally asked my new star player how he was adjusting to the team. He told me how awesome everyone was and how welcome he felt. He also mentioned that he thought he was on the right team, as he had a lot to teach them. Red flag! I explained that he was hired as a peer and that his job was to work alongside them as a unified team.

Despite this clarification I provided, there was still an awkwardness on the team in the months that followed. So, while writing year-end performance reviews, I asked the team members to provide feedback on how well they could work as a team. This question opened the flood gates. All ten team members complained about the new guy's arrogance and expressed difficulty in collaborating with him. He was perceived as dishonest and backstabbing. They felt that he showed me one side and them an entirely, and more negative, side.

This caused me to look at him in an entirely different way moving forward. Of course, when I provided him with this feedback, he acted surprised. I gave him the benefit of the doubt, only to find that in the months that followed, he retaliated against the team for ratting him out. Needless to say, I never promoted him into the management role for which he was being groomed.

At this point in the process, you have a strong sense of what you want to be known for and how others might perceive you. Now it's time to go outside of your comfort zone and get real feedback directly from the source.

BLIND SPOT CHALLENGE #4

Get a 360-degree view

Have you ever had the opportunity to take a 360-degree feedback assessment? I've found that most young professionals have not had this opportunity. In fact, most organizations only offer these powerful, and often expensive, tools to high-level leaders.

There are two ways to get this kind of feedback. The first is to ask others directly, and the other is to use an anonymous tool. Career Revolution has designed such a tool specifically for young professionals, which I'll provide information about in the second option in this challenge.

IDENTIFY TRUSTED ADVISORS

Before you solicit feedback, you need to determine who you're going to ask. I like to call this group, your Trusted Advisors. Make a list of people who have worked with you for at least six months and can really speak to your work style and results.

Think about people who you respect, trust, and of course, those who can support your career ambitions. The obvious choice is your direct supervisor, as well as anyone who has managed you in the past. Your Trusted Advisors can also include co-workers, project leads, professors, or even friends and family. I recommend selecting at least three and no more than eight people.

FACE-TO-FACE FEEDBACK

You can ask your Trusted Advisors questions that promote open and honest feedback. You want to avoid broad questions such as "What feedback do you have for me?" or "Can you give me some feedback?" The ones below have proven effective. They will help you validate your positive attributes as well as learn about developmental opportunities.

- What are three words you would use to describe my work style?
- What's the best thing about working with me?
- If I were to improve one or two things that would make me even more effective, what would they be?
- What could get in the way of my continued success?
- If you were me, what one thing would you do differently?

When asking for feedback, you don't have to schedule a formal meeting in a conference room. In fact, people tend to be more relaxed and open in other environments. Instead, you can get together over coffee or even on a hike. Just be sure to start the conversation by letting the other person know that you are seeking their insights and feedback to help you improve yourself. You can even send your questions to the other person in advance so they can come prepared.

Also, if you receive some feedback you didn't expect or don't agree with, this isn't the time to argue. As difficult as it may be, if you really disagree with the feedback, now's not the time to defend. If you do so, you likely will shut the door to future feedback. Instead, just listen, absorb, and say, "Thank you for the feedback."

And remember, feedback isn't a fact—it's a perception. Your job is to look for trends and themes to uncover your blind spots.

When it comes to asking someone to give you direct face-to-face feedback, you always run the risk of people not being straightforward with you. Maybe they are afraid of how you'll react, don't want to damage the relationship, or simply aren't comfortable giving feedback in general.

To combat this and have a safe and proven way of getting honest feedback, there are online tools designed to solicit feedback anonymously. This is the most powerful option in this challenge.

USE A 360-DEGREE FEEDBACK INSTRUMENT

To help you uncover your blind spots, we have a tool called the *AccelerateME™ 360 Feedback Assessment*. It was designed to help emerging professionals assess themselves on the behaviors most rewarded with career opportunity and promotion. The assessment is designed around *The 7 Mindsets*, a unique model outlining the beliefs and related behavior of the most successful young professionals.

Instead of asking your Trusted Advisor group for feedback face-to-face, you can have them complete an anonymous survey that asks questions specific to early career success.

The chart below outlines the *Mindset* categories used in the *AccelerateME™ 360 Feedback Assessment*. It is an overview of the thirty-five assessment questions, so you can rate yourself to get a quick snapshot.

If you'd like to take the full online assessment, see the Special Invitation section of this book for instructions.

INSTRUCTIONS

First, rate yourself by indicating the degree to which you agree or disagree with each set of statements.

Then, answer the same questions but from the perspective of your Trusted Advisor group. Based on your conversations with these individuals, select a rating you think the group would collectively provide for each Mindset. In other words, how do they perceive you in each category?

5 = STRONGLY AGREE; 1=STRONGLY DISAGREE

MINDSET	SELF-RATING	ADVISOR RATING
SUCCESS STARTS WITH A BELIEF I know what I want and believe it's achievable. I see my current role as a valuable experience on the path of ongoing success. I approach each day with optimism, am grateful for the opportunities I have and inspire others with my vision and enthusiasm.		
JOBS ARE RENTED—CAREERS ARE OWNED I own my career development and performance, including my failures as well as successes. I have a clear set of goals I regularly review with my manager or mentor and seek advisement from those with more experience. I have an active network I can tap into for a variety of personal and professional needs.		
PROGRESSION IS MORE IMPORTANT THAN PAY OR PROMOTION I'm focused on long-term success instead of instant gratification. I go above and beyond what is asked of me and volunteer to help others with projects or tasks before I'm asked. When I encounter a difficult situation or difficult boss, my first instinct is to work through it rather than change teams, jobs, or even organizations.		
TECHNOLOGY IS ONLY A CATALYST FOR COLLABORATION I'm professional in both my written and verbal communications. I fully explore other's perspectives before I give mine and am non-defensive when others provide me with feedback. I spend time planning important written and verbal communications and have learned to address conflict and disagreement in person rather than digitally.		

WORK AND PLAY CAN COEXIST I know what energizes me and can leverage those strengths daily. I have a clear set of personal and professional priorities, and I manage a healthy balance between the two. I enjoy the work I'm doing and feel energized on most days.		
GOOD IDEAS TAKE INFLUENCE TO IMPLEMENT I have good ideas and suggestions, and they are well received by those with the power to implement them. I demonstrate passion and perseverance when trying to persuade others and can articulate how my ideas will contribute to the team or company's bottom line results.		
YOUR BRAND IS YOUR PROMISE AND YOUR POWER I see myself as CEO of the company of "ME," and I can articulate a compelling value proposition. I know my strengths as well as what I am improving. Most importantly, I understand how others perceive me.		

Now, take a step back and look at your completed chart. Ask yourself the following questions:

- What do you notice about your scores?
- How do your Self Scores compare to your Predicted Trusted Advisor Scores?
- Which mindset categories do you think would be perceived most similarly? Why?
- Which ones do you predict might have the most significant gaps? Why? What do you attribute these potential blind spots to?
- Overall, what do you think are your most prominent potential blind spots?

HOW DO YOU COMPARE?

An overwhelming number of my program participants see the value in getting this kind of feedback so early in their career. Since the data is anonymous and confidential, no one can see your results but you.

I also like to share data from our assessment results to see how they align with the participant's sentiments. From our assessment data, we've found that, on average, young professionals rate themselves higher than their Trusted Advisor group overall. This indicates a blind spot right out of the gate. It points to an inflated sense of perception.

Think back to the story I shared about my summer hire. He was a glaring example of common misalignment. Interestingly, I asked him to take the online assessment. He completed the self-assessment portion but never followed through on inviting others to evaluate him. I interpreted that as him avoiding receiving feedback.

In some cases, Trusted Advisors will rate the participant higher than they rate themselves overall or in a specific Mindset. This is also considered a blind spot. Although an easier one to digest, it still means that there's a gap between how you see yourself and how others perceive you. It indicates that you have more power and influence than you think.

HOW TO ADDRESS BLIND SPOTS

Sometimes, an awareness of your blind spots is all you need to be able to remedy the situation. You see it and stop it the next time around. Other times, it will take a little more effort to change habits as well as the perceptions of others.

Once you are aware of a blind spot, I recommend sharing it with your Inner Circle. This is usually a subset of your Trusted Advisor group. By letting others close to you know of your efforts to change a perception, they can serve as a mirror to reflect your progress along the way and hold you accountable. I recommend focusing on one or two blind spots at a time.

Think of the behavior you'd like to demonstrate to others. It's much easier to start doing something than stop doing something. For example, if you discovered that you talk more than or over people in meetings, you can focus on saving all of your input until the end of a conversation instead of trying to stop interjecting. If you discovered that others think you are constantly challenging their ideas, you might focus on asking questions instead of making definitive statements.

Finally, you can ask for real-time feedback. Think of the new behavior you want to demonstrate. Then, you can target questions in the moment. Your goal is to get quick feedback in small chunks over time.

You might pull your boss aside after a meeting and ask them for a quick reaction. For example, "How did that go from your perspective?" or "What do you think I could have done differently?" By getting in the moment feedback, you can keep a pulse on your progress.

Also, by continuously asking for feedback, you're making yourself be seen as more promotable. You're essentially demonstrating emotional intelligence, leadership, and a desire to improve. These behaviors send the message that you are invested in your own growth.

Identifying your blind spots is not an easy task. To take charge of your career, you must be brave and engage those around you in honest feedback, and then be open and vulnerable to receive it. Regardless of how you seek the input, the goal is to see yourself through the eyes of others—especially those who can support you and influence others on your behalf. Facing your blind spots early on can be the difference between an average career and an exceptional one.

SHORTCUTS

HOW TO UNCOVER YOUR BLIND SPOTS

CHALLENGE #1	**Discover your Energizers in overdrive:** What strengths come so naturally that you may be at risk of overusing them?
CHALLENGE #2	**Draft your ideal reputation:** How do you want to be perceived? What do you want to be known for? How do people benefit from working with you?
CHALLENGE #3	**Consider past feedback:** What feedback have you received over the last year that supports or refutes your ideal reputation?
CHALLENGE #4	**Get a 360-degree view:** Identify between three and eight Trusted Advisors–people who have worked with you for at least six months Seek face-to-face feedback by asking your Trusted Advisors questions that promote open and honest feedback Use a 360-degree feedback instrument such as the *AccelerateME™ 360 Feedback Assessment*

STEP 5:

CONQUER CAREER CONVERSATIONS

In this chapter, you will:

- ❏ Get clear on what you really want from your next career conversation.
- ❏ Identify the resources and support you need to take the next step in your career.
- ❏ Select the most valuable development activities for your specific journey.
- ❏ Prepare your next career conversation using the G.A.I.N. model.

It's time for a career conversation. You're eager to discuss one of the most important topics on your mind right now—your future! You've been with the organization for about a year, and you're ready for an opportunity to engage in work with greater impact that pays more. After all, you have a college degree and big student loan debt to prove it.

Your manager begins the conversation by asking, "How can I help you?" It's a question so broad that you don't know how to answer it. You want to sound confident but fumble a bit while trying to come up with something that sounds coherent. You decide to just go for it, and respond, "I want to do more meaningful work."

In response, your manager stares at you with a perplexed look on their face. Apparently, they weren't prepared for your answer either. In fact, they are taken off guard because they believe the job you're in is indeed meaningful and that it will take a couple of years for you to learn enough to be given more significant responsibilities. As they explain this to you, with what seems like a tinge of parental condescension, you hear, "There are no promotion opportunities for you in the near future." You leave the meeting feeling defeated, and your manager thinks they just solved a problem and gave you great career advice.

I've seen this scenario play out numerous times as I've worked with hundreds of young professionals and their managers. The LinkedIn Report, "*Why & How People Change Jobs*," found that the number one reason respondents left their job was concern about the lack of opportunities for advancement. The number one reason for joining a new company was the hope for a stronger career path and more opportunity. It beat out better compensation and benefits, which was the number two reason.

Most young professionals identify their managers as their primary source for learning and developing skills, but according to Forbes, only 46% believe that their managers deliver on this. My research and experience show that this disconnect has several causes.

Like giving feedback and coaching, leading career conversations is a new skill set most managers haven't entirely mastered. Can you blame them? Their managers probably didn't model it for them. As I've worked with managers over the years, I've learned that many think they're having career conversations, but their employees believe otherwise. Many managers mistake conversations that are part of the company's annual performance management process as career conversations. Those who recognize the difference don't know how to have career conversations or how to prioritize them.

As a company advocate for such conversations, I tried to have quarterly career meetings scheduled with each of my employees when I led a team at Sony. However, the reality was that those meetings would sometimes get derailed to discuss pressing business issues. This was sometimes my doing, but other times it would be my employee asking to use that time for other matters.

In a perfect world, managers would see the importance of leading career conversations and be skilled and make time for them. Since we don't live in that world, it's up to you to get what you need to move your career in the direction you desire. Career development is employee-owned, and it's up to you to share your goals with those that have the power to support you along the way.

All of the work we've done thus far has helped you move toward our last step, which is taking charge of your next career conversation. This is not just any conversation. This one will accelerate your ability to steer your career in the direction you want it to go.

Career conversations are ongoing and meaningful discussions between you and another party—most often, your manager— about your career trajectory, including the direction and support needed to achieve your career goals.

Regardless of whether your next step is a specific transition such as a promotion or job change, or something less definitive, such as exploring managing others or expanding your responsibilities, you need to feel confident initiating and managing those conversations.

A career conversation is when you move from self-reflection and self-analysis to action and execution. If you have a clear direction, a one-year goal, and have identified what could hold you back, all that's left is finding the right resources to help you.

YOUR MANAGER IS ONLY ONE PERSON

How many people do you interact with during any given week or month? Between team members, managers, clients, and vendors, who we communicate with is a big component of getting our job done. Our ability to influence others, especially when we may not have formal authority, can make all the difference in getting what we need and want when it comes to our careers.

Making our careers move in the direction we desire often depends on the number of other influencers that can open doors for us. It could be a manager advocating for our promotion, a peer giving feedback to higher-ups about our performance, or even a mentor being a job reference for us. All of these require us to have essential conversations with the right people at any given time.

When you think about your career goals, whose support do you need? Make a list of all of the people who can support you as you pursue your goals. Identify what precisely you need from them and by when. In most cases, your direct manager will be a crucial resource. Still, you may also find that you could benefit from support from others in your professional network, like a mentor or even friends and family.

For example, if you identified that you want a promotion and realized that you need more opportunities to demonstrate your potential by leading projects or facilitating meetings, who has the authority to make that happen for you? Or, if you want to take a professional development course, who has to sign off on that expense or grant you the time off?

It's important to share your objectives with others and gain their support and commitment to your plan.

WHAT MAKES FOR A GOOD CAREER CONVERSATION?

Before I teach young professionals the strategies and tactics of taking charge of career conversations, I ask them to think of the best and worst career conversations they've had.

Usually, most think of a negative experience first, like when they mustered up the courage to ask for a promotion, and their manager did everything to stop themselves from laughing out loud. Or, when they didn't know what to say when their new boss asked them, "Where do you see yourself in three years?"

Career conversations can be intimidating. This is especially true when we have no idea what they are supposed to look like. It's even worse if your manager doesn't know either. Of course, there are positive experiences as well. When I ask people to share their most memorable and valuable career conversations, they have a few elements in common. Usually, the conversation:

- Was a dialogue, not a monologue
- Felt safe and made it okay to be transparent and vulnerable
- Included more questions than answers from the managers
- Ended with clear action
- Resulted in both parties following through on their commitments
- Focused on development and growth
- Connected the individual's personal goals to organizational goals
- Involved feedback
- Provided clarity and new perspectives

Regardless of your manager's skills, and how positive or negative your experiences have been thus far, you have the power to make your next career conversation work in your favor. To do that, you need to spend some time preparing.

WHAT NEEDS TO HAPPEN BEFORE?

Before you can have any meaningful career conversations, it's essential to get clear on what you really want. That sounds pretty simple, right? And it can be. At this point in the process, you may have a clear idea of where you want to go next or what you want from your manager to support your growth. It's how you frame that conversation and how prepared you are for potential responses you may receive that makes all of the difference.

Imagine that you've been thrown into an impromptu career conversation with your manager, or senior leader in your organization, or one you want to work for. You have one minute to share your career next step. Go!

What came to mind. How prepared did you feel? If you're like most, that was a stressful scenario. By this stage in the journey, you should have some solid understanding of where you might want to go next. But, knowing what support you need from others is a different story.

This is an area where I see many young professionals miss a big opportunity. Jen, one of my program participants, shared with me that her last career conversation didn't go as well as she had hoped. Through her self-discovery process, she decided that she wanted to manage a team. She was energized by people-related strengths and set a vision to be a people leader at her current company.

She was so excited at her clarity and direction that she marched in her manager's office and said, "I'd like to have a career conversation with you." Her manager, although in the middle of finishing a report, was kind enough to stop what she was doing and engage with Jen. Jen enthusiastically shared her journey and desire to become a people manager. She then asked her manager if she could be considered for the next available manager position.

Jen's manager struggled to respond and, after a moment, replied, "I don't think you're ready for such a role, and we have several people on the team who have been here longer who share your aspiration." She concluded, "Let's continue this conversation in a couple of months."

Jen told me that she left the meeting feeling defeated and decided to update her resume. She didn't see any path forward in her current company.

What Jen failed to recognize is that when you ask for something like a promotion, you should be prepared to discuss a strategy to get there. What you're really asking for is support for getting to that next role. Jen's manager was put in a position to say yes or no essentially. Since she couldn't say yes without more dialogue, she said no without offering a more in-depth explanation. Then neither party was prepared to have the dialogue needed to make the conversation more productive.

The challenges in this chapter will help you prepare in a way that doesn't leave you feeling like Jen. Instead, you will be in a position of power and one that sends the message that you're serious about your career trajectory.

CONVERSATIONS CHALLENGE #1

Define where you are headed

Take an opportunity to summarize what you've discovered about yourself from the previous steps. All these elements will help you develop an authentic and actionable path for having career conversations. By doing so, you will have a solid foundation from which to lead a powerful career conversation.

Complete the following statements in the most direct and straightforward way possible. Sometimes, it helps to pretend you're being interviewed and have to respond in a way that someone can remember your responses.

- I'm most energized when I'm…
- The values that are most important to me are…
- My one-year career milestone is to…
- What could get in the way of achieving my one-year milestone is…

The most important element you must clearly articulate is your one-year milestone—how you will define success over the next year. It should sound authentic and crisp. If you're going to get support, you want to make sure it's for something you truly want to achieve.

Knowing that milestone and potential blind spots, you can choose what development will accelerate your growth in the direction you desire.

Some young professionals jump at any resources they can get their hands on without thinking about if it's aligned to what they're trying to achieve. This can be a mistake. Having clarity can be very exciting and can create a lot of energy to move forward quickly. So, it's important to look for opportunities that create movement in the right direction.

CONVERSATIONS CHALLENGE #2

Select the right kind of development

In today's workplace, careers are no longer narrowly defined by jobs and skills, but rather through experiences. That's why it's important to identify the best and most valuable development activities for your specific journey to provide yourself with the most career opportunities possible.

The Development Grid outlines four main goals of professional development, along with specific activities and assignments that best meet each objective.

As you review each, put a checkmark next to any that you believe will support the achievement of your one-year milestone.

EXPOSURE
Create broader visibility into your natural strengths and value.

☑ **Volunteer Projects**

Ask to join a new project as an extra resource to expand your network and contributions to areas outside of your daily responsibilities.

☑ **Peer Mentoring**

Become a mentor or coach to others in your organization. Help them navigate career opportunities and advise them on how to overcome workplace challenges. This will demonstrate your leadership abilities.

☑ **Leadership Presentation**

Volunteer to present on behalf of your team at leadership meetings. Practice skills such as communication, influence, and keeping calm under pressure to demonstrate your skills and get noticed by an expanded set of decision-makers.

RELATIONSHIPS
Expand your network and create new career advocates.

☑ **Formal Mentoring**

Ask someone you admire or someone in a role you'd like to move into to meet with you regularly to discuss workplace challenges and coach you on your career navigation.

☑ **Informational Interviews**

Conduct meetings with those in leadership roles to discover their career path, choices, and overall story. You can ask questions and learn from their experiences.

☑ **Networking**

Join affiliate groups related to your current industry or position, or ones you're interested in understanding better. Attend regular educational and networking events. Connect with other members on LinkedIn to stay in touch and share ideas when needed.

(3)

SKILL IMPROVEMENT
Improve your current skills to be the best at your job.

☑ **Formal Training**

Select and participate in a live or online workshop or course that helps you address performance issues or enhances your skills to become more effective in your role.

☑ **On-the-Job Training**

This can be formal and structured on-the-job training or informal, reflective, self-directed activities. Often the most effective type of learning is in-place.

☑ **Self-Directed Learning**

Undertake a specific project that promotes the expansion of skills and knowledge through self-directed learning or research and produces a final product that contributes to organizational objectives. This often happens without taking time away from your current role.

SKILL ADDITION
Learn a new skill to be considered for more responsibility.

❑ **Cross-training**

Partner with a teammate or supervisor to learn a new skill or activity while keeping your current job responsibilities. In turn, you can teach them skills related to your role.

❑ **Special Assignments**

Perform temporary duties on a full- or part-time basis. For example, lead a cross-functional project, serve on a task force, or work on a community project.

❑ **Job Enlargement**

Stretch your current responsibilities in a way that supports your development objective. It can mean adding tasks to your plate that are at the same level of skill and responsibility or even increasing your responsibility.

Based on what you've discovered thus far, identify one or two development activities that will most support the achievement of your 1-year career milestone. Be prepared to describe how these activities will support your growth.

Let's look at a couple of examples using participants from previous chapters.

MICHELLE'S CAREER CONVERSATION

Michelle's career vision was to be the head of the Strategy Office for an innovative brand. She identified all of the things that would have to be true to make that vision a reality. To start with, she knew that she would need to be promoted to a management role. She then brainstormed all of the things that would need to be in place to be considered for a promotion into management. She listed "receiving a top performance rating," which would require her to achieve more and higher quality work than others on the team. This helped her formulate a one-year goal: *"By the end of the next 12 months, I will feel successful if I'm leading a high visibility project that earns me an 'exceeds expectations' on my next annual performance review."*

When Michelle got to this step in the process, it was easy for her to identify specific development activities that would help her achieve her one-year milestone.

Michelle knew that her manager would need to support her taking on higher risk projects that allowed her to prove her potential and be seen by more leaders and influencers. Therefore, she selected both "Special Assignment" and "Leadership Presentation" as her target development activities for the year. In her next career conversation, she could present these ideas to her manager, explain why she selected them, and then enter into a dialogue to work with her manager to identify a special project. I encouraged Michelle to take it a step farther and find projects that her manager would benefit from as well.

BEN'S CAREER CONVERSATION

Let's go back to Ben, who, if you recall, decided to make a big career change. His one-year milestone was to "be in a new job that allows me to play in my primary Energy Zone and gives me the opportunity to see career opportunities I'm currently not exposed to."

Given the shift he wanted to make, Ben selected "Informational Interviews" as a great development activity for him to move closer to his goal. Given Ben's interest in human resources, he wanted to connect with HR professionals and learn more about what they did.

Once you know what your desired development opportunity is, you're ready to prepare your conversation.

CONVERSATIONS CHALLENGE #3

Identify what you want and who can help

Now that you've selected your development activities, who is the best person to discuss them with? Whose permission or support do you need? If you're currently employed and have selected activities that can happen in your current organization, then your manager is usually the best person to start this process with. However, in cases like Ben's, you may identify someone else, such as a mentor, expert, or former boss.

Before you engage in a career conversation, it's vital to identify what you want and what you're willing to do to get it. Most importantly, be able to articulate how your request will benefit the person you're asking it from.

Use the questions below as a guide to prepare.

- Who will your next career conversation be with?
- What are you hoping to gain from your next career conversation? What does success look like?
- What actions would you need from this person as a result of this conversation?
- How does the other person benefit if they help you get what you need?

- What might prevent this person from saying "yes" to your request? How might you respond if they say no?

Sometimes it helps to see an example.

Priya, a 26-year-old software developer, had been with her company for two years. Through her career development journey, she decided that she wanted to be promoted to a project lead role but wasn't sure how to get there. Priya's one-year milestone was to be seen as a stronger leader and be on her manager's radar for the next promotion opportunity. Here's how she responded to this challenge.

- Who will your next career conversation be with?

  My manager

- What are you hoping to gain from your next career conversation? What does success look like?

  I want my manager to know of my desire to be a project lead. Success will be him agreeing to let me manage at least one summer intern.

- What actions would you need from this person as a result of this conversation?

  My manager would say yes to my request and invite me to be one of the interviewers of the intern program.

- How does the other person benefit if they help you get what you need?

  Managing at least one intern will save my manager time. He will no longer need to meet with them weekly, and I can discuss their progress in my already scheduled one-on-one meetings with him.

- What might prevent this person from saying "yes" to your request? How might you respond if that they say no?

My manager may not have thought of me as a leader before. He may want to think more about this request. He also may want me to learn some management skills before taking on this responsibility. There may be others on the team with more experience who have already made this request of him.

If any of these are the case, then I will ask for another opportunity to be ready to manage an intern the next time around. Maybe take a management course or get a mentor.

Since Ben had a very different situation, let's look at how he approached this step. Ben is a good example because I'm the person he made the request to! Remember, Ben selected "Informational Interviews" of HR professionals as a development activity to move closer to his goal of finding a new job outside of his current field of accounting. Here is how Ben prepared.

- Who will your next career conversation be with?

  Christine DiDonato

- What are you hoping to gain from your next career conversation? What does success look like?

  I want Christine to connect me to HR professionals in companies I may someday want to work for.

- What actions would you need from this person as a result of this conversation?

  I want Christine to send at least three emails to HR professionals in her network requesting they accept an invitation from me for an informational interview.

- How does the other person benefit if they help you get what you need?

  Christine's company focuses on helping young professionals. So, this action will show she's living her mission and values.

- What might prevent this person from saying "yes" to your request? How might you respond if they say no?

  Christine may not feel comfortable making this request of those in her network because she doesn't know me well enough yet. I'm willing to offer to help Christine by doing some work for her company at no charge, like proofreading content or doing research.

G.A.I.N. SUPPORT

Now that you have an idea of whose support you need and what's in it for them to support you, let's look at a model for career conversations.

Career Revolution created a simple four-step model focused on helping professionals get a "yes" to what they ask for. The G.A.I.N. model is an acronym for:

- **G**oal: What do you hope to achieve in this conversation?
- **A**-ha: What are your a-ha moments regarding your development?
- **I**nput: What input and validation can the other party provide?
- **N**ext: What next steps do you want support on?

The first step in the career conversation model is to state your goal. What do you hope to achieve in this conversation? State a clear and realistic objective. Think about this as one of many career conversations. So, try to narrow down your desired results to just one clear goal for this meeting.

The next element in the model is the A-ha step. What are your "a-ha moments" regarding your performance and career? For your next conversation, you have a great opportunity to share key learnings and insights from the journey you've taken in this book. Think about Energizers, values, vision, and blind spots.

The third step is input. What input and validation can the other party provide? For example, if you're meeting with your manager, invite them to give you input on the a-ha moments you shared. Ask for additional feedback and insights that would help or hurt your ability to achieve your goal.

The last piece of the career conversation model is next steps. What next steps do you want support on? Present your ask by sharing your desired next steps. Ask for help in your selected development opportunities. Speak to what's in it for them if your next steps are supported. Share what you're willing to do to achieve your goal. If the answer is yes, ask for specific follow-up actions by both you and the other party. If the answer is no, ask why and what development or next steps they recommend.

Here's an example from a program participant of how it all works together.

GOAL

"My objective for having this conversation is to gain your support for a new development opportunity to help me grow my career and add even more value to the team."

A-HA

"My goal in the next year is to earn an in-line promotion. I recently received feedback via the *AccelerateME™ 360 Feedback Assessment* that others may not see me volunteering to take on the types of responsibilities that would make me considered for such a promotion."

INPUT

"What examples can you share of where I missed an opportunity to take on more responsibility? What do you see me doing that would make me considered for such a promotion? What other feedback can you share that would help me grow?"

NEXT STEP

"Based on my goal and the feedback I've received, I believe increasing the scope of my responsibilities and being able to present my work to the larger team would not only support my growth but also add value to the team. Is this something you can support me on?"

It's your turn now! Complete the final challenge to make sure you're ready for your next career conversation.

CONVERSATIONS CHALLENGE #4

Prepare your conversation

Think about the career conversation that you need to have to advance your trajectory. Now, write a script that supports each question in the G.A.I.N. model.

- **G**oal: What do you hope to achieve in this conversation?
- **A**-ha: What are your a-ha moments regarding your development?
- **I**nput: What input and validation can your manager provide?
- **N**ext: What next steps do you want support on?

CAREER CONVERSATION ACCELERATORS

By now, you are more prepared than ever to move your career in the right direction. However, even with the best intentions, conversations are between people. Research tells us that about 40-45% of miscommunications are due to differing communication styles. This includes how and when we communicate.

To help you avoid having your career conversation become victim to the miscommunication disease, here are some things to consider:

- Send an agenda in advance and include key questions you will ask. You can find a sample agenda at Info.CareerRev. com/Career-Resources.

- Pick a creative space where performance review meetings don't usually happen, such as walking outside or coffee shop.

- Avoid talking about any topics other than your career—this isn't a project check-in or performance appraisal.

- Prepare your key points beforehand and bring notes to the meeting.

- Engage others by presenting how they'll benefit from your development. This means being prepared to discuss how your development activities will benefit the person you're asking support from. In other words, don't make the conversation solely about your personal needs.

- Practice with those you trust. Try running your ideas by a few trusted co-workers or friends before presenting to a supervisor. Get their input and ask them to challenge you on various aspects of your proposal. Use this information to analyze things you might not have considered

- Finally, be sure to follow up, preferably in writing, to remind others of their commitments and demonstrate that you valued their time.

Being aware of the pitfalls young professionals can fall into is just as important as setting yourself up for success. Through coaching and focus groups, managers shared stories of career conversations that went poorly. Below is a list of the reasons managers said why they had trouble supporting their employees.

- Not stating the objective at the beginning of the conversation.

- Impromptu career conversations.

- Expecting the manager to have all of the answers.

- Making demands instead of engaging in a dialogue.

- Not following through on commitments.

Remember, you OWN your career path. This means that sometimes you may run into others that don't take action or make things happen for you. If that's the case, your job is to find alternative solutions and keep your career vision alive.

SHORTCUTS

HOW TO CONQUER CAREER CONVERSATIONS

CHALLENGE #1	**Define where you are headed:**
	Summarize what you've discovered about yourself from the previous steps by answering the following questions.
	• I'm most energized when I'm…
	• The values that are most important to me are…
	• My one-year career milestone is to…
	• What could get in the way of achieving my one-year milestone is…
CHALLENGE #2	**Select the right kind of development:**
	Which development activities will be most helpful to you achieving your one-year milestone?
	• Exposure: Create broader visibility into your natural strengths and value
	• Relationships: Expand your network and create new career advocates
	• Skill Improvement: Improve current skills to be the best at a skill or your job overall
	• Skill Addition: Learn a new skill to be considered for more responsibility
CHALLENGE #3	**Identify what you want and who can help:**
	Who will your next career conversation be with?
	What are you hoping to gain from your next career conversation?
	How does the other person benefit if they help you get what you need?
	What might prevent this person from saying "yes" to your request? How might you respond if they say no?
CHALLENGE #4	**Prepare Your Conversation:**
	Goal: What do you hope to achieve in this conversation?
	A-ha: What are your a-ha moments regarding your development?
	Input: What input and validation can the other party provide?
	Next: What next steps do you want support on?

SECTION THREE:

YOU OWN IT

STRATEGIES TO KEEP YOUR CAREER ON TRACK IN THE REAL WORLD

To get to this point, you've done quite a bit of reflection and challenged yourself to go outside of your comfort zone. As a result, you should have a clearer path forward than when you started.

However, one thing I've learned throughout my career is that even with the most well-intended plans, we can sometimes veer off track. Busy schedules, life changes, or even self-doubt can slow our progress. Since career development is complex and dynamic, this chapter includes six strategies you can adopt at any time to increase the probability of your success.

The strategies and resources I've included are ones I've used in my own career, including a few I've learned from amazing young professionals along the way. Think of them as you think of your health. Most of us try everything in our power to stay healthy. However, in the event we fall ill, have an urgent need, or simply aren't feeling as healthy as we'd like, we have a set of go-to resources to get ourselves back on track. Whether it's preventative steps we take to avoid being sick, or resources we keep handy for emergencies, being proactive about potential solutions is important.

Your career is no different. The strategies in this chapter are proactive. You can use them now to increase the likelihood and speed of your success. They are also reactive. You can use them in the event you veer off track or run into a new barrier.

STRATEGY #1: KEEP YOUR PLAN VISIBLE

To increase the likelihood of your success, I find it helpful to summarize your focus and purpose for the next twelve months. You can use the chart below as a guide to doing just that. The trick is to keep it somewhere you often see, such as on your desk or in your notebook. For a digital template, visit AccelerateME. com/career-resources.

MY ONE YEAR CAREER PLAN

Goal One year from today I will be:	
Gaps I need to develop the following skills, relationships, etc., to achieve that goal:	
Development Activities I've selected the following development activities to help me get there:	
Resources I will need the following resources to achieve my goal:	
Support The people I will need to have conversations with are:	
Celebration Once I achieve my goal I will celebrate by:	

STRATEGY #2: CELEBRATE YOUR WINS

I'd like to point out the last element in the chart—celebration. Many professionals, young or more tenured, forget to recognize their progress and small wins along the way. We tend to only focus on our blooper reel: what didn't go well, what got in our way, and how much longer something took than we expected. Instead, what if we focused on the highlight reel of our careers?

I remember meeting with Ben a year after he made the transition into his first HR role. When I asked him how things were going, he said, "Good, but…" The "but" was followed by a few examples of what he was disappointed by. His learning curve into HR was greater than he thought it would be. He didn't realize he would be the low man on the totem pole in his new department. He didn't know how to move to a new function within the HR department. These were all valid concerns. However, I had a few "But's" in return for him:

- BUT, you made a major career transition.
- BUT, you work for one of the hottest entertainment brands.
- BUT, you got to move to the location you wanted.

I challenged Ben to pause and acknowledge what he had achieved, instead of focusing on what he had not. He took a few big risks over the year. All of those risks came with some short-term downsides. However, in the long run, Ben was on a far more fulfilling path than his previous one. Of course, he would continue to face career challenges. As he had new experiences, he would learn more about himself—his Energizers and values—and he would continue to add to his career vision, setting new goals along the way.

There's one constant in the world, and that is change. Even with the best-laid plans, your plans can change. Sometimes from your own doing and others from forces outside of your control.

STRATEGY #3: CHECK YOUR GUT

The process you've gone through will help you take a step forward, but it doesn't account for the changing nature of life and the complexity of human beings. In other words, you will have new experiences, grow and learn and change, and want to adjust your values, vision, and plan along the way.

You've done deep and practical work on this journey. And the goal is to hold yourself accountable to your values, vision, and goals. However, if along the way you have a new insight that pulls you in a different direction, you don't have to ignore it just to stick with your original plan. I encourage you to use the process you've learned so far and examine any potential changes to ensure you aren't just derailing yourself because of a barrier you're facing.

If you find yourself veering from your plan, you can ask yourself a few questions.

First, is this shift due to discovering a new energizer you didn't know you had before? Could you have misdiagnosed your primary Energy Zone? Once you are aware of your Energizers, you have a heightened awareness back at work. It's not uncommon to start to see them in action to change your selections.

Second, did something happen in your life that impacted how you prioritized your values? Life events, such as getting married, losing a job, or having children, can require a temporary or longer-term shift in our values.

Third, did you overestimate or underestimate how long it would take to achieve a milestone? Sometimes we move faster or more slowly than anticipated and need to adjust our expectations.

Finally, you can ask yourself if you dug deep enough to uncover potential blind spots. If this was the first time you thought about them, you might not have been ready to discover them.

If you answered yes to any of these questions, the
want to adjust your vision, goals and plan to make sure they a.-
indeed authentic and inspiring you.

STRATEGY #4: "LEARN" YOUR PURPOSE AND PASSION

Think about all of your discoveries thus far: Your Energizers
and values, your career vision and one-year milestone, and of
course, potential blind spots that can derail you along the way.
Most of this work was a reflection of a moment in time. We are
complex and dynamic beings who live and work in a world that
is constantly changing. That brings challenges as well as benefits.

This means that your job is to revisit these activities. I
recommend doing this annually, to make sure you're staying on a
productive and positive path.

Throughout my career, I always felt pressured to "find my
passion" and "live my purpose." While these are powerful statements
and there are countless books out there dangling the proverbial
career bliss carrot at us, I've found them to be quite aspirational.
Sometimes, I've even found them to be depressing. What do you
do if you don't feel like you have that kind of lifelong clarity? After
being in the workforce for more than a decade, I finally adapted my
mindset to value learning my purpose and passion.

I recently heard author Elizabeth Gilbert on the TED Radio
Hour podcast where she talked about following your curiosity
instead of passion. I loved her conclusion that those who have a
clear passion are probably already following it and therefore don't
need help finding it. For the rest of us who weren't born with a
singular purpose, the best thing we can do is allow ourselves to
indulge in what we're curious about.

Looking back over my career thus far, I realize that my
greatest successes have been a byproduct of a series of experiences,

mistakes, wins, relationships, good decisions, and most definitely bad ones. What was at the core was, as my mom puts it, being true to myself. Being authentic and making choices based on what I was curious about. Most importantly, they were based on my Energizers, my values, and my vision—not on what I thought I was supposed to be doing or achieving.

In an age of social media, I think this has become even harder to do. Since childhood, you've been inundated with the promise of leading a purpose-driven life that includes feeling passionate about your work. While there are elements of this that are important, how you approach seeking passion and purpose is equally important.

When I was younger in my career, I remember waiting for the magical poof—the moment I would have an epiphany about my singular purpose in life—that one mythical day when I would wake up and have a clear career path. I'm sorry to say that day never came. Instead, and perhaps more importantly, I discovered a series of activities and relationships that have brought me joy—and some moments of pain along the way. As I get older, those things change. Some no longer inspire me, and I've discovered new ones that do.

I could never have predicted that I'd be writing this book. I could never have predicted that I would leave my cushy corporate job and take the road less traveled. Yet, I've never felt more in the flow than I do now. But, working in an environment I didn't love doing some work that I wasn't energized by influenced my current career path. Looking back, it was those experiences that gave me the credibility, a strong network, and resources to live the passion I have now.

I challenge you to look at your career as a journey that will shift and change. Your job is to stay in tune with your deepest needs and wants. Staying on top of what energizes you and what you value will be key. I also advise always having a one-year milestone in front of you, no matter what it is. If you don't have a clear objective, then you are allowing others to make career decisions on your behalf.

STRATEGY #5: CREATE A PERSONAL BOARD OF DIRECTORS

Think of yourself as the CEO of the company "YOU." All good companies engage a board of directors who help them meet their goals by advising along the way. You can do the same as it relates to your career.

To keep your career continuously moving in the right direction, it helps to have a network of people you go to for different needs. In fact, you may be in someone else's group and not even know it. Do you have a friend who comes to you for advice? Are you the go-to person on the team for advisement on how to do something?

Chances are you are already applying this concept in your personal life. At the surface level, you may have a hairstylist, a therapist, a doctor, or even a workout group. Now that you have a career direction, you can expand this concept to identifying people from whose advice you would benefit.

The difference is that your personal Board of Directors will understand your career vision. Think about how you defined career success in this process. Who in your network can be a good resource for you? I have about four people I regularly engage with who all believe in my vision and have my permission to challenge me along the way. In my club, I have one of my first bosses. She was the first person to recognize some of the talents on which I built my career. Another is a good friend who is also an entrepreneur. I go to her to talk through business strategies and lament about the pain points of working for yourself.

To build your Board of Directors, think about people you already go to for advice and ask yourself these questions:

- Are they the right people?
- Have they been able to provide fresh perspectives? Have they challenged you to think differently?
- Who do you need to talk to regularly? How often?
- Who is on an as-needed basis? For what reason?

The people you select should serve a specific purpose directly aligned to your vision and goals. Also, think about what you can do for them.

STRATEGY #6: FORGE YOUR OWN PATH

I've yet to meet anyone who didn't tell me they wanted to grow their career. It really comes down to identifying how you want to grow it. As you continue down the path to your one-year milestone, you may find that you want to change direction or simply explore another avenue. If so, it's important to be aware of the different moves you can make.

Remember, growth can happen by taking a variety of paths. It's just a matter of identifying the one that makes the most sense for you. Be careful not to discount some options because they don't provide instant gratification. Remember the concept of a rock wall. Sometimes moving sideways or even backward will get you to the top faster—and often with less danger. Given your longer-term career vision, which moves might be right for you as you strive toward your goals?

TRADITIONAL

In a traditional career move, you progress upward in the organization or your field from one specific job to the next. Think about in-line promotions from your current level to the next one, such as Engineer level 1 to Engineer level 2.

LATERAL

In a lateral move, you shift within an organization or field to different roles at the same job level. These types of changes are good if your goal is to find new challenges and learn new skills. This could entail moving to a different department or company but staying at a similar or same pay grade or level of responsibility. An example would be moving from a sales associate to a Marketing associate.

BACK STEP

Although sometimes falsely associated with failure, this path can actually be an intentional career move. This might be a choice if you decide that you want to change fields altogether. Taking a step backward can allow you to learn something new that might potentially accelerate you at a later date. An example of this would be deciding to quit your role as a UX designer to take an entry-level role as a sales assistant. You would choose to do this because you discovered that you aren't energized by design but want to try sales.

EXPERT

This path might be a good fit if you recognize that your passion is your technical specialty, and you determine that you want to grow your career without having to become a manager. This means you are striving to progress on the path of an individual contributor.

VALUE

On this path, you recognize that you're not tied to a specific technical area of expertise. Instead, you want to develop a plan that enables you to add value to your field or an organization continually. This is a good path for those who like variety and get energy from continually adding to their toolbox of skills.

The changing nature of our lives challenges us to be more adaptable and flexible to see and sometimes create opportunities outside of a traditional career path.

Whether it be recognizing what energizes you or identifying what's most important in your life, the journey you've taken is all about self-exploration and personal commitment.

By taking the time to create an inspiring career vision, identifying the resources you need, and having the right conversations, you can create an achievable path. Most importantly, it will be authentic!

ALIGN YOUR PERSONAL BRAND

Apple, McDonald's, Amazon, CocaCola, Nike, and Netflix are just a few of the most globally recognizable brands we interact with daily. As consumers, we chose what brands we trust and which ones we don't. This influences daily decisions such as where we do our banking, what food we'll eat, what technology we use, and even what shoes we'll wear. Over time, we encounter images, messaging, and personal experiences that create beliefs and attitudes about a brand.

For example, when people talk about Apple, words such as innovation, simplicity, and user-friendly may come to mind. How about Amazon? I think of words like accessible, fast, and convenient.

To maximize the great work you've done throughout this book, you need to think of yourself as a brand just like the corporate brands you admire. Millennial Branding expert Dan Schawbel describes a personal brand as "unearthing what is true and unique about you and letting everyone know about it," in his book, "Me 2.0." I also like his simple definition: "How we market ourselves to others."

When I think of personal branding, I sometimes conjure up images of salesie, arrogant, or egotistical maniacs who take every opportunity to promote themselves. And I do know some of those people. I'm sure you do too. However, personal branding in the age of social media is no longer a choice, but rather a result. Anyone can quickly search you on Google. I still cringe when I see bad-hair day pictures of the past come up when I Google my own name!

WHAT IS YOUR PERSONAL BRAND?

Your personal brand communicates your potential value to potential employers. Guess what, you already have a personal brand! Whether or not it's intentional or it aligns with your career aspirations is what I challenge you to discover. If I were to peek at your LinkedIn profile or bump into you at a coffee shop, would the impression I leave with align your ideal personal brand?

What do you want people to associate with you when they think of your name? Think of your favorite consumer brand. Why is it your favorite? If you could use three to five words to describe it, what would they be?

As part of discovering your blind spots in Step 4, one of the challenges asked to create your ideal reputation. This question is the starting place for creating a personal brand. In that challenge, how did you describe what you have to offer and how you add value? Take a moment to review that challenge if needed.

Essentially, you've already done some of the heavy lifting and defined your personal brand. That combined with your vision, is information others should know if you want to accelerate your career progression. Outside of the career conversations you're going to have, you also have the opportunity to align this brand when others interact with you. This expands the career possibilities and opportunities throughout your journey.

What are all of the ways people interact with your personal brand? Of course, social media is a major touchpoint. But, so is your presence, including your physical image and your actions. Your personal brand is reflected in how you dress, how you communicate, how you respond to difficult situations, even how your desk looks!

Let's start with the most obvious one—your online presence.

ALIGN YOUR SOCIAL MEDIA PRESENCE

Social media allows us to tell others about our career accomplishments as well as our aspirations. By aligning your career vision and goals with your online presence, you're increasing the chances of attracting the right kind of opportunities and resources.

Of course, a great place to share your career story is on LinkedIn. Here are a few things to consider when aligning your personal brand with your career vision.

PICTURE

Advances in technology mean you don't need a photo taken by a professional photographer. However, make sure your photos reflect the image of someone who has already achieved your vision. If you want to be seen as a leader in your industry, look the part. Avoid blurry or dark photos. Instead, picture it's the first day of your dream job. Snap a picture of what you envision you'd look like on that day. If your industry is casual and creative, then your picture can be the same. If your industry is more formal, then align your image with its standards.

HEADLINE

This can be updated to reflect the bridge between where you are today and where you want to go. For example, if you're currently an individual contributor working as an HR assistant and want to be a leadership facilitator, you can create a headline that spans the gap, such as "Innovative HR professional passionate about helping others achieve their goals."

JOB EXPERIENCE

Although you can't make up experiences you haven't had, you can highlight specific aspects of your jobs that speak more to where you want to go. If your goal is to become a people manager, then you can list some experiences where you've mentored others. You can also highlight volunteer experiences.

ENDORSEMENTS

Ask influential people in your network to endorse you or write a recommendation for skills that reflect where you want to go. Using the previous example, you could ask employees you've supported to endorse you for mentoring them or facilitating meetings.

CONNECTIONS

Connect with people in industries or with expertise related to where you're headed. If you want to switch industries or work for a specific company, connect with people in those spaces. Remember to add a personal note. I get hundreds of requests a week on LinkedIn and, believe it or not, I do remember those who send me a personal note.

CONTINUED LEARNING

Share learning resources and events you're participating in. It could be a book you're reading, the course you're taking, or degree you're working toward. Post learnings that demonstrate to others that you're actively building new skills. For example, if you have a goal of expanding your expertise from a graphic designer to a user experience or interaction designer, you can complete courses showing others that you have the formal training to do so.

COMMUNITIES

Join groups or follow top influencers in your field of choice. Comment on other's posts and articles.

EXPERTISE

Social media provides a great opportunity to share your expertise with others. You don't have to turn into a full-time blogger, but a few minutes a day or week of sharing relevant content and ideas with like-minded professionals will grow your network slowly over time. You can start by just sharing posts of people or topics related to your career vision.

This seems like practical advice. However, I continue to be shocked when colleagues share stories of employees, or prospective employees, misconduct concerning social media.

I'm sure you've seen or heard them too. Job candidates posting their interview stories and it being seen by the recruiter who was courting them. Disgruntled employees ranting about how much they hate their boss and forgetting that they invited their boss to join their network a year ago. That doesn't even begin to cover the multiple stories I've heard from hiring managers checking out job candidate's social media, such as Instagram or Facebook, only to find photos of their "gone wild" spring break trip or illegal drug use.

Whether we like it or not, what we post is part of our personal brand.

REVIEW YOUR PRODUCT

Picture yourself as a product on Amazon—Product YOU. Your target customers are prospective employers and influential leaders. Product YOU has been rated by past and present employers, co-workers, bosses, friends, and family. What do you think your overall rating would be? How many stars would you receive? What reviews would be posted?

Now scroll down and read the comments. What would your best ones say? What about the worst ones? Take a moment to write your ideal review—the one you want others to take note of when making a decision on whether or not to promote or hire you.

TAP INTO A HUMAN NETWORK

A recent LinkedIn report found that younger professionals are the most comfortable using online career channels. No surprise there. However, they also found that the number one way those in North America heard about their next job was through personal referrals.

So, how can you bridge this gap? Building your network must go beyond who you connect with virtually on LinkedIn. Most people have thousands of connections and don't know most of them personally. Your human network is more about quality than quantity.

When I think back to my biggest career breaks and opportunities, I can attribute several to my relationships with people I'd worked with. I remember applying online for a leadership role that was bigger than anything I'd done before. The job description read like my career vision, but I didn't have enough of the qualifications. I decided to send my resume through the company's on-line job board, despite being underqualified.

As I expected, weeks went by, and I heard nothing, so I put it out of my mind. About a month later, I received a call from a consultant my current company had hired a year or so ago. I worked alongside her for a few months and had great respect for her experience and insights. She told me that she was now consulting for the company I had applied to. They received so many resumes for the job that they hired her to pick the top five resumes from a pile of a hundred or so.

She called to inform me that I would be contacted to schedule an interview! She said that when she saw my resume, in the "B" pile, she pulled it out and put it on top. She told the department head that she had worked with me personally and that although I didn't have all of the qualifications, I was easy to work with, a quick study, and would be a good culture fit—all elements that wouldn't be known just by applying online.

I'm proud to share that I got that job! Her feedback not only gave me a shot at an interview, but I'm sure played a role in how they perceived me, even before I interviewed.

Imagine that you are in a similar situation and that someone you worked with in the past has influence over your next opportunity. If they saw your resume in a pile, what reaction do you think they'd have? Would they move it to the top or bury it at the bottom? The answer to that question lies in the reputation you've built, with or without even knowing it.

YOU ARE ONLY AS GOOD AS YOUR WORD

How you show up to others plays a key role in opening up— or closing—doors in your career path. This topic is one I talk about a lot in my training, as I've personally experienced both sides of this coin.

I'm energized by helping and developing others, so much so that I built an entire company around it. I get excited when I see a young professional have personal breakthroughs that change their career trajectory in a more authentic direction. This means that I've volunteered endless hours to provide as much support as possible to this mission. Whether it be mentoring emerging talent, or providing feedback and coaching to new entrepreneurs, I continue to burst with pride as I see many achieve success beyond their wildest dreams.

However, for every wonderful, ethical, and talented young professional I've had the honor to collaborate with, I've sadly experienced several examples that left me with a bad taste in my mouth. In the spirit of developing a personal brand, I'd like to share one recent story that left me particularly disappointed.

Years ago, I met a young woman at a Marketing agency I hired to support my business. She was sharp and talented and continued to impress me with her follow-up and customer focus. I couldn't believe she was only in her late twenties. My first impression was that she was going to go places.

Shortly after my project ended with that agency, she reached out to me to share that she wanted to do something similar to what my company did. She envisioned writing a book and helping college students find their purpose before they graduated. I could hear the passion in her voice and was willing to support her in any way I could. Over the next year or so, she reached out regularly to ask for advice and guidance. I made professional introductions, reviewed her new content, and invited her to special events where she could observe and network—all of which she expressed much verbal gratitude for.

I admired her follow-through and tenacity. She was a real go-getter. So much so that she finished her book in record time and had booked a few volunteer speaking gigs.

In our last meeting, she confessed that although she had achieved a lot, it was hard for her to make money on her own and wondered how I had so many active clients. After giving her some advice, I told her that although I had a lot of wisdom to share, she possessed some skills and experience that I could benefit from. She was an expert in inbound Marketing and social media—a skill set that I didn't have.

I shared with her a specific Marketing challenge I was facing that was time sensitive. It was a problem that she could help me solve as well as make some income in the process. She expressed an eagerness to help, especially the opportunity to make some money. She would put pen to paper and use her Marketing expertise to outline an approach and recommended strategy. We set a deadline and hung up.

About a week past our agreed deadline, I was surprised I hadn't received anything. So, I shot her a quick email to make sure everything was okay. Given the follow-through I'd seen her demonstrate scheduling meetings with me and submitting content for me to review, I started to worry that something was wrong.

About an hour after I emailed her, I received a multiple paragraph response that is now burned in my brain. It spoke to all of the projects and activities she was engaged—her book launch, design of a new course, and podcast. She explained that she was really sorry, but due to her current workload, she didn't have time to take on a consulting project. She concluded by saying that she hoped this didn't impact our relationship that we could continue to work together in other ways. I later heard a voicemail from her expressing the same sentiments.

I was totally shocked when I read her email. First of all, she sent it more than a week after the date she agreed to present me with a strategic proposal. So many feelings and thoughts went through my mind. I felt used. I felt like she didn't think my time was as valuable as hers. I had spent numerous hours responding to her request for help and, until now, had asked for nothing in return. Now, that the tables were turned and I asked for her help, I learned that the relationship wasn't reciprocal. Second, it's one thing not to be able to do something, after all, we all get busy. However, it's another not to let the other person know. In the time I waited for her to fulfill her commitment, I could have engaged other resources. So, not only did I feel used and ignored, but her inaction also impacted my business timelines—a double whammy.

Once I had time to digest this unfortunate situation, I realized that this person is still talented and skilled. I don't believe she meant any harm by dropping the ball. I don't even think she's aware of the negative impact this had on her reputation and credibility in my eyes. The biggest loss that this situation yielded was actually to her reputation.

Although I would never bad mouth her in professional circles, I'm no longer comfortable putting my reputation on the line to ask valuable connections for favors on her behalf. This is not to penalize her. However, advocating for her now poses too much risk for me and my own credibility. I saw this play out when I had to turn down a speaking opportunity due to being double booked. I could have recommended her in my place. This would have provided her a well-paid gig that she was seeking. However, I hesitated because I didn't want to risk my own reputation should she demonstrate the same behavior with my client.

When I thought about this full circle, it was quite a lesson on personal brand. She couldn't fulfill her commitment to me because she was overwhelmed with all of the work it was taking to build her own business. By her not fulfilling her commitment to me and leaving me hanging, I then couldn't recommend her for the very type of opportunity she was seeking.

Sometimes, we get so focused on our success and related challenges, that we lose sight of the bigger picture. The lesson I'm hoping you take away is that your personal brand is determined by what you do and don't do. It's the things you say and don't say. Your reputation is a big key to your long-term success.

IT ONLY TAKES SEVEN SECONDS

We've all heard the saying, "You only have one chance to make a good first impression." Research teaches us that within the first seven seconds, we form a solid impression of a complete stranger. Some research suggests it takes even less time to determine how trustworthy we think someone is.

Whether we like it or not, when we show up, people make judgments about who we are and the value we bring. We are judged on our personal image—the way we dress, talk, walk, and other non-verbal cues.

Essentially your personal brand is the whole representation of yourself, including your image. The way you communicate, verbally, and non-verbally, combined with your physical appearance, should align with the personal brand you've created. The goal is to project one unified brand that helps you stand out and achieve the goals you've set for yourself.

I've conducted hundreds of job interviews, and I can think of many examples of job candidates whose presentation didn't match their stellar resumes—think chewing gum, wearing wrinkled clothing, using slang or looking disheveled. I remember being so disappointed when my top candidate told me about their "like" career goals and their "like" awesome experience and "um" desire to "um" apply their "um" skills in the "like, um" job they were "um" interviewing for.

This disconnection is a misalignment between someone's personal brand and image. To maximize the opportunities available to you, you must think about all of the aspects of how others experience your personal brand.

I'm imagining this is pretty self-explanatory. I would venture that most of us are aware of this and avoid the obvious examples I just presented. With that said, there are a few traps I've seen young professionals fall into that can negatively impact their personal brand. So, what image cues make someone want to invest more time with you or run for the hills?

YOUR PERSONAL STYLE

Studies have shown that non-verbal communication accounts for 70% or more of how we communicate. So, what someone sees when they first meet us, such as our hand gestures and facial expressions, send more of a message than the actual words we use. This means that within seconds of meeting you, someone has decided what you are like and how they will react.

If I perceive you as unapproachable or cocky, I'm less likely to want to engage with you or get to know you better. Whereas if I see you as friendly or trustworthy, I'm more likely to invest more time to ask you questions and give you an opportunity to share more about what you have to offer.

Think about the first visible signals you send to the world on any given day. A smile is a universal sign of connection. It's also a great and easy way to leave a good impression. When someone smiles, most of us can't help but smile back. When you're smiling, you're often portraying openness, warmth, and even confidence. Others immediately feel comfortable around you and are, therefore, more willing to engage you in dialogue.

Second, is your overall appearance, what you're wearing, how well-groomed you are, and your overall style. There used to be clearer norms in the workplace related to dress code—men in suits, women in skirts and pantyhose. Thank goodness that time has passed! We have many more opportunities to dress as we'd like in our own style and comfort. However, that freedom has also caused employees to fall into a few traps.

Some people have misjudged casual workplaces and unknowingly damaged their personal brand by being overly casual. One of the questions I often get from young professionals is how to dress professionally while remaining true to their personal style. I always tell young professionals that the goal of their appearance is to be taken seriously while feeling true to yourself.

This means that you should dress in a way that balances fitting into your environment and what feels most authentic to you. If you work in a formal setting and are vying for a promotion, look around at what your company leaders are wearing. Find one or two whom you really admire and then identify the attributes of their appearance that you like. If they wear suits, try stepping up your wardrobe a bit. Whereas, if you work in a more creative environment and see that your company leaders are quite casual, experiment with casual pieces that still send the message that you are ready for the next step in the company.

I remember working at a company that had casual Fridays. We all loved the opportunity to take it down a notch at the end of the week. I remember a team member coming to my office asking for more opportunities to be seen by the higher-ups. She and I agreed that I would have her present to the executive team in our next Friday meeting. However, I was perplexed that she showed up in worn running shoes and denim shorts on Friday. She wasn't breaking any dress code rules, but she wasn't exactly sending the message that she was influential.

A great rule to follow when it comes to appearance and career growth is to dress for the job you want versus the one you have.

SLANG AND FILLER WORDS

One of the most common image traps young professionals can fall into is using slang and filler words. Whether that be "likes," "ums" or other non-word words, the way we speak has a big influence on how credible others perceive us to be or not.

I had a very intelligent and motivated employee who loved training and teaching. She told me she had a lot of practice and was ready to be in front of real clients. So, I gave her a shot. I could see that she had some legitimate skills. She made eye contact, had a strong voice, and knew the right questions to ask. However, all of that was overshadowed by her constant use of "um." I counted twenty in just a few minutes. My client noticed it as well and pulled me aside, asking why I brought someone who wasn't qualified to teach.

It was an interesting conclusion she drew. She equated the use of filler words with experience. The facilitator was actually very qualified—she just happened to insert a filler word in between sentences. This became a distraction and pulled attention away from her real talents. This small habit was impeding her ability to be seen as qualified at her job.

I remember the first time I saw myself presenting on video from a talk I gave early in my career. I practiced and felt very confident in my delivery. When I watched the video, I almost died! I had a couple of nervous habits, of which I was entirely unaware. I inserted the word "totally" dozens of times! It was distracting and pulled attention away from my important message.

Have you ever filmed or recorded yourself in a meeting? I highly recommend it. Most of the time, we are completely unaware of some of our communication habits. Once we're aware, we can find ways to address it.

Next time you get ready for a job interview, networking event, or even a meeting, ask yourself:

- Does my image align with my personal brand?
- Does my image match the way I want others to perceive me?

When you can answer yes to these questions, you will feel confident, and those around you will see you that way as well.

Creating the right personal brand will help you be seen as credible and increase the number of right opportunities available to you. A personal brand isn't a one-time action or decision. Your personal brand will continue to evolve and change. The key is to tell the story of who you are, what you value, and where you want to go in a consistent and compelling way.

CAREER TROUBLESHOOTING

During my career, I've fielded hundreds of questions from eager and sometimes frustrated young professionals seeking career advice. They range from how to interview for a new job and negotiate first salaries to dealing with annoying co-workers or improving presentation skills.

Once emerging professionals complete the *AccelerateME*™ Career Development course, their questions become very specific. Often, they focus on challenges and roadblocks that can result from doing the tough work of identifying Energizers, values, and a career vision, or uncovering blind spots and engaging in career conversations.

In this chapter, I've included the most common questions I've heard from young professionals after they complete the steps outlined in this book. I've categorized each question under the chapter in the book it relates to most. If you have questions related to your own personal journey, look for those that are similar to yours to find potential solutions that might also work for you.

TROUBLE SHOOTING: ENERGIZERS

Q. What if I'm in a job that doesn't align with my Energizers?

This is one of the most common questions that arise after participants complete a strengths assessment or identify their primary Energy Zone. Once we become aware of what brings us energy and what comes most naturally to us, we look at the world differently. We can explain why we're unhappy in our current job.

To address this, I recommend two approaches. The first is to look for ways to apply your natural Energizers in your current job. This entails looking for opportunities to do what you do best more often.

Even if you find a job that leverages more of your strengths, there will still be things that drain you. The goal is to showcase what you can do more often. This will bring you more joy, and others will notice and give you more of the work you want.

Here are a few tips on how best to do that.

1. **Share your Energizers with your manager.**
   Tell them that you will volunteer to participate in work that falls into your primary Energy Zone, even if it's not part of your job.

2. **Partner with co-workers with opposing Energizers.**
   If you are energized by coming up with new ideas and problem solving, but drained by presenting those ideas, see if you can find a project team member who can present. Just make sure they give you credit too!

3. Carve out time to be drained.

I realize this one sounds a little wacky. Once you know that something drains you, it's sometimes easier to digest. It is what it is. This means you can expect to be exhausted and schedule a time to do the job that needs to get done. I am drained by the need for perfection and detail when building a budget. However, as I moved into senior leadership roles, I had to manage large budgets. Each month I would schedule a two-hour time block where I would lock myself away in a quiet space and just knock it out. I would then engage a co-worker who was energized by this activity and treat them to a nice dinner out each month if they would double-check my calculations.

The second option is to look for new jobs that enable you to play to your strengths more often. This is not an immediate fix, but sometimes you realize that your current situation will never energize you. For example, if you discovered that you're energized by regularly interacting with people and find yourself in a job or company that has you working alone most of the time, then it may be time to make a change.

In this scenario, I recommend updating your LinkedIn headline and resumé and spread the word that you're seeking a more social culture or industry. Of course, it wouldn't hurt to give the first strategy a shot while you wait for your next opportunity. Try and participate in extracurricular social activities that fuel your fire.

Q. What if I find that I'm energized by work that's included in a co-worker's job or a different department within the organization?

This can be a tricky situation. But it can also be a great realization while you have connections within the organization. Here are a few steps to give yourself the best shot at transitioning to a more energizing role without having to leave the company.

1. **Share what energizes you with your manager.**
   You don't necessarily need to share what drains you. Letting your manager know the types of activities where you add the most value will help them with future delegation.

2. **Ask co-workers if you can help them with projects and tasks that energize you, even when they don't fall into your responsibilities.**
   This isn't about taking over their jobs but instead saving them time by taking tasks off of their plate. They will especially appreciate this if they are drained by those activities.

3. **Participate in formal training for any new skills you will need to apply your strengths at work further.**
   For example, if you are energized by project management but won't be considered for such work until you have a certification, then take it upon yourself to obtain it. You may even be successful in getting your organization paying for it if they see it as an opportunity to leverage your skills down the road further.

TROUBLE SHOOTING: VALUES

Q. What if my current job doesn't support most of my values?

Once you've identified your top values, you may recognize that you are not living them as fully as you'd like. If that's the case, you have an opportunity to make some changes, small or large.

The first step is to identify what's within your control. What might you do differently to live a specific value more fully? This means you will have to challenge your current thinking. Sometimes it's hard for us to see where these opportunities for change exist because we've been doing things a certain way for a long time. If this is the case, it can help to seek advice from someone we trust or someone who we admire for the way they live the value we're struggling to prioritize.

I remember one time I was struggling to find time for health and fitness. I was working long hours and felt like every time I scheduled a workout class during lunch, my boss would call me into a mandatory meeting. I felt stuck and couldn't see a way out unless I quit my job. I noticed a co-worker who was very fit and working the same hours I was. So, I asked her how she fit fitness into her schedule. She shared with me that she works out every day before coming into the office. She also fell victim to the meeting schedule and realized that she had to work out before the day could run away from her. I decided to adopt her strategy and try this just three days a week.

I also decided to share with my manager that I was struggling to balance my personal priorities with my workload. I received a high-performance rating and figured I had earned enough credibility to share my challenges. Although my manager still changed meeting times last minute from time to time, she also tried only to call me in if I was really needed. She knew of my goals and became more mindful.

Q. What if my values are conflicting? What if by trying to live one more fully, I jeopardize another?

This question can come up in a variety of situations. In a recent coaching session, someone shared that as part of exploring a new career path, they were going to lose something important to them. They struggled as to whether or not it was the right move.

They were in the final interview process for a new job at a new company. This job would enable them to spend more time doing work they were energized by and reduce their commute time. This meant they could be home earlier and spend more time with family. This was a core value of theirs that wasn't being met in their current work situation. However, in the final interview stages, they learned that the new role would mean a slight pay cut. This was disappointing as they also identified financial stability as an important value.

In our quest to more fully live our values, we may find that we have to give up something. In this situation, you have to ask yourself what's truly most important to you in the next one to three years and what you're willing to trade to get it.

In my coachee's case, she had to figure out if the reduction in pay was worth gaining more time with family and more energizing work. Could she sacrifice money in the short term?

If you're struggling with a similar situation, here are some questions you can ask yourself to help make an informed decision.

- What are my "must-haves"? What are the top two to three values that must be met for me to make a change?
- What am I going to gain by this change?
- What short-term sacrifices am I willing to make?
- What long-term sacrifices am I willing to make?
- Can I eventually recover what I'm sacrificing in the short-term?
- Can I live with what I'm giving up?

Another way to determine if this is the right decision is to make a list of pros and cons. For example, by making this change, which of your top values are you going to live most fully? Financial stability? An opportunity to help people? Spending more time with family?

On the other hand, what values may not be supported? More commute time? More travel and less time for family or hobbies? Could you lose stability?

There is no right or wrong answer to these questions. Each of us has different needs and goals that can shift throughout our life. Think about what's most important to you in the next one to three years and decide based on your values, needs, and career goals. If you do that, you can't go wrong.

TROUBLE SHOOTING: VISION

Q. What if I'm still not clear on my long-term vision?

Vision is often the most difficult step in the process. Sometimes we simply don't have a clear vision. This can make it difficult to set goals and take control of our path. If, after completing all of the challenges in Chapter 5, you are still unclear, then I recommend focusing on a short-term goal instead. Instead of feeling overwhelmed with a broader vision, think about what success might look like in the next six months.

If you're feeling stuck regarding what your vision is, try working backward and identifying what you don't want.

Picture yourself six months from today. What would you hope would be different than how things are today? How do you want to feel? What type of work would you like to be doing more of or less of? What would your ideal day look like in comparison to what it looks like today?

Once you have a few ideas, you can identify one or two that you'd like to make progress on over the next six months. Whether that be living a value more fully or participating in more energizing work, a great start is to move forward in just one area. By doing this, you ensure you're headed in a positive direction, and you may be surprised at the clarity and inspiration you might find along the way.

Q. What if my vision is no longer inspiring to me?

Your vision may change over time. What you may have identified as a success one day might shift as you learn and grow. That's not a bad thing. In fact, it's common for your vision to change and refine over time. What's most important is that you acknowledge it and make the necessary adjustments. As I mentioned earlier in the book, many of the activities you completed should be done annually.

If you wake up one morning and realize you're no longer inspired by the larger direction you set for yourself, it's time to carve out some time to retake the challenges in Step 3. I recommend going through the visualization activities again to re-picture your perfect day. What's different about it? What shifted?

Don't worry about making it perfect. Instead, focus on the next year. What would need to happen for you to be successful one year from today? Now write it down! Remember to work backward and list all of the milestones you would expect to complete to meet your one-year vision of success.

TROUBLE SHOOTING: BLIND SPOTS

Q. *What if I disagree with the feedback I received?*

If you followed the challenges in Step 3, then you've solicited feedback. Asking others to provide input on your actions and behaviors can be scary. So, what if the feedback you get doesn't sound accurate to you? Maybe it's wrong or unfair. Perhaps the person or persons sharing it don't see the bigger picture or all of the facts. Any of these circumstances might be true. However, how you navigate this situation is critical to your success in uncovering blind spots.

The first step is to remember that you asked for feedback. This means that even if you disagree with it, your job is to simply say, "Thank you." Essentially this person has given you a gift—albeit wrapped in ugly paper. The only move you can really make is to be gracious, even if you have to grit your teeth in the process.

Second, is to make sure you don't act defensively. You don't have to agree with them, but you also can't argue. This means checking your body language as well as the tone of your voice. If you come across as angry or argumentative, the chances of people continuing to be open with you will decrease.

Instead, you can ask clarifying questions to make sure you truly understand the feedback. Start by repeating back what you heard. "I understand that you don't see me as a team player." Then follow-up by asking them to share an example.

"Can you share a moment when you saw this happen?"

Then, even if you still don't agree, say, "Thank you."

Lastly, remember that when you ask for feedback to uncover blind spots, you will receive pieces of data that together tell a story. Your job is to put the pieces together. When I receive feedback, I have a big fan and a big critic in the mix. My fan thinks everything I do is fabulous and never sees room for improvement. Whereas, my critic only sees my deficiencies and weaknesses. Therefore, if I really want to get a balanced perspective of myself, I eliminate both of their feedback—unless the feedback they've shared is mirrored from the people in the middle.

Look for trends in all of the feedback you receive. If you hear from multiple parties that you are perceived as someone difficult to work with, then you have some data you may want to pay attention to. This is especially true if you participate in a formal 360-degree feedback assessment, like our *AccelerateME*™ assessment. When you dig into your personal data, you will see trends that help you focus on the areas you will benefit from developing.

When receiving feedback, the key is to take a step back and be as objective as possible. This can be really difficult given that the feedback is about you, and it's normal to feel an emotional, rather than logical, response. Take a deep breath and remember that you and only you have the power to make meaning of the feedback provided. Only hold on to that which will benefit you and throw out the rest.

Q. *What if I uncovered many blind spots and now feel overwhelmed or defeated as I'll never improve or don't know where to start?*

If you took the brave steps to uncover your blind spots, then you took a leap of faith and solicited feedback. To your surprise, you opened Pandora's box and are now aware of several things about yourself you hadn't seen before. If this happened to you, it's normal to feel overwhelmed or even defeated.

First of all, you should celebrate that you did something so brave. I've worked with several leaders who never took such a brave step early in their careers. Instead, they were forced to get developmental feedback to move into management roles. Believe me, when I tell you, it feels much more powerful when you take these steps on your own terms and when no one else is viewing your feedback.

Now, take a deep breath and step back to see the bigger picture. Group your feedback into themes. If you completed the *AccelerateME*™ *Feedback Assessment*, your report will do this for you. If not, write down all of the blind spots you think you've identified. Did you uncover that you aren't as influential as you thought? Do your team members not invite you to brainstorm new ideas because they believe you'll try and negate anything new? Whatever your specific themes are, it's helpful to see them all in one place—even if the list is long.

Once you have it all in one place, you can prioritize it. What is your career vision? How did you define success in the next twelve months? Your job is to select one or two blind spots that you think are most impeding your ability to achieve your one-year milestone. Although it's tempting to want to address all of them, I recommend focusing on a couple first. Once you make progress on these, you can re-assess and move on to the next set you think will most help your career.

TROUBLE SHOOTING: CONVERSATIONS

Q. How transparent or honest should I be with my manager?

Once young professionals have completed the five-step Career Acceleration Formula, they are often excited and ready to take action. If you're employed, you've likely identified your direct supervisor as someone who can be a great asset to you in this journey.

So, what if you discovered you might be a better fit for a role outside of the team? Or that much of your current work activities don't fall into your primary Energy Zone? Knowing what is safe to share with your manager can be tricky. After all, no matter how friendly they might be, they are still the person with direct authority over your performance rating and compensation.

There's no one-size-fits-all answer to this question. It's going to take some judgment and a little risk to navigate this. To help you determine the best path for you, here are a few questions you can ask yourself.

1. **How much trust exists between you and your manager?** To answer this, think about what personal information you've shared with them before, and how much personal information they've voluntarily shared with you. These are good indicators as to how trusting of a relationship the two of you have. If they've been fairly open with you in the past about their family life, health, and personal career ambitions, that's a sign that you might also be able to share the same with them safely.

2. **What has been the nature of previous career conversations?**

If you've had career conversations in the past, perhaps you've already built a foundation for deeper ones. If this is your first conversation with your manager, you might want to start with a more general conversation and then work your way up to riskier and more vulnerable topics in the future.

3. **What's the worst-case scenario of openly sharing?**

Think about the best and worst case that full transparency could result in. Could you be fired? Could it impact your ability to get a raise? Could it open up new doors that might not have been previously open to you? However, you answer, be prepared for the worst case scenario if you decide to be transparent.

4. **What are the consequences of not being transparent?**

This question is about what you're willing to lose to gain what you really want. If you don't share your aspirations or challenges, how much longer can you really tolerate the status quo? Is the risk worth the potential reward?

Q. What if my manager said "no" to my career ask? For example, I asked for a raise or promotion and didn't get it.

You mustered up the courage to ask for what you want finally, and you got a less than enthusiastic response. Most of us have been there. This can be especially disappointing when you feel clear and passionate about your career next steps or support you need.

When you get a "no," you may want to act out or even quit altogether. Occasionally this may be the right option for you. But, before you take that route, there are a few things you can do to ensure you're making the right step.

First, ask yourself if you were prepared. Did you have clarity on what you were asking for? Did you speak to the benefits to the team, organization, or specifically your manager? How will you save money, time, or improve quality? I've found that sometimes, we get so excited when we have clarity for ourselves that we forget the principles of strategic influencing.

Second, is the "no" negotiated? Meaning, are there any factors that could alter that outcome? Is the "no" about timing? It's always good to ask a powerful question to really understand how your manager sees the outcome. You can ask, "What factors did you consider when coming to this conclusion?" This question will help you understand how your manager sees your request. You can get inside their head and get a breakdown of their decision-making criteria.

Another good one I've used is, "What would have to happen or be in place to get a yes?" This will force your manager to think about the future. If we ask someone a black and white question, we get a black and white answer. If you got a "no," then the conversation can be dead in the water. Asking an open-ended question will force your manager to think about how "no" can become a "yes." This usually results in a deeper conversation.

If you ask the deeper questions, be prepared for additional feedback. You may uncover a blind spot you didn't expect in the process!

Q. What if my manager doesn't seem supportive of my career goals or aspirations? How can I work around them?

Maybe your manager always cancels or postpones career conversations. Or perhaps they smile and nod, but never actually follow through. Gaining the support of your direct supervisor can be an important step in growing your career.

When thinking about this topic, I'm reminded that managers are people too. Meaning that they are not all built the same.

Some never had anyone support their careers. Others struggle with managing their time. And some are just bad managers.

At the end of the day, if you're manager isn't supporting you, you have to take control of the situation. After all, it's your career, and if you don't take charge of it, no one else will. After years in leadership development, I find that there are four primary reasons managers don't support an employee's career aspirations. I've also included a few tips to overcome each one.

1. A narrow view of the next steps.
Many managers share that their employees came to them with a very narrowly defined plan for their careers. This meant that the only way to support that employee was to say yes or no to the actions laid out in the employee's plan.

I advise young professionals to stay focused on the bigger goals, like a raise or promotion, and be open to various ways of getting there. You may think that you need to take on a direct report, but your manager may have other ideas on how to support you. Keep your eye on the prize and be open to a variety of paths to get there.

2. Timing is not in your favor.
Sometimes, your manager's hands are tied based on what's going on in the larger organization. They may be privy to information they can't yet share with you. When you ask for their support, think about what's going on in the business that might affect their ability to help you. Is there an annual process when managers can advocate for career moves?

A great way to figure this out is to observe how other people have gained support for career growth. Think of someone you've seen take the steps you're seeking and ask them to tell you their story.

3. **Your manager is overwhelmed in their job.**
   It's possible, even if they won't admit it to you, that your manager isn't being supportive because they're simply struggling to keep up with their own workload. They probably won't tell you that's the reason they aren't focused on your career development, but you can look for signs that tell you otherwise. Perhaps they cancel meetings last minute or highjack current meetings to address challenges in everyday work.

   If this is the case, your best bet is to acknowledge it. You can wait a little bit for the storm to pass or if this seems to be the new norm, tell them that you are having trouble having a meaningful career conversation with them due to what seems to be other business priorities. Sometimes simply saying it out loud will help them realize that they are neglecting you.

   You can also ask if the two of you can meet after work, for lunch or even a coffee. By taking the conversation out of the office, you may have a better shot at getting the support you need. If you've exhausted all options and are still not getting their support, you can tell your manager that you're interested in working with a mentor that can add additional insights to help you grow your career. This will take the pressure off of them and open the door for you to get additional support.

4. **You don't have a strong business case.**
   Let's say you've gotten time with your manager, explained your vision, and still haven't gained their support. If so, it's possible, what you've presented might be a good move for you, but doesn't align with the business you're in. For example, you might feel that you're ready to be promoted into a leadership role, but the business simply doesn't have any available opportunities for you. Or you've discovered

you want to take on more activities and projects that play to your natural Energizers, but the business doesn't need you to do so.

In these types of cases, you may find that your manager can't support you because there is no business need to do so. If you find yourself in one of these situations, it's best to have a heart-to-heart with your manager to really understand what options might exist for you in the future. You may find yourself opening up to career opportunities outside of the company. If so, think about what you can learn in your current role that can prepare you for new opportunities elsewhere.

YOU'RE AWESOME

By participating in the activities and challenges presented in this book, you have rolled up your sleeves and done a lot of work. Some steps may have been more difficult than others, but you persevered.

The changing nature of the world you live in has made the workplace more difficult to navigate. The key to accelerating your path and finding joy along the way requires self-awareness, authenticity, and the ability to adapt when needed.

Whether it be recognizing what energizes you, identifying what you value most, getting clear on where you want to go, or identifying what can get in your way, this book is all about helping you get what you want in the timeframe you want it in.

I recommend revisiting the challenges in each step at any point during your career when you start to feel anxious or wonder if you're making the right decision. If you skipped a step or specific challenge because you just weren't ready for it at that moment, revisit it at a later date when you may be more prepared.

By taking the time to do some self-exploration, identifying what support you need and having the right conversations, you can put yourself on a career path that's authentic and achievable.

As you seek to live your best life, I'm honored that you chose this book as a trusted resource. I hope the content I've covered helps you be in the driver's seat of your career path.

I also encourage you to connect with me on LinkedIn. I'd love to have you in my network and hear about your experiences and success stories.

I look forward to learning of your awesome career!

Christine DiDonato

TOOLS & RESOURCES

Now that you've completed the AccelerateME™ process, I recommend the following tools and resources to keep your momentum going.

COMPANION WORKBOOK

"The Get There Faster Workbook" includes each activity and challenge discussed in this book, along with space to record responses as well as several bonus activities. Available on Amazon.

CAREER RESOURCES AND TEMPLATES

Visit AccelerateME.com/career-resources to access the following tools and more.

- Career conversation agenda
- Career conversation template
- Hacks for how to ask for a raise
- Career goal worksheet
- One-year career plan template

AWESOMEBOSS.COM

If you manage people sometimes you need a little help keeping your team engaged. AwesomeBoss.com is designed to help managers reward and recognize others as well as take the guesswork out of giving and writing feedback. Assessments

ASSESSMENTS

AccelerateME™ Values Assessment

Access to the online Values Assessment can be found in the companion resource, the "Get There Faster Workbook". Available on Amazon.

AccelerateME™ Career Feedback Assessment

Go to AccelerateME.com/feedback-assessment to request a complimentary discount code.

LINKEDIN LEARNING

Premium LinkedIn members have access to the following courses on Linkedin.com/learning

- Take Charge of Your Career
- Negotiating Your Job Offer

ACCELERATEME™ WORKSHOPS

Career Revolution works with organizations to provide onsite and live-virtual programs for employees. We also conduct master certifications so that employees can facilitate the program for their organization. For more information send inquiries to Support@CareerRev.com.

WHO IS CHRISTINE DiDONATO

An innovator in the space of emerging leader development, Christine DiDonato is the founder of Career Revolution, Inc. and CEO of AwesomeBoss.com. As a former talent management executive for Sony Electronics, Christine focused her passion and research on developing the youngest employees to become the next generation of leaders.

To help young professionals take charge of their careers, she created the AccelerateME™ Career Development Program and related feedback assessment. These tools are specifically designed for today's emerging professionals to get the feedback they crave and take greater ownership of their career path.

Christine is a LinkedIn Author and seasoned facilitator who partners with clients to move beyond theory and academics to create tangible solutions that address the challenges of our new workforce. Her contributions as a leading expert in her field can be seen in popular media sources such as TIME, Money, Inc., Forbes, and, USA Today.

When not facilitating, writing, and consulting, you can find Christine in the kitchen cooking family recipes from generations of her Italian heritage and entertaining friends and family over a bottle of wine.

Christine calls San Diego, California, home, but you will often find her traveling to visit clients and friends.

STAY CONNECTED

LinkedIn: linkedin.com/in/christinedidonato/

Career Revolution Inc: CareerRev.com

Instagram: @careermindset

Twitter: @careermindset

GRATITUDE

Thank you to my amazing network of friends and family for a lifetime of support and love.

To my mom, Nancy, for being my biggest fan and go-to phone call whenever I felt stuck or just needed a pep talk.

To my little sister, Lisa, for being the big sister I never had. Your calm and rational advice continues to keep me grounded.

To my fierce and funny friends who keep me laughing, even when I shouldn't be. Lori, you remind me to see the glass as half full. Megan, you snap me back into reality when needed. Juan, you have translated my wacky ideas into works of art for almost a decade now. Robb, your patience, and deep friendship keeps me grounded. Without all of you, life would be dull.

To my editor, Annie, you inspired me to stay true to my voice. You made it fun to write this book and made sure I didn't veer from my authentic vision and message.

Lastly, a big shout out to the amazing young professionals who share their hopes, dreams and pain points with me. Thank you for trusting me. Your stories inspired this book. It would not exist without you.

I'm one lucky woman!